D1744011

Stuart Holroyd, sceptical, open-minded and well-informed, became observer to a remarkable US group of psychics headed by a famous American scientist and an English aristocrat. Their claim was that they had made contact with galactic intelligences, and their 'evidence' was astounding . . .

Did three 'selected' minds help to avert a world disaster?

Were the group in constant communication with extraterrestrials?

Was it possible for these alien intelligences to effect a landing on earth?

Had they, in fact, already visited earth in previous centuries?

Did the group's meditations avert Kissinger's assassination and a Middle East holocaust?

# Briefing for the Landing on Planet Earth

## Stuart Holroyd

**CORGI BOOKS**
A DIVISION OF TRANSWORLD PUBLISHERS LTD

Briefing for the Landing on Planet Earth
A CORGI BOOK 0 552 10997 5

Originally published in Great Britain
by W. H. Allen, London

PRINTING HISTORY

W. H. Allen edition published 1977
Corgi edition published 1979

This book is set in Monotype Plantin 10/11 pt.

Corgi Books are published by Transworld Publishers Ltd.,
Century House, 61–63 Uxbridge Road, Ealing, London, W5 5SA

Made and printed in Great Britain by
Richard Clay (The Chaucer Press), Ltd., Bungay, Suffolk

And I took the little book out of the angel's hand, and ate it up; and it was in my mouth sweet as honey: and as soon as I had eaten it my belly was bitter. And he said unto me, Thou must prophecy again before many peoples, and nations, and tongues, and kings.

*Revelation*, 10, v 10–11

# Contents

# Author's Note

This book is about people going through a very testing and unusual experience, and I want to express my appreciation to the principals, both for their unstinting co-operation and for permitting the personal aspects of the story to be told. One problem in writing about contemporary events of this kind is that words tend to fix and finalise things, and I should like to stress that this is an ongoing story, and that in the three years that have elapsed since the events here reported some of the people involved have undergone considerable and beneficial personal changes as a result of their experiences and their strange guidance; others have chosen to drop into the background. However, in these three years the communications have continued, further elaborating the themes introduced in this book and broaching some new ones. This book is only the beginning, and a book on the extraordinary events and communications subsequent to the April 1975 climacteric will follow.

To reproduce verbatim the material on which the book is based would require three or four volumes of the present length. So the material as presented in these pages is edited. I have omitted repetitions and some digressions, and have tidied up grammar and syntax where necessary, simply in order to make the narrative readable and to include as much of the very varied material as possible.

My thanks are due to Nada-Yolanda and Mark Age, Inc., of Miami, for permission to quote from their publication, *Visitors from Other Planets*, and to Brad Steiger and Prentice-Hall, Inc., of Englewood Cliffs, New Jersey, for permission to quote from *Revelation: The Divine Fire* by Brad Steiger.

# Introduction

The subject of UFOs – flying saucers – used to be a matter of violent controversy. Now the argument has subsided into a kind of sullen deadlock. The people who read *Flying Saucer Review* are more certain than ever that the phenomena are genuine – whether or not they are really 'visitors from outer space'. The sceptics now simply decline to discuss the matter, as if it were really too silly for words. Yet if they were not hopelessly intolerant and narrow-minded, the present book would lead some of them to agree that 'ufologists' are not all cranks and gulls.

The central figure in this book is Dr Andrija Puharich, an electronics engineer and inventor, described by Aldous Huxley as 'one of the most brilliant minds in parapsychology'. Puharich is probably best known for his 'discovery' of Uri Geller, the Israeli psychic who was launched to fame in the early 1970s when he bent spoons on British television. By that time, Puharich was already the author of two remarkable books: *The Sacred Mushroom*, describing his investigation of a Dutch sculptor who produced detailed memories of a 'past life' in ancient Egypt, and *Beyond Telepathy*, a balanced account of some impeccable experiments with well-known 'psychics'. No 'psychical researcher' in England or America had the slightest doubt that Puharich was a serious and totally honest observer of parapsychological phenomena. And when his book *Uri: A Journal of the Mystery of Uri Geller* was published in 1974, everyone expected it to be another cautious and well-documented account of laboratory investigations into Geller's powers. What actually appeared left everyone staggered and bewildered. According to Puharich, strange voices spoke out of Geller's mouth – or from above his head – declaring themselves to be 'Space Intelligences' who had selected Geller to be their Messenger in Chief to the human race. And the rest of the book was a catalogue of preposterous marvels, with the 'Space Intelligences' causing car engines to stop, making objects appear and disappear, even 'teleporting' Puharich's camera case several thousand miles . . . Critics decided there could be three possible explanations: (a) Puharich had been hoodwinked by Geller; (b) Puharich was lying; (c) Puharich had gone mad. Even the most ardent ufologists found the book impossible to swallow, for the catalogue of marvels simply went on too long; it left the head spinning.

Having met Uri Geller myself, my own theory was that he was undoubtedly genuine and had some odd ability to produce 'poltergeist phenomena'. Poltergeist means 'rattling ghost', and among the thousands of cases on record, some date back to the Middle Ages. At a fairly early stage, people noticed that the disturbances – objects flying through the air or loud bangs and crashes – usually occurred in the neighbourhood, of a disturbed adolescent, often an epileptic or hysteric. Nineteenth-century investigators were inclined to believe that such people were 'natural mediums', through whom 'spirits' wished to communicate. Then, in the 1880s, Freud 'discovered' the unconscious mind – or at least, popularised the concept – and the Society for Psychical Research quickly saw that this could be a plausible and natural explanation. Of course, it left unexplained the question of *how* a person's unconscious mind could cause objects to sail through the air; but it seemed a step in the right direction. In fact, since then, 'split brain research' has taken an even more important step towards an explanation; researchers have discovered that we have *two* people living inside our heads, in the left and right sides of the brain. The left half is the rational, logical person you call 'you'; when someone asks 'you' questions, this is the part that replies. A few centimetres away, in the right cerebral hemisphere, there is another 'you', a dumb, instinctive 'you' who operates almost entirely by intuition. If the two halves are split – as they sometimes are in epileptics – the left half ceases to know what the right half is up to, which explains how a person can cause poltergeist effects without having the least idea that he (or she) is responsible. Almost certainly, the right half is the culprit, together with its various allies in the older parts of the human brain.

On the strength of Puharich's earlier books, I am inclined to believe that he, as well as Geller, has a highly active unconscious mind. And this could explain the storm of 'psychic phenomena' that began to occur as soon as the two got together. This is the theory that I have suggested in my book *The Geller Phenomenon*. I should add that both Geller and Puharich, while not actually discounting it, are inclined to be doubtful. But then, they would be. The Uri and Andrija I have talked to live in the left side of their heads. . . .

All of which brings me to another old friend, Stuart Holroyd, the author of this book. I have told elsewhere (in *Voyage to a Beginning*) how we became literary allies in the 1950s, and how the mutual stimulation led me to write *The Outsider*, and Stuart to write his own first book *Emergence from Chaos*, a study in poetry and religion. My book was the first to appear, in May 1956, and it made me an overnight reputation; moreover, since it appeared on the same day as Osborne's play *Look Back in Anger*, I found myself linked with Osborne as an 'Angry Young Man'. We achieved overnight notoriety and a great deal of publicity. Stuart's book appeared a few months later. It was less successful than my own, partly because by this time he was also known as an Angry Young Man, and the highbrow critics were already sick of the absurd publicity we were receiving. Still, it made Stuart a secure reputation, and a play called *The Tenth Chance*, presented at the Royal Court, made it clear that he also possessed a true dramatic talent. He followed this up with a book that combined philosophy and autobiography (*Flight and Pursuit*, 1959), and then abruptly left London and the literary scene, married, moved to the south coast and established a language school, which he ran for fourteen years, in which time the only books he produced were on English literature and history for the educational market, and an autobiographical novel, *Contraries*, describing the old 'Angry' days of the fifties and the love affair that led to his second marriage: a book which revealed that in the 1970s he was writing with a new kind of assurance.

In early May 1974, a friend who runs a Dutch 'occult' magazine rang me from The Hague to ask me if I could attend – and report – a series of lectures on paranormal phenomena in London. (I had written *The Occult* in the late sixties, and it had gained me a reputation as some kind of authority on the subject). I said it was impossible at such short notice, but that I had a friend in Hastings who was a good writer and a conscientious reporter. He was not – as far as I knew – interested in the 'occult', but might be willing to take on the job . . . In fact, Stuart agreed, and attended the May Lectures, organised by Puharich and Sir John Whitmore. His report appeared in the Dutch magazine *Bres*, and was reprinted in a book *The Frontiers of Science and Medicine*, the editor, Rick Carlson, commenting that 'Holroyd's material is, to some extent, duplicative, but the duplication is worth it; first, because the subjects are complex and occasionally arcane and second because his insights are incisive and his writing lucid'.

As a result of attending the Lectures, Stuart became as fascinated by the subject as I am myself. And for the same reason. Both of us are centrally preoccupied with religion and mysticism – that is, with human consciousness, and the insights it can achieve. Both of us had formerly been inclined to dismiss 'occultism' as wishful thinking, and to regard its exponents as cranks. Yet *if* the roots of mystical revelation lie in the unconscious mind, as I am relatively sure they do, then there is an immediate connection between these and so-called 'paranormal powers'. Hindu mystics have always recognised this; the power to perform strange 'miracles' is just one of the less important by-products of the path to sainthood. And once we begin to talk about well-authenticated instances of telepathy, second-sight or fore-knowledge, we are also asking fundamental questions about the universe we live in. For example, *if* there is even one single provable instance of a glimpse into the future, then there is something basically wrong with our notion of time. And since the existentialist philosopher wants to know who we are and what we are doing here, paranormal research immediately becomes an important possible source of information.

Stuart Holroyd plunged into the subject with his customary passion and enthusiasm. The result was a remarkable book, *Psi and the Consciousness Explosion* that appeared in 1977. By that time, he had also turned his wide-ranging knowledge to account by writing no less than four books on paranormal subjects – telepathy, dreams, magic, astral projection – for a series I was then editing.

In the present book, he tells of his meeting with Whitmore and Puharich in America, of how he became aware of the astonishing continuation of the 'Space Intelligence' communications, and how he was persuaded to make his own assessment. It seems to me that Puharich showed considerable wisdom in agreeing to Stuart's writing the book, rather than writing it himself. He is too eccentrically brilliant to make a good writer; he gives the impression that his mind is moving twice as fast as his pen. But, more important, Stuart Holroyd is uninvolved. As a writer, his interest is in human psychology; therefore it would not make any basic difference to him if Puharich, Whitmore and Phyllis Schlemmer all turned out to be insane; the story would be equally absorbing. Yet, as will be seen, the one thing about which he has no misgivings is that of their sanity. Beyond all doubt, *something* very strange has been happening, and is continuing to happen, even as I write these words. It would be absurd not to acknowledge that it *could* be a matter of genuine extra-terrestrial communication. Yet on the present showing, there is simply not enough evidence to give real support to that possibility. Then what the hell *is* going on? I would agree that the remarkable events described in this book cannot easily be explained in terms of my 'poltergeist phenomena' theory either. Strange entities, claiming to be super-beings from 'another dimension', warn us that the planet earth is close to a serious crisis, and that this is why they have been forced to intervene so directly. Much of what

13

they say strikes me as convincing, and all of it is interesting – far more so than the majority of 'spirit communications' of the past. Could it be, perhaps, that the original poltergeist theory was correct, and that poltergeist phenomena *are* due to 'spirits' who operate through human 'mediums'? I have suggested elsewhere that the 'spirits' who communicate at seances may be the crooks and con-men of the spirit world, habitual liars with nothing better to do. Could this explain why the landing on planet Earth has not yet materialised?

In this book, Stuart Holroyd has presented you with all the facts, upon which you can make your own judgment. He has told the story with honesty, clarity and intelligence, and brought to bear on it his immense knowledge of this strange field. Whether or not you find the story of the Space Intelligences totally unacceptable, I think you will agree that it is an absorbing and disturbing narrative.

COLIN WILSON

# CHAPTER ONE

## *Preposterous Propositions*

How this bizarre story is going to end is, at the time of writing, anybody's guess. But let me go back to how it began, at least for me. On a visit to the United States in January 1975, I was staying with a friend in Rockland County, some thirty miles up-river from New York, and happened to mention that a friend in London had given me the phone number of Sir John Whitmore, who was living somewhere in New York State, at a place called Ossining. 'That's just across the river,' my friend said, so we called up Sir John and arranged to go over to Ossining for lunch the following Sunday. In the spring of 1974, Whitmore and others had organised in London a symposium and series of public lectures on 'The Frontiers of Science and Medicine', which I had attended in order to write some article on the proceedings. I had met John (in future references I'll drop the honorific, as he has chosen to do) several times in the course of the May Lectures, and subsequently on one or two occasions, but at the time I knew little of his background or work. We were not close acquaintances, but since we were, as I thought, fortuitously in the same area, it seemed natural to pay him a social visit.

Ossining. The name rang a bell, but I couldn't recall in what connection. I kept scanning my memory banks for the connection on and off all through the Saturday, but it continued to elude me. I didn't worry too much at it, though, particularly as the Saturday drew on, for my host, Richard Connolly, and I spent the afternoon and early evening at the High Tor vineyards as guests of the viticulteur, Father Tom Hayes, who plied us with his excellent High Tor wines, which

15

we contentedly discussed, drank and compared for hours, sitting cosily round a log fire, while outside snow lay thick on the hillsides. Which may seem a digression, but when you're into something as weird as I am at the present time it can be helpful to establish your credentials as a fellow with a taste for normal, earthy and rational pursuits, such as drinking and talking about wine.

The combination of jet lag and Tom Hayes' High Tor reds ensured me a good night's sleep on the Saturday. So on Sunday we arrived in good time for lunch at Ossining. When I saw the mail box outside the house we had been directed to bore the name 'Puharich' the connection that had eluded me came back in a flash. This was the home of Andrija Puharich, the maverick scientist who had brought Uri Geller to America and whose book, *Uri*, which I had read some months before, recounted some very queer goings-on at Ossining, such as materialisations and disappearance/reappearance events, as well as telling a very tall story about communications with extra-terrestrial intelligences and sightings of UFOs. I had met Puharich briefly in London at the May Lectures, where he had given a literally incredible talk in which he solemnly declared that he and Geller had been contacted by extra-terrestrial beings to bear witness to their existence and their powers, and to prepare mankind for a meeting with these beings at some unspecified future date when they would make mass landings on Earth. Subsequently I had done some homework on Puharich in order to write my article and also because my interest in the man was aroused, and found that he had done some very original and impressive parapsychological research work on correlations between environmental electromagnetic field forces and processes of paranormal cognition, had scientifically investigated some of the outstanding psychics of recent years, such as Eileen Garrett, Peter Hurkos and the Brazilian miracle healer, Arigó, and had invented an electrical device for applying radio waves of controlled frequences directly to the skin, which could be used for alleviating deafness, accelerating healing of bone fractures and controlling blood clotting. The man was clearly a highly original, gifted and versatile scientist and, I would have thought, nobody's fool, but it was equally clear that he had made something of a fool of himself, in the eyes of the scientific community, by writing as sensationally as he did about Geller and UFOs and contact with beings from other parts of the cosmos. I had heard various opinions of him expressed, ranging from admiration to regret ('a good mind gone off at a tangent') and derision ('a classic case of omnipotence fantasy'), but I didn't know what to make of the man. It would be interesting to meet him again on his home ground, though. I filled Richard in on some of this background as we drove up to the big detached house and while we waited for someone to answer our ring at the door.

John Whitmore answered and welcomed us warmly. John is tall, athletic, fair-haired, about forty, wears a neat beard, talks and moves energetically, and has successfully shed his past personae of public schoolboy, Sandhurst subaltern, professional racing driver, country gentleman and international tycoon. His manner and dress are casual, his speech is English English with some American overtones and turns of phrase and he's outgoing and enthusiastic. Some people also think he's crazy, but that's a point on which I think we had better withhold judgment.

So John took us into a big sitting-room where there were some plush couches and chairs and the atmosphere was a bit unlived-in and lacking the clutter of a home, except that a solitary bottle of Vick vapour rub stood out conspicuously on a low table. He introduced us to a pretty, oriental-looking young woman named Melanie, whose manner was almost overwhelmingly effusive, intimate and caring right from the first moment but who for the rest of the day kept getting my name wrong and calling me Stephen. John mentioned that Melanie had worked with Andrija and Uri, and I recalled that she was frequently mentioned in Puharich's Geller book.

Puharich himself wasn't around. He was in bed suffering from some minor malady that we gathered Melanie thought was symptomatic of nervous exhaustion and overwork, and for which she had prescribed total rest. So he wouldn't be down, which was a pity. Though if he had been I wonder if he would have got a word in, for as soon as we had got through the initial pleasantries John launched into what was virtually a monologue which was to keep Richard and me pretty enthralled for the next three hours. The enthralment, in fact, might have been total if we had had a bottle of High Tor to pass back and forth and some definite prospect of the lunch we had been invited for. Noises suggestive of preparation for the latter event emanated from a distant part of the house – clattering of crockery, chattering of women's voices – but nobody came in to announce that lunch was served. A toddler came into the room a couple of times in the three hours, and a young woman – presumably the mother – appeared and whisked the child away.

There were four women in the house, John explained, and three of them were psychics, who were helping with the work. They lived as a community, and he had bought a neighbouring house, which he would show us in due course. The two houses comprised a small estate, and they were putting two acres of land under cultivation so that they could grow their own food. Their ultimate aim was that the community should be as self-sufficient as possible. They had even installed a generator and laid down several thousand gallons of diesel fuel. The purpose of all this was that if any crisis arose they would be able to continue with the work they were engaged on.

Richard and I were intrigued. What work could involve a renegade and prodigal English aristocrat and a maverick American scientist shutting themselves away in Ossining with four women? Well, John said, he was going to tell us, because although a lot of the work was still highly confidential the time was coming when it would have to be more widely known. Even though those involved still had some doubts about the source and nature of the information they had got, they felt the time had come when they had to lay their reputations on the line and, with appropriate reticence, seek means of getting the information across to more people.

Maybe I would be able to help. John had liked the fair and open-minded way I had written up the May Lectures material, so at the risk of sending us away thinking him nuts he was going to tell us.

I was familiar with the general situation already, having heard Andrija's talk in London and read his book on Uri. But Andrija had only told a fraction of the story. Since March 1974 they had been in constant contact with 'the Management', i.e. the extra-terrestrial intelligences, and they now had tape recordings of over one hundred hours of communications with them.

I recalled that in Andrija's book there was quite a lot about communications with extra-terrestrials. Andrija and Uri had found that if they placed a tape-recorder on a table between them and waited, sometimes the 'start' button would be pressed down by some paranormal agency and a message would be imprinted directly on the tape. Two-way conversations had also been held in this way, some of which Andrija had transcribed verbatim in his book, but unfortunately none of these recordings were available for others to hear, for as soon as Andrija had transcribed their contents the cassettes had dematerialised. Very conveniently, Andrija's critics had mocked, but that was a point which I had wondered about. If Andrija were simply a liar, he could, with his expertise in electronics, quite easily have produced some recordings of synthetic speech to support his claim. But by claiming that these beings he was in contact with first directly imprinted speech sounds on tape then made the cassettes dematerialise he was compounding improbabilities and certainly not speaking in a manner calculated to enhance his own credibility. I had puzzled over that without reaching any plausible explanation of Andrija's motivation other than the most absurd one that he was telling the truth. But now, it seemed, the Management had become less coy and had allowed one hundred hours of their communications to remain intact on tape. That really was rather interesting, because to synthesise that much speech out of electronic signals would have been no mean task.

But John explained that it wasn't exactly like that. In the present case, the Management had preferred to use human 'channels', that is, mediums in deep trance. That, I thought, was disappointing. I had read quite a bit about trance mediumship and spiritualism, and knew that although there were a few classic cases that still defied explanation, most of the phenomena could be explained in terms of abnormal psychology or extra-sensory perception. A century of psychical research and tens of thousands of hours of communications with alleged discarnate spirits had failed to turn up any really conclusive evidence for the existence of such entities, and it seemed to me that the existence of the Management, if it was attested only by mediumistic phenomena, must be equally if not more dubious.

I kept these thoughts to myself, because you don't argue rationally with a man once you begin to suspect he's just a misguided crank. But John must have either anticipated or intuited my objections, for he went on to explain that he had gone through months of doubt and suspicion, during which he had examined every possible explanation of the communications that he could think of – that they emanated from the mediums' subconscious minds, that they came telepathically from the participants, particularly Andrija, and even that the whole thing was a hoax designed to relieve him of some of his considerable inherited fortune – and finally he had had to reject all these normal explanations and accept the communications at their face value. Of course, he expected others to have the same problems and questions as he had had, and he didn't expect others to make the same kind of commitment as he was making, for as he saw it he had nothing to lose except his money whereas others might well feel that commitment would put their reputations, their careers and even their family lives in jeopardy. Andrija was a case in point. He had lost much more than he could possibly have gained by his involvement. His professional credibility was tarnished and his previous work in this area had not helped his marriage. There were in fact quite a few eminent people who knew about the work and would probably become active in it at the right time, but who for the present had to sit on the fence in order to safeguard their professional integrity and credibility. As far as he himself was concerned, John felt that the wealth he had inherited, and the freedom of movement and independence it had given him, had been a preparation for the role he was to play.

The main thing that had convinced him that the communications were not a run of the mill psychical phenomenon but emanated from an external source was the range and variety of the information they conveyed. The Management had been observers of the Earth's history for millennia, and had intervened in it on several occasions in the past, and their communications contained a wealth of detail about the origins and progress of civilisations, the origins of languages and mythologies, and the roles of historical figures. Also there was an entire cosmology, comprising information about five different extra-terrestrial civilisations, their inter-relations, their technologies, and about how the Earth related to this cosmic scheme. The Management knew about contemporary political situations and events on Earth, and sometimes gave some intriguing information about what went on behind the scenes, and they were particularly concerned about the Middle East situation. And there was much more, there were other areas and subjects, there was a lot of wisdom and coherent teaching, and it was inconceivable, John thought, that all this could have emanated from the mind of the medium or any of the participants, or even from them all collectively. He had asked all the obvious questions about the provenance of the material, and now he was ninety-five per cent satisfied that the communications were what they claimed to be, and he was prepared to put in abeyance the residual five per cent of doubt, or rather incredulity, and come right out and declare in appropriate circles in the near future that he and the others at Ossining were in contact with beings from another part of the cosmos who were benevolently disposed towards the inhabitants of Earth and were going to be among us in the near future in order to provide the guidance that we urgently needed at this critical juncture in history.

Richard and I, as may be imagined, were somewhat stunned to be regaled with all this instead of with the anticipated lunch. It was a fascinating experience, something it would be fun to write home about, and I enjoyed the novelty and irony of being able to do the old British act of showing off one of our aristocratic eccentrics to our American cousins in a situation that had the additional piquancy of taking place right on the American cousin's doorstep. Well, we all have our subjective defence mechanisms against novelty and strangeness, and mine were such thoughts as these. The Queen in *Alice in Wonderland* reproached Alice for not having had enough practice in believing impossible things, and boasted that she sometimes believed as many as six impossible things before breakfast. Well, we were being asked to believe as many before lunch, and although I at least had had some recent practice in suspending disbelief, I was still far from graduating in sheer credulity, and certainly wasn't prepared for the challenges of this particular wonderland. My sympathies were with Alice.

About three o'clock Melanie came in and asked if anyone would like to eat, as if it were a novel idea that had just occurred to her. So we went into another room where about ten people were already assembled around a big table colourfully laden with wholesome salads, cheeses, fruit and home-baked brown loaves. Conversation over lunch was largely about the absent Andrija, about how he tended to take too much on himself and how other members of the community might in future unobtrusively relieve him of some of the work. I sat between John and an elderly lady who turned to me once and volunteered the information that some days ago she had seen a cigar-shaped UFO hovering over Manhattan, and was silent throughout the rest of the meal. After lunch John took us round the estate. His own house was about two hundred yards from Andrija's, down a driveway, and between the two lay a small lake. Adjoining his house there was a large barn which was in the process of being converted into a studio-office with living quarters for guests. The house, the conversion, the big generator, the tanks of stored fuel, the land under cultivation, all bespoke a substantial capital investment in the work.

Finally we were shown the place where it all happened, the 'cage'. I had read in Andrija's book, *Beyond Telepathy*, about the use of a Faraday cage in his experiments with Eileen Garrett, but this was the first time I had seen such a structure. Their Faraday cage is a rectangular metal box of dimensions $8 \times 8 \times 12$ feet, which is lined with copper and placed on insulating supports and constitutes a complete electrical vacuum. When the door is shut no electro-magnetic waves can penetrate the cage, and the electrical environment within the cage can be controlled for experimental purposes. Inside the cage there were three chairs and a table on which stood some expensive-looking recording equipment and a small portable TV set. John demonstrated the electro-magnetic shielding property of the cage by switching on the TV set and slowly shutting the door of the cage. The picture remained on the screen up to the point when there was just about a quarter-inch crack for the signal to get through. Then John sharply pulled the door shut, the screen became blank, and I caught in Richard's eyes a fleeting expression of claustrophobic alarm, which I confess I momentarily felt too. I thought of Kurt Vonnegut's Billy Pilgrim in the novel *Slaughterhouse-5*, who had been kidnapped by the little green men of the planet Tralfamadore and caged in their zoo.

There was an interesting story about how they had acquired the cage, John said. Some time ago, they had been having some technological difficulties in the communications sessions, and the Management had indicated that some protective improvements had to be made in the system. The following day, out of the blue, Puharich had received a call from a company that was going bankrupt and wanted to dispose of a Faraday cage cheaply and quickly. They had bought it and instantly found that their channelling problems were solved and the communications came through much more easily when they held their sessions inside the cage. This was one of many synchronistic events (Jung's term for events that are meaningfully but non-causally connected) John said, which regularly happened in connection with their work, and which for them constituted further evidence of the objective reality of the Management.

When we were back in the sitting-room and John had talked some more about the work, he finally got round to saying that he wondered whether our visit at this time was just a chance social call or another of those synchronistic events. Perhaps the Management had their eye on me, he said with a laugh; perhaps they were behind this seemingly casual visit; perhaps they wanted to use me in some way. I wasn't very comfortable with that idea, which again reminded me of Tralfamadore and the fate of poor Billy Pilgrim.

That was that. I was in the States for a couple of weeks, but didn't pay another visit to Ossining. The visit had been an interesting experience, something to file away in memory for possible future use in some form or other. A few days after it I had lunch in New York with a scientist from the Stanford Research Institute. I knew he was familiar with the Ossining set-up, and I asked him what he thought of it. 'It's either the most bizarre and crazy thing happening on this planet, or it's the most important,' he said. He was one of the fence-sitters John had mentioned. To me, 'bizarre' seemed just about the right word.

That was just over a year ago from the time of this writing. I had a busy year, having contracted to complete three books, and had virtually forgotten about Ossining and the Management when, one day in September 1975, I received a transatlantic call from John. The work we had talked about that Sunday when I visited, he said, had been progressing, and they had received definite indications from the Management that it was time for a book about the communications to be written and published. Would I be interested? Of course, I didn't have to commit myself on the information I had at that time, but if I was interested in principle he would send me some tapes of the communications to listen to and we would be able to meet and discuss the project in a few weeks' time, when he would be in England. I agreed, considering that I had nothing to lose and it would be interesting anyway to hear some of the communications, and a few days later the tapes arrived, together with some written background material about how the whole thing had started and the people involved in it.

I received some odd looks and comments from my family

in the course of the next few days. On several occasions my wife or one of the children came into my study while I was listening, and on hearing the queer sounds emanating from my hi-fi quite forgot the purpose of the call. I'm regarded by friends and family as a fairly rational, intellectual type, and for me to be listening to communications with alleged 'Space Gods' was considered amusingly off-beat. They soon became used to it, though, as I became used to the initial strangeness of the tapes. The strangeness is in the language, the syntax, the tone of the communications delivered through the channel (the medium Phyllis V. Schlemmer), and also sometimes in the manner of the communicants, who are mainly John and Andrija, which can be embarrassingly deferential and awed. I felt sometimes that I was eavesdropping on a very private ritual, and sceptical questions kept occurring to me. Were these two clever men the dupes of a cleverer woman? It was a strange inconsistency that in many of the communications there was an excess of 'thats' and 'ofs' and a number of circumlocutions which sounded like a deliberate attempt to avoid literacy, whereas in others the language was incisive, uncluttered and sometimes even quite eloquent and aphoristic. Also, when John or Andrija asked a difficult question, the voice often said, 'We will consult', and there followed a long pause during which the spokesman for the extra-terrestrials was supposed to be telepathically communicating with his peers, but which could be a pause to give Phyllis an opportunity to think up an answer.

As Thomas Aquinas said (though not in so many words), it is unphilosophical, unscientific and ultimately unintelligent to invoke a supernatural explanation of a phenomenon before you have eliminated every natural explanation. When confronted with the weird and wonderful, a man's first reaction tends to be to try and rationalise it, and that's what I was doing all the time I was listening to those first tapes. I eventually became quite satisfied that the minimal hypothesis, that of a deliberate fraud or hoax, could be ruled out. I had some biographical material on Phyllis, and a tape of her talking about herself and her life, and I was satisfied not only that she could not possibly possess all the knowledge that she channelled but also that she could have nothing to gain by deception, particularly as the sessions often severely depleted her physical and psychic energies.

So my first hours of exposure to the communications convinced me that they were genuinely paranormal and of great interest. But the second minimal hypothesis was not so easily dismissed as the first. The second would be that they were normally paranormal, that is to say, attributable to telepathy or the emergence of a secondary personality in the medium's trance state. There are many precedents in the annals of psychical research of mysterious communications of considerable length and showing great ingenuity and powers of invention, which have come through mediums in trance. There is the 'Patience Worth' case, recorded by Dr Walter Franklin Prince, in which a St Louis housewife with an eighth-grade education produced over a period of five years a million and a half words by automatic writing, including long novels and poems and a wealth of aphoristic wit and wisdom, all in highly literate and colloquial seventeenth-century English. There is the contemporary case of the Brazilian trance author Chico Xavier, who has produced something like one hundred and thirty books, allegedly posthumous works of known Brazilian writers, which are consistent in style and subject matter with the works those authors wrote while alive. There is the book, *A Vision*, which the wife of the poet W. B. Yeats wrote in trance, and which contains a cosmology, a philosophy and a wealth of imagery that the poet drew on in composing some of his greatest work. And there is the case of the Rev. Stainton Moses' *Spirit Teachings*, which has some remarkable correspondences with the Ossining communications. Between 1872 and 1883, Stainton Moses filled twenty-four notebooks with automatic writing. His communicators purported to be illustrious Biblical characters, and they informed their amanuensis that a missionary effort to uplift the human race was being made in the spirit realms and he had been chosen as a channel for their communications. These are four classic cases of automatism, and there are scores of others, and the conclusion that Prince reached in his study of the Patience Worth material applies to all of them: 'Either our concept of what we call the subconscious mind must be radically altered so as to include potencies of which we hitherto have had no knowledge, or else some cause operating through, but not originating in, the subconscious of Mrs Curran [the medium] must be acknowledged.' The Ossining communications, it seemed to me after I had heard some hours of the recordings, posed the same dilemma.

But this case differs from the other cases of paranormal communications above-mentioned in that the objective reality of the communicators is theoretically verifiable, for they claim to be actively engaged in the affairs of our world, to intervene in certain ways, and to be able to predict future events. And as we shall see in later chapters, some of the statements, and particularly some of the predictions made in the communications, are very impressive.

Another thing that puts this case in a different category from others is the amount of correlated activity the communications have already engendered. Among the first batch of tapes I listened to was one about a trip to the Middle East which John, Andrija and Phyllis made in November 1974, at the request of the Management. The purpose of the trip was nothing less than to help avert an imminent crisis in the Middle East by influencing the Russian leaders in Moscow *by meditation*, and the instructions of the Management were that the three should make a crescent-shaped tour, keeping within 1,500 miles of Moscow, and should engage in meditation periodically in order to transmit the required psychic energy. To undertake such a trip obviously demanded a considerable investment, not only of money but also of faith and trust, and on the face of it the entire enterprise would appear to be crackpot and incredibly presumptuous. But the Management said it was necessary, so off the three went from New York to Helsinki, then to Warsaw, Ankara, Tehran, Moscow and back via Copenhagen, where they were assured that their mission had been a success. In explaining their strategy of psychic influence, the communicators showed a shrewd insight into the Russian mind. They said: 'It is an emotional mind. But with great love and strong meditation a simple mind may be made to feel, and then in turn come to some sense. There is a difference between a simple mind that thinks it is intelligent and a simple mind that is simple in ignorance and with emotion. The Russian leaders are more emotional, and with meditation and strong prayer and a link with all, we can work on the emotion to stabilise it. The problem with Russia has always been the emotion.' That's not a bad assessment for an extra-terrestrial.

So the quixotic travellers completed their journey, but they had no way of knowing for certain that their money and faith had been well invested, for at the start they had only the Management's word for it that a crisis was imminent, and at the end they only had the Management's assurance that they had been instrumental in averting it. However, it is perhaps relevant to recall that there is a meditation room in the United Nations Building in New York, and also that the great modern Indian saint, Sri Aurobindo, a man of no mean intellectual capacity, claimed that the strengthening of the Russian resistance during the siege of Stalingrad was due to the power he generated through meditation. The idea of psychic influence on world events is not exclusive to our extra-terrestrial friends and their Ossining confederates.

I have mentioned the 1974 Middle East adventure as an example of an action initiated by the communicators. There are other types of such actions, or rather programmes, for work in these several areas is continuing. There are investigations of children who can produce the 'Geller effect' of bending metal, there is work with psychic healers, and there is a research programme involving dolphins and porpoises (aquatic superminds also allegedly 'in service' with the Management). The work of the community and their associates ramifies in many directions and involves activities all over the world, some of which have been topics of public attention and debate over recent years. To pursue the ramifications of their story is to see emerge a portrait of an age, our age, a portrait in which are delineated its deepest concerns, its discoveries and adventures, its fears, hopes, longings, and yes, perhaps also its follies. Even if the questions of the provenance, the authenticity and the veridical content of the communications were put aside, the story would be worth telling just because it focuses and inter-relates aspects of the emergent new consciousness of this end-quarter of the twentieth century.

But in the end the most exciting part of the story is the part that is most contentious, dubious and hard to swallow. When the parapsychological and socio-cultural aspects of the case have been thoroughly explored, there remains to be considered the question whether the communications can conceivably be what they purport to be. Is there even a remote possibility that our planet has long been under the surveillance and occasionally under the direct influence of intelligent forces from some other part of the cosmos? To do the communications justice, we have to venture into this area where speculation is rife and hard facts are difficult to come by. There is a vast literature about UFOs and extra-terrestrial visitors to our planet, and to judge by the success of the books of Erich von Daniken, Pauwels and Bergier, and Brinsley le Poer Trench, there is a large public avid to believe in the existence of the 'Space Gods'. The unscholarly and wildly conjectural approach adopted in most of the UFO literature has tended to polarise attitudes towards uncritical belief on the one hand and total rejection of the possibilities on the other. Rational men who want no truck with the 'lunatic fringe' can scarcely be prevailed upon rationally to consider such evidence as there is for the existence and activities of extra-terrestrials. Some may go as far as Carl Jung went in his 1947 essay, *Flying Saucers*, and concede that UFOs have a kind of objective existence as psychic exteriorisation phenomena, and that the world-wide sightings of them over recent decades are symptomatic of 'a wave of hope in the reappearance of Christ'. Religions, of course, have always taught the existence of a supramundane intelligence, and divine intervention in human affairs and history, so the idea is not unfamiliar. And if we take a look beyond the popular literature and the scholarly acrimony it has engendered, and shelve the plausible Jungian hypothesis for a time, we find that a surprising number of people who are in a position to be better informed than most do not find the idea of the existence and interventions of extra-terrestrials inherently implausible.

When I had listened to the first batch of tapes and had begun to take seriously the possibility of venturing upon the present book, I sought through books immediately to hand in my own modest library and within half an hour turned up a number of facts that began to erode my basic scepticism about extra-terrestrials. I found, for instance, that in 1971 an international conference, sponsored jointly by the American and Russian Academies of Science, had been convened in Armenia and had launched 'Project Cyclops', an international research project on the practical possibilities and foreseeable consequences of establishing contact with extra-terrestrial beings. The following year a symposium entitled 'Life Beyond Earth and the Mind of Man' was organised by Professor Richard Berendzen of Boston University. Professor Berendzen, an astronomer, stated that recent developments in the sciences 'strongly indicate the high probability of the existence of extra-terrestrial life'. He had also suggested, I learned, that an effective way of communicating with extra-terrestrials might be through psychic channels. And in a book co-authored by Professor Carl Sagan of Cornell and Professor Josif Shklovsky of Moscow University, entitled *Intelligent Life in the Universe*, the suggestion is put forward that the ancient Sumerians may have had contact with the space people. The researches of the philosopher-mathematician Dr Charles Muses into ancient mythology and symbolism point to the same conclusion.

Furthermore, the sober calculations of astrophysicists and exobiologists of the possibilities of the existence of intelligent life elsewhere in the universe are staggering. Dr Frank Drake of Cornell estimates that one in ten million stars possesses a detectable civilisation. This modest figure would yield a total of between a hundred thousand and a million in our galaxy alone. That a proportion of these should be older and technologically more advanced civilisations than ours is a possibility that can hardly be dismissed out of hand without incurring a charge of narrow-minded planetary chauvinism. Our own space technology is barely fifteen years old, and the Apollo project of landing men on the moon was accomplished within six years of its inception, so who is to say that other civilisations possessed of aeons of technological expertise in advance of ours might not exist and long ago have conquered interstellar space and evolved technologies beyond the boldest imaginings of our scientists and science-fiction writers?

These were some of the facts and arguments that disposed me to take more seriously than I had on the day I first visited Ossining the idea that the communications may not be fraud, delusion or a parapsychological phenomenon but precisely what John and Andrija believed them to be: messages from the space people. I could think of a score of reasons why the proposition was absurd, but if there was the remotest possibility that it might be true, it was obviously worth investigating the evidence more deeply. When I accepted the invitation to be the chronicler of the Ossining group's adventure, I confess that just for a moment I entertained the thought that it would be stupid to pass up a possible opportunity to be a witness to a new apocalypse. But I suppressed the thought no sooner than it surfaced, well aware that of all the tutelary spirits I could choose to accompany me on this particular venture, the most inappropriate would be those that bore the names 'faith' and 'hope'.

Since the above pages were written nine months have elapsed, I have listened to the recordings of all the communications, participated in some myself, and completed this book, and I would now like to add a few pages to this introductory chapter in the light of these experiences.

I was apprehensive, when I embarked on this book, that I might reach a point where I could no longer continue with the work. It was possible that when I had heard more of the material and had analysed it and thought about it, I would become convinced that a perfectly normal, or what I have called a normally paranormal explanation of it could be plausibly adduced, in which case I would be obliged by the ethics of intellectual integrity to wield Occam's razor and cut out all extravagant hypotheses such as the existence of extra-terrestrials. But this hasn't happened. Increasing familiarity with the material of the communications and with the people involved has only consolidated my feeling that this is one of the most remarkable true stories that any writer ever had dropped into his lap, and also increased my puzzlement as to where the communications could emanate from if not from the alleged extra-terrestrial intelligence.

When I first visited Ossining and John said with a laugh that he wondered whether my appearance at that time was as casual as it seemed and whether the Management might not have a plan to use me in some way, I frankly thought him crackers. But when I listened to the tapes I understood why the thought might have occurred to him. Two days before I visited Ossining, in fact on the very day that I arrived in New York and before I had contacted John, he and Andrija were told in a communication: 'There will be those that will come to you this weekend that will be of benefit. There will be a time when they will walk away moving their heads back and forth and will not understand. But then they will sit and they will think and they will have an experience and they will begin to understand. And then they will work with you. We have decided that those that work with you must begin to have experiences for them to have understanding. There are not many in your physical world that operate on faith, as you do, Sir John.'

When I asked John whether anyone else had visited Ossining that weekend, he couldn't recall whether anyone had but he was certain that no one had visited who had later become involved in the work. He had quite forgotten about the prediction in the communication held on the Friday, but when I drew his attention to it he said, 'I'm sure that was intended for you.' Well, maybe. After listening through all the tapes I have become inured to the shock of seeing an extraordinary prediction fulfilled.

The rest of the above-quoted prediction is true, too, that is, if it was intended for me. I did walk away shaking my head, and I did have a couple of experiences of seemingly para-normal effects, though these did not contribute to my under-standing so much as to my perplexity. I will relate them because this kind of thing is an integral part of the story, and I trust that what is straight reportage will not be misconstrued as advocacy. These things happened, and nothing remotely like them had ever happened in my experience before, but the only grounds I have for associating them with the Manage-ment is that they happened when they did.

The first was a 'poltergeist' type of event. It happened in October 1975, not long after I had received the first parcel of specimen material from John and at a time when I was debating with myself whether I could undertake this book. Late one night I, my wife and a friend watched a television programme in the sitting-room of my home. The programme had a soporific effect on the other two, but I watched it through and at the end walked across the room and switched off the set. I then turned and spoke to the others and our friend woke up, and at that moment a potted plant on the mantel-piece behind me literally jumped out into the room and landed at my feet. When I realised what had happened, I said to our friend, 'Did you see that?' He said yes, he had seen it, the plant had jumped off the mantelpiece. We sought a normal explanation. The only possible one was that I had knocked the plant off after switching off the television. But to have done so would have required a most unnatural up-and-round swing of the arm, which I was certain I had not performed. More-over, the plant, which I later ascertained weighed just over five pounds, had not been toppled, but seemed to have been lifted, for it landed upright two or three feet away from the mantelpiece, and the saucer in which it stood was undisturbed. I remembered some of the tales I had heard about paranormal events at Ossining and around Uri, and I wondered.

The second event occurred when I had already begun working on the book. I played through one of the cassette tapes of a communication, making notes and transcribing rele-vant portions as I did so. I left the cassette in my player and did some writing, then later in the day I wound back to check a point, but now the track was completely blank. It certainly could not have been erased normally in the interim. And it was not until later that I discovered that this particular communication was one of the very few of which there existed a duplicate copy, which suggests that it was deliberately selected for demonstration purposes. I was impressed, much more impressed than I had been by reading Andrija's accounts of the more sensational teleportation and dematerialisation events that had occurred in connection with Uri, which is the reason I don't expect anyone else to be particularly impressed by these two anecdotes, though I think I had to report them as they were events that influenced my attitude to the work and the communications.

Another influence has been my own experience of communication sessions. I have participated in seven sessions over the past nine months. This is not the context to report them in detail, but perhaps a description of what a typical session is like will help the reader to have a mental picture of what is going on when communications are summarised in later chapters.

The first communication I participated in was at Orsett Hall, the former Whitmore ancestral home in Essex, now owned by John's close friend Tony Morgan. Phyllis had arrived from New York the previous day. Through listening to the tapes, including the one of her life story, I had formed an impression of a capable, resourceful, extrovert and probably rather formidable woman. To my relief I was wrong. Unostentatiously casual in dress and manner, rather short of stature with short blonde hair styled for convenience, talkative, fun-loving, down-to-earth, Phyllis seemed as normal and nice a person as one could meet. She is, but she's also something more.

She prefers to work late, so it was about one o'clock in the morning when she, John and I left the other members of the weekend house party talking in the drawing-room and went upstairs to Phyllis's room. She and John made the necessary preparations, arranging three upright chairs in close proximity, fixing the recording equipment, and putting on the copper bracelets that they have been instructed always to wear during sessions. During and for some time after these preparations, we continued the conversation we had been engaged in downstairs, which had nothing to do with our present purpose. Then John said we had better begin, Phyllis stubbed out her cigarette, composed herself in an upright posture with her hands resting on her knees and said she was ready, whereupon John switched off the room lights and placed a small torch in a position where it afforded us dim illumination but did not cast a direct light in Phyllis's direction. Phyllis began counting down from forty-five, her voice becoming softer and slower until she fell silent, her head slumped forward and to the left and her hands fell loosely down at her sides. She remained thus for a minute or two and then, very slowly, her head rose, her back straightened and her forearms came up to a horizontal position so that she was sitting as if holding a tray but with the palms of her hands turned inwards towards each other. Then her voice whispered, 'We are here', very low, completely exhaling on the last word. John said, 'Greetings Tom', and introduced me. 'Tom' is the name that the spokesman for the communicators has adopted for convenience of address, and here and in the sequel I shall also use it for convenience. Phyllis's voice soon became stronger, and through her Tom delivered a courteous, indeed flattering, long speech of welcome to me. The ending of the speech and the invitation to put a question were indicated by Phyllis's hands being lowered to her knees and Tom saying 'Yes.'

I was impressed by Tom's eloquence and I was both impressed and surprised to be told at one point in the communication precisely what I was thinking. Tom said, 'Now into your mind at this moment comes the thought that you wonder what you are doing communicating with us, and if it is in truth another from a distant place that is speaking to you.' That was indeed what I was thinking.

The main subject of this communication was the present book. I was given to believe that my meeting John when I did was not fortuitous, and that I could bring certain qualities into reporting the communications which someone more closely involved would not be able to contribute, not the least among which were doubt, scepticism and objectivity. 'You will be able to put the questions that will occur to people,' Tom said. This is a point I have continually borne in mind while writing this book.

Probably the main initial credibility hurdle for readers of this book will be that communications from an extra-terrestrial intelligence should come through a trance medium, and to conclude this chapter I propose to make a few observations on trance mediumship in general and on Phyllis's in particular.

What we are asked to believe happens when Phyllis is in deep trance is that she leaves her body and that Tom, the spokesman for the communicators, takes over control of her body and her vocal mechanisms. What we see happen is certainly consistent with this explanation, and the content of the communications is certainly such as to make nonsense of any simplistic sceptic's suspicion that it is all clever play-acting on Phyllis's part. But neither the content nor the observed events, nor the combination of the two, conclusively proves that this is in fact what happens, so we have to consider whether we have available any way round a simple 'believe it or not' option, to ask whether there is any other evidence we can call on which may at least affect the balance of probabilities even if it does not constitute a final elucidation of the truth of the matter.

We have three categories of such evidence: well-authenticated precedents from the literature of psychic research, certain statements that Phyllis has made about her trance experiences when she has returned to a normal waking state of consciousness, and relevant statements made in the communications themselves. Let us then see how the balance of probabilities is affected if we consider in turn the separate statements, (a) that Phyllis leaves her body during trance, and (b) that Tom takes possession of her body and control of its functions.

We have ample evidence for the reality of out-of-the-body

experiences, or to use an older and today less fashionable term, astral projections. The voluminous case records and scrupulous analyses of Dr Robert Crookall, the testimonies of experients such as Sylvan Muldoon, Oliver Fox and Robert Monroe, and the recent experimental researches of Drs Puthoff and Targ at the Stanford Research Institute and of Professor Charles T. Tart at the University of California, not to mention the many testimonies of people who have undergone pseudo-death experiences and been brought back to life, have established beyond doubt that there is a component of human personality – 'the bit of me that counts', as one experient called it – that in certain circumstances can separate from the physical body, leaving the latter merely an 'envelope' or 'shell'. The experience of separation of our essential self from our physical body that occurs somewhere between the many unseen bodies that are said to exist, such as the astral and the etheric, is in fact by no means uncommon, and although for most people who have them such experiences are involuntary and rare, some people have learnt and developed techniques for effecting separation at will. So the claim that during trance Phyllis leaves her body is neither outrageous nor inherently improbable.

'Most times I am not anywhere,' Phyllis says, referring to the times when she is in trance. She usually returns to normal consciousness as from a deep and dreamless sleep. She never has any recollection of the words she has spoken, but sometimes she retains vivid impressions of places she has visited while out of the body. And very often her post-session reports of her out-of-the-body experiences closely correspond with the information contained in the related communications. Some examples of these correspondences will be brought to the reader's attention in later chapters. The point I want to make here is that they constitute at least *prima facie* evidence for the authenticity of both the information and the post-session report.

If we accept on the basis of the evidence of psychical research and of her own testimony that Phyllis may indeed leave her body when in trance, the next question to consider is whether the vacated body and its functions can be taken over by an external agency. On this subject a very interesting statement was made by Tom in a communication in January 1975:

'The one whom we communicate through is a physical transmitter, and it has to be a being that is willing, that will become passive in order for us to become active . . . in order to communicate with you, we must take over the subconscious of the being, and at the same time control the physical body. We must, with great effort, maintain a balance in the body. We must cause the body to have its heart operating, its lungs breathing and all its major organs functioning. The reason for the drain of energy many times from the two of you is that we are maintaining the body in a suspended state.'

The second occasion when I personally participated in a communication was at a remote old house in South Herefordshire, and when Phyllis was coming out of trance she moaned, sobbed, rolled her head and screamed in a way that I found most alarming. John, who had conducted the session, did not appear to be perturbed by this performance, however. He held Phyllis's hands firmly and said, 'I command the immediate release of this being', and the symptoms of distress very quickly abated. 'Tell us what happened,' John said when Phyllis was fully conscious, and she told us a harrowing story about having to battle with another entity for possession of her body when she returned to it. 'They're still all around us,' she said, and I confess I looked around the room with some apprehension, but of course saw nothing. I asked what were all around, and Phyllis explained that when a human channel is opened scores of spirits and elementals rush to the spot like wasps to a jam pot, seeking to take possession and get back onto the physical plane. John added, I thought with impressive nonchalance, that there was nothing to worry about really because the physical is always stronger than the psychical and the would-be intruders could be driven off with a few well-chosen words. Which I thought was nice to know and could come in useful some day; but the point of this anecdote is that for Phyllis the possibility of possession by alien entities is very much a reality.

It has been a reality, too, for many people involved in

psychical research. To survey the evidence here would require too long a digression, and I can only recommend anyone concerned to pursue the matter to consult Richard Hodgson's report on the Lurancy Vennums (the 'Watseka Wonder') case or Dr Ian Stevenson on the case of Jasbir Jat. James Hyslop, who was Professor of Logic and Ethics at Columbia University as well as a notable psychical researcher, wrote that although he had fought against the idea for ten years he was finally unable to reject the conclusion that: 'In a number of cases, persons whose condition would ordinarily be described as due to hysteria, dual or multiple personality, dementia precox, paranoia, or some other form of mental disturbance, showed unmistakable indications of invasion by foreign or discarnate agencies.' Hyslop meant spirits, but his 'foreign agencies' could just as well have been extra-terrestrial intelligences.

In the light of the evidence surveyed in the above paragraphs, I suggest that we may consider the antecedent improbability of the propositions that in trance Phyllis leaves her body and Tom takes over, greatly diminished. If the reader agrees, he will have cleared the first of the credibility hurdles. And if he stays with this narrative the exercise will serve him in good stead, for there are and much bigger hurdles to come.

CHAPTER TWO

# The Forming of the Triangle

To put it baldly and boldly, this book is a story of a scientist, a psychic and an aristocrat who were brought together in order to help bring mankind through a time of crisis.

Though formed by widely different backgrounds and experiences, the lives of Andrija Puharich, Phyllis Virtue Schlemmer and Sir John Whitmore converged early in 1974 through a series of events so extraordinary that they could not but see them as a part of an organised plan. With but little demur they fell in with the plan, the fruition of which lies ahead of the time covered by this narrative, but to date the scientist has seriously damaged his reputation, the psychic has seen the collapse of her family life and former business interests, and the aristocrat has spent a substantial portion of his patrimony. So at first sight the story is one of an immense and presumptuous folly.

Some would put it down to omnipotence fantasy or delusions of grandeur, and the possibility of casting two of the protagonists into the stereotypes of the deranged scientist and the prodigal heir to a distinguished lineage lends some plausibility to this view of the matter. But really it is too glib a view, which leaves too much out of account. If we must go in for psychological speculation – which we must if only because everyone else will, rather than accept the story at its face value – it would, I think, be subtler and more apposite to think of these three not as seeking the satisfaction of exercising power but rather that of being exercised by it. The sense of being in service to a cause, of having a personal destiny bound up with the destiny of something greater and more significant than self, is surely an under-acknowledged component of the motivation of much extraordinary behaviour. By any standard, the behaviour of these three people has been extraordinary. Whether they were chosen or self-elected, guided or deluded into embracing their exacting and strange mission, may be moot points, but a point there can be no doubt about is that they have had the rare and heady satisfaction of believing themselves to have been recruited into service. By whom or what, and what purpose they have served, could be questions of concern to all of us.

Phyllis's parents were hoteliers in Pennsylvania, and they entrusted her upbringing up to the age of twelve, when she went into a convent school, to her grandparents, who were Irish on her father's side and Italian on her mother's. She lived mainly with her Irish grandparents, the Virtues, but spent the summers on her Italian grandparents' grape farm. Both of her grandmothers, she says, were psychic, and her Italian grandmother was also a medium, and she recalls vividly the experience that, considered retrospectively, was the beginning of her own mediumship.

She was five years old when her Irish grandfather, Thomas Virtue, died in 1934. He had eleven children, most of them daughters, and when he was dying the family came home from all over the world. In the middle of one night, Phyllis recalls, she was awakened and taken down to her grandfather's bedroom to say goodbye to him. Everyone in the room was weeping and mourning, and when she went in she wondered what was going on because she could see her grandfather standing beside the bed. On the bed was a big doll that looked like him, and she couldn't understand why they were all crying and what they were doing with the big doll. 'You must feel gran'pa's feet, then you'll know he's gone to God,' said her aunt, and she was lifted up to touch the ice-cold feet of the doll and to kiss its cheek, and she was puzzled because all the time there was the living form of her grandfather standing beside the bed. As not all members of the family had been able to get home in time, the corpse was laid out in a downstairs room for four or five days before the funeral. In the middle of the night, Phyllis would get up and go to the room and try to lift the doll out of its box, and she would talk to her grandfather, whom she frequently met wandering around the house. The family thought that she was undergoing a traumatic experience and refusing to accept her grandfather's death, and on the day of the funeral she was not allowed to go to the cemetery or to the mass. 'I member distinctly the day of his funeral,' she says. 'I was out playing hopscotch, and he was playing hopscotch with me. I thought this really great, because he'd never been able to play hopscotch before because his legs hurt. And I remember when they were bringing the coffin out my uncle Tom picked me up and moved me off the sidewalk, and I said to my grandfather, "Don't you want to go with the big doll?" And he said no, it was okay.'

Her family didn't allow Phyllis to talk to her grandmother until the day after the funeral, for they felt that grandma Virtue had enough to cope with emotionally and shouldn't be further distressed by the child's seemingly wild talk, but when Phyllis did finally talk to her and told her that gran'pa wasn't dead but was right there with them, her grandmother, she says, 'immediately recognised what was going on'. She considers that she was fortunate, on this as on later occasions, to have someone to reassure her that what she experienced was at least a known phenomenon if not a common one.

At the convent she was made to feel guilty for professing to see auras and spirits, and she had one experience that made her withdrawn and fearful of her own apparent powers. She had a quarrel with a nun and in anger told her that God would punish her, and the evening of the same day the nun had a seizure as she was going into church, collapsing and foaming at the mouth. If she could do such things to people, Phyllis felt, those who said she was a witch and evil must be right, and it wasn't until some years later that she confessed her fears and their cause to the Mother Superior, who told her that the nun was an epileptic and it was no doubt just an unfortunate coincidence that her seizure at the entrance to the church had occurred after their quarrel.

Phyllis had to learn to live with her faculties of paranormal perception, and there were times when it was not easy, and throughout childhood and adolescence she was very much a solitary. She could not conceive of devoting her life and her abilities to the service of the Church, though she was at times put under strong pressure to do so, for there were those in her family who believed that if with her endowment she did not serve God through His Church she must perforce serve the Devil. She did in fact on occasions serve the Church in an unofficial capacity, by accompanying priests who performed exorcisms. She recalls one particular priest who, when she was a college sophomore, she accompanied on several (unofficial) exorcisms, and who, after solemnly performing the rites, would turn to her and say, 'Has it gone, Phyllis?'

At college she studied science subjects because she wanted to be a doctor, but she left before graduating in order to get married. Four years of domesticity (she had two children) and business (she and her husband owned three restaurants) followed, but when she was twenty-four the marriage broke down and she took the children to Miami, where, starting from scratch and after some arduous years, she gradually built up her business interests and her reputation as a psychic. One of her businesses was a salvage company, and it prospered so rapidly because of her ability to locate sunken vessels psychically that a rival sabotaged their salvage boat.

For the sake of the growing children, she moved from Miami to Orlando, Florida. She also married again, and her husband, Norman Schlemmer, helped with her business interests. As a psychic, she was engaged by many corporations and also did medical diagnostic work. She assisted police, mining companies (she once psychically located coal in Ohio), and had a successful television series, but her main interest and occupation was her work at the Psychic Center of Florida. The Center, which Phyllis established, was a school for the development of psychic faculties, and her courses soon became booked to capacity.

In January 1974, a young man who for the purposes of this narrative will be known as Bobby Horne started attending a course at the school. Bobby, a short order cook from Daytona Beach, some sixty miles from Orlando, had come to Phyllis's attention some two months before, when she had been prevailed upon to go to his home to try to put a stop to some poltergeist-type events that had been happening there. She had apparently been successful, and some days later she had received a call from Bobby begging her to let him join one of her psychic development classes. She had told him he couldn't join before January, thinking that his enthusiasm might wane before then, but promptly on the first day of the new year's first session Bobby turned up for class. He had only been attending for two or three weeks when he became the central figure of attention, for things began happening around him.

Phyllis says that she first realised that Bobby had ability as a psychic healer when she 'saw the healing aura around him'. He was sitting in class next to a woman who was due to have an operation for an eardrum perforation which made her completely deaf on one side. On Phyllis's instructions, Bobby attempted a 'laying on of hands' type of healing, and within two days the woman's hearing was restored. Another class member had a diabetic ulcer, which was disposed of within four days of Bobby's treating it. Paranormal healing was not a novel phenomenon in Phyllis's experience, but Bobby's abilities profoundly impressed her.

She was even more impressed when, on 21 February, Bobby came to her with a story and evidence of a healing he had performed out of class. A friend of his named Reg, who was a welder in a workshop near his home in Daytona Beach, had come to him two days before and asked him to drive him to hospital. He had had an accident at work with an acetylene torch and had suffered a third degree burn on the underside of his right arm. He had covered the burn with grease, but he was in great pain and needed treatment. When Reg appeared at his house, Bobby was outside taking photographs of his children, and when he saw Reg's burn he wondered whether his new-found healing abilities might be effective on it. Reg just wanted to be taken to hospital, but Bobby persuaded him to let him try just at least to reduce the pain by laying his hands over the burn for a few minutes. As his loaded camera was to hand, Bobby took some pictures of the burn before he attempted the healing. For about eight minutes he held his hands over the burn, and when he removed them, to his own astonishment as well as Reg's, the arm was completely healed. Instead of grease and charred flesh there was clear and intact new skin which was distinguishable from the surrounding skin only because there were no hairs on it. Bobby took some more pictures, and a couple of days later went to Phyllis with his amazing story and photographic evidence. Phyllis checked Bobby's account of what had happened with his wife and with the healee, who both substantiated it. She was personally sufficiently satisfied that the story and the pictures were authentic that she decided this was a case worthy of the attention of the famed investigator of the outstanding healers and psychics of the age, Dr Andrija Puharich, whom she had met at a conference some years before and on a number of occasions since.

To judge from his own accounts, Andrija Puharich must have seen more miracles, and a greater variety of them, than any living man in our Western culture. To hear him talk about them, in his gentle, unemphatic, matter-of-fact way, is to experience an unnerving distortion of one's sense of reality. Short of stature but powerfully built and barrel-chested, with a shock of thick greying hair and a bristly grey-black moustache that curls up at its extremities, he looks like a gnomic Einstein. He is professorial and dry and wears half-moon spectacles when he is lecturing from notes, and many audiences who have heard him speak in recent years have experienced the difficulty of reconciling his manner and appearance with the way-out content of his talk.

His academic and career credentials as a scientist are impeccable. He has been prolific of invention and innovation in the fields of medical electronics, neurophysiology, biocybernetics, ESP research, and holds fifty-six US and foreign patents for his inventions. Such work could only have been accomplished by a man who was scientifically scrupulous, patient, diligent and attentive to detail. But aside from his orthodox scientific work, Andrija Puharich has, over a period of thirty years, applied his scientific expertise to a study of parapsychological and paraphysical phenomena which has involved him in close co-operation with and observation of some of the most gifted psychics of the period.

Eileen Garrett, Peter Hurkos, Harry Stone, Arigó, and Uri Geller comprise, as anyone familiar with the literature of parapsychological research will know, a formidable group, and that one man should have worked with all of them is itself remarkable. No pattern of life experiences could more thoroughly have prepared a man to take prodigies in his stride and to accept a role as nuncio and intermediary in man's cosmic connection. It almost appears contrived; like a planned process of gradual initiation, a process of gentle persuasion leading by degrees from the improbable to the imponderable. His work with Mrs Garrett and Peter Hurkos was in the comparatively respectable area of ESP research, studies of paranormal mental faculties such as telepathy and clairvoyance. With the Indian scholar, Dr Vinod, whom he says he met by chance in New York in 1951, he had his first experiences of the physical phenomena of mediumship such as materialisations, and also through him obtained his first intimations of the existence of non-human intelligences. Then in 1963 he was in Brazil on a mission connected with the US National Aeronautics and Space Agency, and again 'quite by accident' he heard about the phenomenal psychic surgeon José Pedro de Freitas, known as Arigó, who with any rusty old knife and no anaesthetics or sutures would perform in rapid succession a series of operations each of which an entire hospital team would normally take twenty times as long to perform. Puharich paid several visits to Brazil to study and film Arigó in action, and it was during these visits, he says, that he first became aware of UFOs, and actually photographed some. Shortly after Arigó's death in an automobile accident in 1971, Puharich heard about Uri Geller and went to Israel to meet him. He later brought Geller to Europe and

46

the United States for investigation by scientists, and he reports having witnessed phenomena that make the famed spoon- and key-bending feats look like child's play, such as Geller's being teleported in a flash from East 57th Street in New York City to the verandah of the Ossining house.

Depending on your point of view, Puharich's career as a psychic investigator may look like a process of preparation for his extraordinary ambassadorship or one of gradual decline of sense and judgment. One fact that may favour the former view is that the motif of the cosmic connection has come through apparently independently of Puharich in several of his investigations of these remarkable psychics. Geller hypothesised that his powers had been invested in him by extraterrestrials, and that as a child while playing in a garden he had been struck unconscious by a blinding ray of light emitted from the head of an immense figure that had appeared. To almost any other psychic investigator but Puharich such a claim would have seemed preposterous, but by the time he met Uri, Puharich had had some experiences of UFOs and had had some communications with an alleged cosmic intelligence through the mediumship of Dr Vinod.

In 1952, Dr Vinod had channelled a series of strange communications full of complex scientific and mathematical concepts which purported to come from 'The Nine'. On a visit to Puharich's research laboratory in Maine, this Indian sage and psychic went into a trance and suddenly started speaking in a voice totally different from his own. The communications began: 'M calling. We are Nine Principles and Forces, personalities if you will, working in complete mutual implication. We are forces, and the nature of our work is to accentuate the positive, the evolutional, and the teleological aspects of existence. We propose to work with you [addressed to Puharich] in some essential respects . . . We want to begin altogether at a different dimension, though it is true that your work has itself led up to this . . . We have designed to utilise you and thus to fulfil you. Peace is a process and will be revealed only progressively. You have in plenty the patience which is so deeply needed in this magnificent adventure. But today, at the moment of our advent, the most eventful and spectacular phase of your work begins.' These communications, which were never published, continued for many months but terminated when the attendant group split up and Dr Vinod returned to his home in India.

That was nearly twenty years before Puharich met Geller and twenty-two years before regular communications with 'The Nine' were resumed, and in the interim Puharich's research work did indeed become increasingly spectacular, though some who would use the word would intend it pejoratively. Meanwhile he continued his more orthodox scientific work and consolidated a reputation as an innovator in electronic medical technology, thus maintaining the respect of his scientific peers despite his eccentric excursions into the dubious peripheries of the paranormal. But through his involvement with Geller and the publication of his book on him in 1974, he went right out on a limb, apparently deserting science for science fiction, declaring publicly that he and Uri had been in direct contact with an extra-terrestrial civilisation and were the appointed harbingers of a forthcoming mass landing of UFOs on Earth. The message, however, didn't get across, even though Uri became internationally celebrated for his psychokinetic feats. If it was a PR operation by extra-terrestrials, the Geller episode was misconceived and mismanaged, for people failed to see the connection between paranormally bent cutlery, space beings and the role of man and the planet Earth in the cosmic scheme. Puharich arranged for Geller to be investigated by reputable scientists, such as the physicists Harold Puthoff and Russell Targ of the Stanford Research Institute, both in Europe and America, and though a number of distinguished men were impressed and prepared to attest to Geller's paranormal powers, they were understandably sceptical about his claims as to whence those powers derived. Geller became disillusioned and headstrong and in 1974 he and Puharich went their separate ways. The cosmic connection, it seemed, had been severed.

Knowing about Puharich's work in medical technology and

his investigations of the healing work of Arigó, and knowing from her conversation with him when they had met that he would be interested in the case, Phyllis sent Andrija the photographs Bobby had taken of Reg's arm before and after his attempt to heal the burn. As it happened, Puharich had scheduled a trip to Miami early in March 1974, so he was able to meet Bobby personally and hear his story. It was routine procedure in Puharich's investigations of psychics to put them into a hypnotic regression in order to see if any information could be gleaned from their subconscious as to the source of their paranormal abilities. He did this with Bobby in the presence of Phyllis, and although Bobby had never been under hypnosis before he immediately went into a trance state and began to channel coherent intelligence of a kind that amazed them both. Though the conscious Bobby knew nothing of Puharich's erstwhile cosmic colleagues, the entranced Bobby became a spokesman for an extra-terrestrial that identified itself as 'Corean', which it later transpired was the name of a civilisation and not an individual.

'There will be a time we will be many on your Earth,' announced Corean. 'We wish to be welcomed when we come. We wish to come. We bring no harm. We have come before. We feel the Earth people cannot accept us, accept what is happening. We have chosen some as channels. Your people have to see to believe.'

Bobby, they learned, was one of the chosen channels. He had been led to Phyllis because, with her psychic diagnostic experience, she could guide his healings. But he was not strong, and in order to enable him to channel the energies required for healing, his physical body needed to be specially treated and equipped.

That information particularly interested Phyllis, because in her psychic development class some days before she and some other members of the class had witnessed a weird phenomenon. It had looked as if wires were being inserted into Bobby's neck and throat. 'Did we see it right, Corean,' Phyllis asked, 'was it an electronic circuit?'

'In your terms, yes,' the voice answered. 'This is what it

was. He is being, as you call it, wired.'

Andrija asked, 'Can you estimate how much longer it will take to completely heal his physical body and prepare his conscious and unconscious mind to be your servant?'

This brought a gentle rebuke from Corean: 'He is not a servant. He is a channel we shall work through.'

Andrija apologised for misconstruing the relationship, but asked another question: 'Can you in any way indicate what the purpose of your landing will be so that we can better understand and prepare man for that event?'

Corean replied: 'Man is confused. The Earth is in great trouble. We come with love to help. It will be difficult for you to prove to your man of our existence. There will be many things occur prior to our coming and at our coming, as proof, so that we may be allowed to help. Bobby is one . . . There will be many who will not believe. You must help find a way to prove to them we come with love and there have been many times we have tried and failed, for man does not believe, only what he can see. We will show many things.'

Andrija and Phyllis were instructed to proceed cautiously with Bobby, not to tell him all at once about the source of his powers and the nature of the task that was being performed through him. His conscious mind as well as his physical body needed to be prepared for undertaking the work. They would have to be discreet and patient, and Phyllis should speak to his wife in private, for he would need her help and strength. And for the present it would be unwise for Bobby to hear the tape of this communication.

Slumped in a chair, his head lolling loosely to the right, Bobby uttered these instructions which, out of trance, he would have no knowledge of. After arranging with Corean to have another communication the following day, Andrija brought Bobby back to a normal state of consciousness, and asked him how he felt. Refreshed and relaxed, Bobby said, but what had happened? Andrija told him he had just proved himself a gifted channel as well as a healer.

Both Phyllis and Andrija were concerned about the instruction not to tell Bobby the whole story at this stage, and they spent some time that night discussing the ethics of this. They came to the conclusion that they should go along with the request at least for a short time and see what happened. Andrija, Phyllis noticed, was both impressed and eager to continue. He said that it was as if Bobby was taking over where Uri had left off. In the last communications channelled by Uri from the space people they had started giving information about their proposed landing.

So they told Bobby that in trance he had functioned as a channel for an intelligence that they couldn't at present identify but that could possibly be from another world. Bobby was excited, and keen to continue working with them. And there were some questions he would like them to ask on his behalf. The first concerned his fear of death. He had had a conviction for so long that he couldn't remember how and when it started, that he would die on his thirtieth birthday, which would be on 18 June next. One night he had dreamed very specifically that he would die in a green car with a brown interior. He was so convinced that his fate was so predetermined that he would do crazy things, like walk blindly across a busy highway, convinced that nothing could kill him until the appointed day. His belief was only strengthened when his wife inherited a green car with a brown interior.

When the three assembled the following evening, Andrija began, after putting Bobby in trance, by asking about this conviction and fear of his death.

Corean answered that he would not die in a physical sense. 'He will be completed, be healed. We will have him completely ready for this work.'

That was good news. It was more a question of being reborn than of dying. 'I think we can explain that to him satisfactorily,' said Andrija. But there was a second question. Bobby wanted to know why he had been chosen as a healer.

Rather incoherently, Corean explained: 'We chose . . . many years . . . this will . . . his life will change, a new life, a continue of life in his next age . . . He was chosen many, he was chosen before. He will soon understand and know. He was with you before.'

This was the first intimation of a fact that was to be repeated frequently in future communications: that the group that was convening for the present enterprise had worked together in previous incarnations. 'Could you tell us where and when,' Andrija asked, stressing that it was not particularly important for him to have this information, but it might help Bobby to accept his role.

'We feel at this time, his consciousness would not accept the truth,' Corean answered. 'He is not ready, his consciousness would only be more confused to know of when he was with you before.'

'We need something to tell him,' Phyllis protested, but she received only the assurance that he would know and accept everything soon. They were obviously going to get no further on that tack, so Andrija took from his pocket a list of questions he had prepared. First, was Corean aware of his own connection with Hoova?

Hoova was the name of the extra-terrestrial civilisation that he and Geller had been given to understand they were in contact with. Corean answered: 'There are many who work with many on your planet . . . You have been contacted . . . You have done much already. We will advise you soon of what we ask you to do.'

Was Corean aware of who Uri Geller was? Andrija asked. Were they connected with the space people who used Geller as a channel?

'We know of this,' was the answer. 'We do not work with him now.' And to Andrija's further question whether they communicated with the group that worked with him, Corean replied, 'Yes. We are many groups, and we are one.'

Returning to the subject of Bobby, Andrija asked if Corean had been responsible for the supposed poltergeist effects around him some months before.

'Yes. Just like the burn brought you here, these things brought Phyllis here.'

'Pretty tricky you are!' Andrija said with a laugh. 'You have been very clever in bringing Bobby, Phyllis and me together. Are there any other people we should move out towards, or be aware of, that you could identify or name?'

'The arrangements will be made for you to meet another,' Corean answered. 'You will be meeting number three soon.'

Andrija had a number of questions about the types of healing that Bobby would be capable of and the strategy they should pursue in publicising his abilities. He mentioned the international conference on healing, the May Lectures, to be held in London in two months' time, and asked if it would be a good idea for Bobby to attend and demonstrate his healing powers.

'These are the ones who will aid you, yes,' Corean said, referring to the doctors and other interested parties who would be attending the conference. But the most important thing was not to rush Bobby, not to demand too much of him too soon, to be content initially with convincing only a small nucleus of people of his abilities. Ultimately, if with care he could be made physically and mentally strong enough, he would be able to heal any condition. 'There is nothing that cannot be helped, there is nothing that cannot be corrected. But we will not again, now, do a work like the burn which was to draw you. We will start easy, we will start with lesser work to see how this can be accepted. If this is accepted, then things like you speak of will be accepted, and done.' It was going to be Phyllis's task to guide, control and pace Bobby's healing work, and to help his wife to understand him and to give him her support.

'You must try to explain to her that this work will not take away from her, but will add,' Corean said.

Phyllis promised to try, and after an exchange of cordialities and thanks – 'Wonderful talking to you,' said Phyllis, and 'A great privilege,' said Andrija – Bobby was brought out of trance and the session ended.

In view of the proposal that Bobby should go to London for the conference on health and healing in May, Andrija wanted to arrange for the organiser and major sponsor of the conference, Sir John Whitmore, to meet him. John was going to be in New York at the beginning of April, together with his friend the English author and biologist Lyall Watson, who was also going to participate in the conference. So Andrija arranged for Phyllis and Bobby to be his guests at the same time.

When John and some friends in England conceived the idea of giving London a taste of some of the positive developments on the counterculture scene, Andrija was the first person he thought of as a potential contributor. He had heard him lecture in California a couple of years before, and had been impressed both by Andrija himself and by his talk, which had been about his work with Arigó. He had approached Andrija and had found him not only willing to be a contributor but enthusiastic about the whole project and immensely helpful with suggestions and introductions to other potential participants. So when Andrija told him about Bobby Horne and the strange communication that had come through him and the proposal that he should participate in the conference, John was keen to hear more.

The best way to put him in the picture, Andrija suggested when John arrived at Ossining with Lyall on 7 April, would be for John to listen to the tapes of the two communications with Corean that they had had in Orlando three weeks before.

When he had heard the tapes, John's mind raced with questions, doubts and suspicions. Who was fooling who? he wondered. Or was it a case of collective delusion? Or a practical joke played by discarnate beings, spirits of the dead who were mischievously sporting with the living to pass their time while they were waiting to reincarnate? This was perhaps a wild idea, but there had to be some explanation, and at least the existence of spirits was better substantiated than that of space beings.

Bobby had to be the number one suspect, since he did most of the talking, or channelling as they called it. Suppose that he was only pretending to be in a trance state, or even that he really was in such a state and it was his unconscious that was engaging in the dialogue? The story of the burn healing was suspicious, particularly as the main evidence for it was the photographs that Bobby himself had so conveniently taken before and after the event. But for Bobby to have invented and to masquerade as Corean, and to fool two people as experienced in psychic studies as Andrija and Phyllis, would have required knowledge, cunning and ingenuity surely quite beyond Bobby's capability.

When they had met the previous day, Bobby had made John nervous, probably because he was so obviously nervous and out of place himself. He was tall, lithe and dark-skinned, he moved awkwardly and spoke hesitatntly and softly with a Southern drawl. Much of the conversation that had taken place in the house those two days seemed to go above his head, and though he was clearly excited at being involved with these people and a focus of their interest, he was worried about having left his wife and child behind in Daytona Beach. He just could be pulling a hoax, John thought, but he couldn't understand how, if that were so, Bobby could have spontaneously produced a scenario that so neatly tallied with Andrija's previous communications with extra-terrestrials announcing a forthcoming landing and soliciting help in preparing mankind for it. He couldn't have read Andrija's book on Uri, for that was still in the press and not to be published until May.

But if Bobby could be eliminated as either a deliberate or unwitting hoaxer, what about Andrija? The way the Corean communications dovetailed with the communications he and Geller had experienced, and the fact that Bobby had come into Andrija's life so soon after the split with Uri, just as Uri had come in soon after the death of Arigó, were factors in the situation that had to be accounted for and naturally aroused suspicion. Did Andrija possess such great telepathic powers that he could project through a sequence of mediums – for before Uri there had been Dr Vinod – a complex and consistent scenario that served only to flatter his own ego? The facts certainly supported such a hypothesis. The trouble was that the facts were equally compatible with the hypothesis that the communications *were* from extra-terrestrials who had chosen Andrija to be their ambassador. On that supposition, it would be logical that Andrija should have been led to one medium after another, and that after the misfiring of the Geller project the space people should adopt a representative endowed with paranormal powers more useful to mankind than an ability to bend metal. Phyllis, who seemed a sensible and capable woman, had testified that Bobby had already effected some quite remarkable healings, and that was a fact that didn't fit in with the Andrija-as-telepath theory. The alleged communications and the healings were separate phenomena and not necessarily connected, and for that matter there was no necessary connection between the communications received and the powers exhibited by Geller. But if there wasn't a necessary connection, there certainly was a meaningful one, what Jung would have called a synchronistic one. To maintain that the communications were a product of Andrija's unconscious, and that Uri's psychokinesis and Bobby's healings were phenomena unconnected with each other and with the communications, would surely be to practise a kind of philosophical caution and hairsplitting more likely to obscure the truth of the matter than to elucidate it.

Such were the perplexities that John grappled with after hearing the tapes of the first two communications. They were mind-boggling and, he thought, quite insoluble in the present state of his knowledge. He would have to learn, see and hear much more before he could hope to make sense of the whole situation. There had been three more communications in the previous fortnight, and he now proceeded to listen to the recordings of these. The experience did nothing to alleviate his bewilderment, but on the contrary increased and complicated it, for these communications brought Phyllis into prominence and under suspicion. He had liked Phyllis immensely when they had first met the previous day. Though, with her blonde hair-do, heavy make-up, smart clothes and feminine small-talk, she didn't fit his preconception of a spiritually developed person, she was warm and communicative and in this situation reassuringly normal. But the recordings he now listened to utterly confounded these first impressions of Phyllis.

Andrija had left Orlando after the second session with

Bobby, but before going he had given Bobby posthypnotic suggestions to enable Phyllis to put him into trance just as he had done. This she did the following day, 19 March. The ensuing communication was largely about some events that had occurred in Phyllis's class and about how she could help Bobby's work as a healer and gain his wife's support, but in the middle of the session there was a description by Phyllis of an operation being performed on Bobby, and though Phyllis's voice was level and matter-of-fact, what she said was too fantastic, too like hallucinatory raving, to be believed. John hadn't paid much attention to the talk in the previous communications about preparing Bobby's physical body for his healing work by equipping it with a kind of electronic circuitry, but now Corean announced that further adjustments were to be made in Bobby and the present was a good time to make them, and that if Phyllis wished to watch she could do so. Phyllis said she would and that she would describe what she saw happening so that Dr Puharich could listen to the description later.

'Yes, this is what we desire,' said Corean. Phyllis's description followed:

'As I'm watching and observing Bobby, his head has been turned towards his right shoulder, about a 45 . . . I'm sorry, 30 to 35 degree angle, and from his left temple to his neck area, to his collarbone, there is a glow; and behind his left ear there appears to be a filling out in the neck area. His colour is changing, his aura is changing. It seems to be giving an electrical surge of energy. There appears to be wires going into his hands, very fine gold wires, and they . . . metallic bands of some sort, about a quarter inch, right, it's beginning to circle his head. There appears to be a swelling in the left side of his neck muscle, a little to the rear and below the ear, and there appears to be a rod of some sort, that's also glowing. And then there's a glowing light like a pencil, a pen light, which seems to be coming half way up his left ear, about two inches to the rear in his hair. His watch is starting to magnetise, to glow on its own. I think perhaps in the future we should remove the watch. When I'm in his aura, in his vibration, and can pick up the physical condition, I can feel it in my own back, a group of wires, it seems to be; although I cannot observe this, I can feel it. Things seem to be going through the spinal cord, starting at the base of the spine. Bobby's head is now starting to turn around. Now there is a band glowing underneath his shirt, around his chest area. Now all that seems to be done, and he seems to be relaxed and in a deep sleep, and around his throat is a very bright reddish type of vibration or aura. The adjustments seem to have been made.'

This talk of rods, wires and glowing metallic bands was just too bizarre. Had Phyllis really seen such things? Would he have seen them if he had been present? Would Andrija? Wasn't this whole idea of mysterious processes of bio-engineering a bit too reminiscent of a science-fiction TV movie? Yes. But after the session, when Bobby was out of trance, he and Phyllis had examined his body at the points where she had seen some of the 'adjustments' being made, and their conversation had also been recorded. They spoke of visible puncture marks and lines like thin scars on Bobby's hands, chest and head. And later the same day Bobby had done a healing on Phyllis's husband, Norman, and during and after the attempt, apparently, the red puncture marks on his hands had become much darker and more prominent. If that were true, it certainly seemed to indicate that something had happened to Bobby during the earlier session, and that Phyllis's observations couldn't be written off as hallucinations.

Soon after this, Andrija had returned to Florida, and a curious event – which was eventually to prove more significant than they realised at the time – had taken place at the Miami home of a friend of Andrija's, Count Pino Turolla. The count was something of an eccentric, an independent scholar and explorer, and he had recently returned from Ecuador and brought with him a number of artifacts, one of which, a small figure, Phyllis was given to hold in order to see what psychic impressions she received from it. A thing unprecedented in Phyllis's experience had happened while she was holding this object. She had fallen into an involuntary trance and begun to chant, in a high-pitched voice, in some strange language. The count, delighted, seized a native whistle and tried to play an accompaniment. Andrija politely thanked the entity communicating through Phyllis for the beautiful chant, and tried to get it to identify itself. The voice said 'Akee ah', and there followed a flood of rapid, speech-like sounds. Andrija assumed that 'Akee ah' was the name of the god-figurine that Phyllis was holding and that the language was that of an ancient civilisation. More chanting followed. 'Thank you for that beautiful blessing,' Andrija said with John thought, incredible composure, as if being entertained by an ancient god was an everyday occurrence. Then he asked permission to call on one of Phyllis's regular guides to explain in English what had just happened, and after a pause a totally different voice emanated from Phyllis and said, 'Hello. This is Tom.' Andrija recalled that Phyllis had told him that she had on several occasions in the past, channelled an entity named 'Tom', whom she had assumed was the spirit of her grandfather Thomas.

At Andrija's request, Tom obligingly explained that the language they had just heard came from some 34,000 years ago, and that at that time there were 'Three cultures, three divisions from three areas of the universe. One came with love, one came to own, and one came to observe.'

'Please continue. This is very enlightening,' Andrija said.

The entity that had spoken through Phyllis, Tom further explained, was 'a being that gathered all three together to discuss an amnesty. The one that observed recorded it, the one that possessed controlled the minds. The being that came tried to prevent . . . There was a massacre . . . A much more advanced civilisation began then was lost.'

Asked by Andrija to identify in modern geographical terms the place on Earth where this first intervention by the space people had taken place, Tom gave the figures 40 and 79, which Andrija then ascertained were the latitudinal and longitudinal co-ordinates. Then Tom said he had to leave, but would return another day, and when Andrija brought Phyllis out of trance she said she wanted to cry and felt that she hadn't finished, which, though nobody realised it then, was probably the understatement of her life.

John had been in some bizarre situations before, but by the end of his first day at Ossining he was beginning to think that this was rapidly building up into his most way-out experience ever. It wasn't only the tapes. The people and their conversation, the house and its surroundings, all contributed to a general eerie effect. The house seemed so isolated and old-fashioned, and the great mature trees in the grounds and the heavily wooded hillside rising sharply to the rear, with a mysterious derelict stone tower standing in the middle of it, constituted a setting pregnant with suggestions of the supernatural and in keeping with the activities of a mad scientist. The domestic arrangements were looked after by two young women. One was quiet, observant, and moved with a captivating feline grace, the other was excitable and she kept professing to see and experience things that, so far as John could make out, nobody else did. He was quite comfortable with the idea that his own perceptual mechanisms were comparatively crude and limited and that some people were gifted with greater psychic sensitivity, but her tangential relation to ordinary reality and sustained hypersensitivity were, he thought, possibly more symptomatic of insecurity than of any paranormal endowment.

Phyllis, on the other hand, seemed disposed to hide her psychic talents under a veneer of ordinariness. But after dinner on the first day she gave a spontaneous demonstration which John found impressive. Lyall Watson had been talking about his observations of the work of the psychic surgeons in the Philippines, where he had recently seen things fit to elicit wonder even in the presently assembled company. On a string round his neck, Lyall wore a black stone, which he said he had picked up in a stream in the Philippines. At Andrija's suggestion, he handed it to Phyllis to see if she would receive any psychic impressions from it. Holding the stone, Phyllis closed her eyes, and while they waited for her reactions John wondered whether she was going to break out into song in a strange language. But she didn't. She said, 'Heat, fire, moving through space.'

'Interesting,' Lyall said, and when Phyllis handed the stone back to him he told her that it was in fact a piece of a meteorite. Whether Phyllis picked up her impression by psychometry from the object or by telepathy from Lyall, it was a convincing demonstration of her psychic abilities.

It was Phyllis, too, who had introduced the first intimation that this was not going to be any ordinary house party when, shortly after their arrival, she gave Andrija a cassette which she said contained a message from an entity with a name that sounded like 'Ryr' and which had spoken through her during one of her class sessions on the first of April. Everyone listened to the message, which went: 'We speak of three, of three, one of three recent, not one of three. Of three, of three centre, bring one more, become three, surround core. We meet with third within your eight, then that completes your three.'

Ryr, whoever or whatever he or it was, clearly had problems with the language. Well, it was unreasonable to expect busy extra-terrestrials to be polyglots and he was no doubt doing his best, but what could this cryptic jargon mean? Phyllis, who had had time to think about it, recalled that in one of the communications channelled by Bobby, Corean had stated 'You will be meeting number three soon', and they had been told pretty clearly that three people, apart from Bobby, would make up the group to undertake the work of receiving and pro- pagating the message. Ryr's communication would tie in with this, Andrija agreed, and the statement 'We meet with third within your eight', probably meant that within eight days the meeting with the third person would take place. It was now the sixth day, he pointed out. John and Lyall, the two newcomers on the scene, exchanged a glance and knew that they were both thinking the same thought and it wasn't by telepathy. John noted, too, that the Ryr communication had been received on April Fool's day.

A rich man with a reputation for prodigality and an open- ness of demeanour that can easily be taken for naïvety is a natural candidate for paranoia. John lay awake long that night, reviewing what he had seen and heard during the day, and reviewing also the events in his life that had brought him to this place and among these people. What he feared above all was that he might be made a fool of, exploited, ripped off. It had already been mentioned that the work Andrija, Phyllis and Bobby were embarked on would need money. It was scarcely conceivable that the whole story and the supportive tape recordings had been cunningly contrived for his benefit, but on the other hand the story itself was inconceivable and the truth had to lie somewhere. Much as he abhorred the idea of being exploited or made a fool of, the idea of exercising in any life situation a corrosive scepticism and negativity cut even more deeply against the grain of his beliefs and of the personality he had cultivated over the years since he had sold his ancestral estates and opted out of the status game and the rat race. By temperament and conviction he was a yea-sayer, but he was not fool enough to be unaware that a disposition which is an unqualified virtue in the poor may be an irresponsible folly in the rich. The admirable ethic of his class, which he had imbibed at Eton and Sandhurst, the ethic of *noblesse oblige,* did not, he was well aware, go so far as recommending the dissipation of the capital upon which *noblesse* itself rested. Having reneged on the responsibilities of primogeniture, he had put himself in a vulnerable position and had had to construct a personal ethic that took account of that vulnerability, and he had learned to consult his intuition, his gut feeling, in situations which, like the present one, confounded rational judgment. He consulted it now, and decided that the situation, bizarre as it was, felt right, and that to act on the assumption that these people were bent on ripping him off would be to succumb to paranoia and to repudiate the positive orientation and personal philosophy that he had based his life on during the past few years. He could at least ride along with it for a while and see what happened. For what if it turned out that this was precisely the point that all he had done, thought and experienced had been leading up to?

That was quite a thought. Well, according to the communications, the coming together of Bobby, Phyllis and Andrija had not been a matter of chance. If he was destined to play a part himself, and this visit was part of a plan, then the planners must have conceived the May Lectures project to bring him and Andrija together. He could have sworn it had been his own idea, but the way the theme and timing of the May Lectures coincided with the nature and development of Bobby's healing powers made him wonder.

Jim Hurtak could be part of the plan, too. Certainly the weeks he had spent with Jim Hurtak the year before had contributed a lot towards preparing him psychologically for the present situation and ensuring that he wouldn't be immediately thrown by it. Hurtak, who had held the post of Professor of Oriental Studies at the California Institute of the Arts at Valencia, was not so much a teacher as an experience, a guru-figure whose teaching was not an explanation of objective reality but a spontaneous creation of ideas and experiences that made his students explore new areas for themselves and in themselves. Dressed always in a crumpled suit and wearing a black beret perched on the back of his head, Hurtak held classes which sometimes ran as long as eight hours, during which he would alternate between reading long passages of scripture and delivering rambling commentaries on them. The commentaries were always fascinating and provocative, but how they were connected with the readings was a mystery to John. He sometimes spoke about UFOs and about his personal contacts with extra-terrestrials, who, he said, had often intervened in Earth history since prehistoric times, when they had first established a civilisation in the Tarim Basin to the north of Tibet. Many of his students recorded his every word, except on occasions when he made them turn off their machines while he gave them some devastating piece of cosmic news that only he was privy to and which he said he was now allowed to share with them.

John recalled his first meeting with this strange man, when he had gone along uninvited, unannounced and unknown to one of his classes and was greeted by the professor with a vigorous handshake and the words, 'Good. You've come. I was expecting you.' After that he had become a disciple, regularly attending his classes and joining the groups he took on weekend field trips, sometimes visiting scientific research establishments, where they were often unaccountably rather coolly welcomed, and on other occasions going to some 'power spot' where they would meditate or listen to Jim preach. It was one of these field trips that had finally led to his moving on from the Hurtak experience. They left Valencia at dawn in several cars and drove for several hours before turning onto a sandy track. This led at last to a white-domed building surrounded by a barbed wire fence on which hung a sign that read: 'College of Universal Wisdom'. A mile or two beyond this they came to a run-down desert café, where Jim introduced them to a grey-haired, stocky man named George Van Tassel who was the presiding genius of this desert ashram, and presumably the possessor of universal wisdom, though on this occasion he didn't dispense much of the latter commodity but talked at length about his contacts with UFOs. Then in the stifling heat of the desert afternoon the groups sat perched some twenty feet up on some rocks in a semi-circle around Jim, who regaled them with an unabridged reading of the Book of Isaiah. At dusk they all traipsed deep into the desert on foot to a spot that Jim said was special, though nobody else could tell how it differed from any other sandy waste, and Jim recited a Hebrew incantation which he said would summon UFOs. As the sky got darker and the stars brighter, Jim hailed a distant moving light in the sky as their first UFO sighting. Then other members of the party began to see them too, and to utter appropriate expressions of rapture and awe, but try as he may John couldn't convince himself that they weren't normal aerial phenomena.

He had stopped being a disciple of Jim Hurtak's after that experience, but he had remained grateful to him for the expansion of awareness and the sense of the existence and importance of non-ordinary realities that being exposed to the Hurtak personality for two months had given him, and he retained a suspicion that Jim-as-guru had his own ways of disengaging his disciples when their time to move on had come, and that the last field trip he had participated in had perhaps not been as mad and unscheduled as it had appeared at the time.

And now it seemed that the Jim Hurtak episode was fitting in with the unfolding pattern of his life. He remembered that in the conversation over dinner Lyall had asked Andrija whether he had checked out the geographical co-ordinates that had been given in the communication Phyllis had channelled as the location of the space beings' first landing on Earth. Andrija said he had, and it turned out to be a place called the Tarim Basin, which was to the north of Tibet. This correspondence with Jim Hurtak's information could hardly be put down to either coincidence or contrivance, and it was one of the first things that disposed John to believe that the communications might really be from an extra-terrestrial intelligence.

After a short and fitful sleep, John awoke to the sound of voices downstairs. Dressed only in underpants, he went sleepily down to the kitchen to see what was happening, and was greeted with laughter by Andrija, Phyllis, Bobby, and some other members of the household who were sitting around talking and smoking. He gathered that Bobby and one of the girls had been up in the woods together and had had an experience. Well, that's nothing unusual, he thought, but it turned out that they were talking about something else, and now Bobby suggested that they should all return to the spot together, so they all went and put on warm clothes because there was a chill in the night air, and ten minutes later they were crashing through the woods up the hillside towards the mysterious tower. The time was 3.15, the night was still and brightly moonlit and at intervals there was a sound like the hooting of an owl. The atmosphere was certainly eerie, but so far as John was concerned the nature of the experience they were supposed to be having remained a mystery. Bobby told them all to wander around and pick a spot that felt comfortable. Comfortable for what? he wanted to ask, but he didn't want to spoil it for anyone else so he found a comfortable tree to lean against, and waited to see what would happen next. About half an hour passed in silence, then they reassembled, summoned by a few shouts, and trekked back to the house. Returning to the kitchen, they sat and talked about what it had all meant. Bobby certainly seemed to be profoundly moved. For John it had been too reminiscent of one of Jim Hurtak's crazy excursions. He returned to bed cold and confused and this time slept deeply and long.

The following morning he wished he hadn't left the gathering so soon, because apparently shortly after his departure Bobby had fallen into trance and a communication had taken place. In it, Andrija said, there had been a strong intimation that John was to be the third member of the team. John was disappointed to have missed that, but he didn't have to wait long for a repeat performance. That evening he, Andrija, Phyllis and Bobby went to Andrija's room, and after Andrija had spent some time tinkering with complicated recording equipment and setting up an infra-red camera, the lights were turned low and Bobby settled in a wooden armchair facing the three of them. Slowly he began to count backwards from thirty-one, and before he reached ten his voice was barely audible and he was slumped heavily. Then his head rose and he appeared to be having some difficulty with his breathing, but Andrija and Phyllis showed no concern so John assumed that all was well.

'We welcome you,' said Andrija, after a pause.

'We come in love,' said Bobby, hesitatingly.

A shiver ran down John's spine. The idea that these words might have originated in a source beyond Earth, or in another dimension, was awesome.

Corean began by referring to a message for Bobby which, apparently, had been communicated the previous night but Phyllis had neglected to pass on to him, although she had promised to do so. Phyllis explained that although they all remembered that there had been a message, it hadn't been on the tape when they played it back.

'We did not ask the message to be taped, we asked you to deliver the message,' Corean said. Phyllis apologised, and Corean went on: 'We do not ask for your apology. We only ask that this time you will keep your word.'

So gentle, so loving, but firm as a rock, John thought. He was already impressed. This brief initial exchange implied that Corean knew that the message hadn't been delivered, and therefore must have had Phyllis and Andrija under observation since last night's communication, and also that it had the ability to interfere with the tape-recording process, presumably by stopping the tape running whenever there was something to communicate which it didn't want recorded.

Corean then announced that some more work was going to be done on Bobby, and that Phyllis should describe what she saw. Andrija asked, and was granted, permission to take infra-red pictures. Then Phyllis began to describe another weird operation in which silver rods and balls went into Bobby's body and there was wiring all over his face. John could see nothing, nor, he suspected, could Andrija, though he was snapping away with his infra-red camera as fast as he could.

Phyllis had moved forward a little and apparently encroached on Bobby's aura, for Corean said 'Do not touch.' Then five minutes or so passed in silence and Corean announced that Bobby's breathing would have to be stopped for the next part of the adjustment, and to John's amazement Bobby abruptly stopped breathing and remained immobile and breathless for what seemed an age but turned out to be just forty-five seconds. Then he resumed breathing and Corean, speaking through him, got down to the business of the evening:

'We feel the three we ask for may be assembled. We feel you have done extremely well with no more help than you have asked for. Please do not touch. We feel you have talked. We feel there is a decision the three must agree before we may continue. We feel you have come a long way to reach this decision. John, you are not aware that we speak to you?'

'No, I wasn't,' said John in a small voice, momentarily thrown by being unexpectedly addressed by name.

'We feel you three are what we asked to be assembled,' Corean went on. 'We ask that you harmonise, agree on a direction, on a director. Then we may complete our third meeting ... We ask that you three sit as one and agree.'

'You want us to make that decision now, Corean?' said Phyllis.

'We ask that a talk ... We wish you to take all the time

you need to make this decision.'

So it was decided that the three should adjourn for their discussion, and Corean said that while they were having it Bobby should ponder the message, which was now repeated and went: 'To give in humility and to receive in humility is the same. One without the other has no meaning and no purpose. It is no greater to receive in humility and no lesser to receive than to give.'

'We leave now, in love,' said Corean, and Bobby began to count up out of trance. He opened his eyes, rubbed his hands and looked at them. They felt like wax, he said. He had feelings of tingling, burning and stiffness in various parts of his body. He pulled up his shirt. There was a red mark and a bump on his chest, and what looked like a bunch of pin-pricks where Phyllis had earlier described silver wires going into his body.

Andrija repeated the message about giving and receiving in humility, and elaborated on the theme a bit to be sure that Bobby understood its implications. He did, and he was moved. He said:

'Last night on the hill, I was trying so hard to find the words to tell. I wanted to give something, I wanted just to give. And it's like that. These things in people really embarrass me. They say "That was really wise, what you said," or "That was really great, what you did." I can't even take credit for being alive; how can I possibly take credit for any of this, for anything I say? I really feel like it's not me saying this because I'm not intelligent enough to say anything that would have any real meaning. I realise that it's not me doing any of this, and I don't really want anyone to say thank you. It embarrasses me, because I know who they should be thanking and it's embarrassing that they don't know who to thank.'

After some more discussion of the message and its meaning, they left Andrija's room and went down to the kitchen. At the top of the stairs, Bobby stopped. 'My leg feels different,' he said. 'It feels like it's not mine.' He poked his hip with his fingers. 'It's me up here,' he said, then moved his finger down a couple of inches, 'but not here.' This was his right leg, which had been injured in an accident, and he had been having some pain in it. He tried it out on the first stairs then ran down the rest. 'It feels great!' he said with excitement. In the kitchen he sat down and rolled up his trouser leg. He looked at his knee and said, incredulously, 'I have a new leg. There used to be a scar here and it's gone.'

It was obviously an emotional moment for him and not an appropriate one to ask the question that John would have dearly liked answered: had anyone else known about the scar? Would there, perhaps, be some hospital record of it?

Andrija, Phyllis and John had their discussion, which was chiefly about the question of commitment. They shared their thoughts and feelings, both the emotions and the doubts that the situation aroused in them, and John was reassured to find that the others felt about it much as he did. Bobby was recalled and through him contact was re-established with Corean. Andrija reported:

'Our decision was in the affirmative, to go ahead and do all that is necessary. The direction we have chosen is to help Bobby along the areas which have been indicated, with his conscious, his physical, his subconscious, and all the things that go to make up his life, to keep him in good form, in harmony and happiness, while he does his work. We intend to carry his work to parts of the Earth, and to those people who should know about it, in order that proof may be given, so that people may accept your coming and your presence. We realise that, sooner or later, we will have further discussions and you will inform us about your plans, and we expect, of course, to meet your people, or people from your part . . . We expect further plans to develop, and we are prepared to follow these out. We have decided rather quickly and easily, that I should carry on as the director, based largely on my experience in this sort of situation. That is, in substance, what we have come to, in complete harmony, and our faith, I'm sure, will grow, as we ourselves get stronger in our knowledge and our convictions and in our actual operations.'

Corean has just one small objection to this statement. As the partnership was now cemented and formally entered into it was not appropriate for Andrija to speak of 'your plans', meaning Corean's. 'We ask that this part be changed to "our plans".'

'We accept that as a very beautiful gesture,' said Andrija.

Corean said, 'We come to you with love. We ask much of you. We are now one. We are very happy with the results, with the decision, with the harmony of the major three. And we thank you.'

The session ended with an exchange of thanks, mutual compliments and assurances. 'This is not the last meeting,' said Corean. 'There will be more when they are needed. We will meet again in love.'

It was an emotional moment. John felt moved to say, 'I don't know how to thank you enough for the extraordinary honour you have given us to be a part of this.' But even as he spoke the words, the thought popped into his mind, 'If this is a hoax by spirits, they must be convulsing themselves at this moment.'

The spirit-hoax hypothesis was his main residual doubt, but it was overwhelmed by the thought that if it were not the explanation, then this was surely the most exciting project to be engaged in on the entire planet at this time.

## CHAPTER THREE

# *A Change of Channels*

A word of explanation is owed to the critical reader who asks, 'How do you know?' I am well aware that this story as it progresses will read more and more like fiction, and that some readers will be disposed to categorise it as such. That was my reaction when I read Andrija's book, *Uri*, which seemed to me to have more in common with Robert Heinlein's science-fiction novel, *Stranger in a Strange Land*, than with any sober and considered work of psychical research. To categorise the book as fiction was the most convenient and comfortable way of dealing with its content, and I'm sure that many readers besides myself reacted in this way. It was not the reaction that Andrija sought, however, nor is it the reaction I seek to the present narrative. Frankly, I don't want to make it easy for the reader to get on comfortable terms with material that has caused me a great deal of discomfort, and indeed still does. Which presents a curious problem, for the story has the momentum, coherence and roundness of a good tale, and to tell it convincingly requires rather the deliberate flaunting than the careful exercise of the principles of narrative art. Lest the reader should settle down to enjoying the yarn, and should merely suspend disbelief instead of exercising judgment and intelligence to assess the facts, I propose to interrupt the narrative flow from time to time and put in an appearance *in propria persona*. This will enable me to raise, and at least to discuss if not to answer, questions that will occur to the critical reader, and will also afford me opportunities to reassure all readers that I am still around and have neither taken leave of my senses nor suffered my narrative to be taken over by its protagonists, as novelists are said sometimes to do.

To the question, 'How do you know?' I should like to be able to answer, 'I was there. I saw and heard and can vouch for it.' But this is true only of a very small portion of the events covered by this narrative. My sources are the tape recordings of the communications, John Whitmore's written account of the early stages of the work (on which the latter part of the previous chapter was largely based), and the oral testimonies of the people involved, all of whom have been as co-operative and frank as could be wished. I have been able to visit most of the places where the events I record took place, and to obtain and correlate different people's accounts of the events. So I have a vast and indeed daunting body of material out of which to compose this narrative. There is certainly no need for embellishment or invention, and even subjective statements of the type, 'John thought . . .' or 'Phyllis felt . . .', are always based on the subject's own testimony and should be understood as a convenient ellipsis for 'John told me that he thought . . .' etc. I conceive my job as to tell the story as simply and intelligibly as its complexity allows, to maintain an objective viewpoint in presenting the material, and to do the reader the honour of leaving to his own intelligence the decision as to what he should believe.

When I was asked, in 1974, to report the May Lectures for the Dutch magazine, *Bres*, I devoted one of my four articles to the lectures given by Andrija Puharich and Lyall Watson, and began it with a paragraph which is, I think, germane in the present context:

'Anyone who writes, reads or thinks about parapsychological phenomena has at some stage to confront the problem of his own credulity threshold. He is going to be asked to believe some quite incredible things, so he needs to be clear at least about two things: how exacting are his own standards of proof? and to what extent is his intellectual assent influenced by emotional or temperamental factors? Man needs beliefs – and the bored, the underprivileged, the unqualified, the disaffected, the social misfits and the rebels are all strongly disposed to believe in anything that mocks orthodox science or religion and its custodians.'

There is perhaps a touch of mandarin *hauteur* in this. When the counter culture emerged in the 'sixties I was not particularly enthused. By temperament and education a bookish man with a respect for intellectually achieved order, I tended to regard it as a refuge of mediocre minds, and a residue of that attitude is to be seen in the above paragraph. My recent research and literary work has caused me to modify that attitude to the counter culture and has raised my own credulity threshold, but the cautionary remarks with which I prefaced my first brief excursion into reporting Andrija's work are still, I think, relevant. There are many people, I know, who will have much less difficulty than I have in giving credence to the content of this book, and one thing that worries me is that there are many who will believe it for the wrong reasons.

In one of the communications held at Ossining the month before, Corean had indicated in reply to a question of Andrija's that at the time of the May Lectures Bobby may be able to give a convincing demonstration of his healing ability before the assembled doctors and scientists. So Bobby and Phyllis had come over to London with Andrija, and had been spending the week quietly in a house on the outskirts of London, at Mill Hill, loaned by a financier friend of John's, Ian Wasserman. On 20 May, after the first day of the programme, Andrija and John went out to Mill Hill and held their first communication since the one in which they had entered into their commitment. Since then, John learned from Phyllis, Bobby had completed two quite remarkable healings in Orlando. A young man suffering from pancreatitis, who had been able to eat only baby food and had had no energy, had been completely cured after seven treatments, and a woman scheduled for a cyst operation had been able to cancel it for after three healing sessions with Bobby there had been no sign of the cyst. Bobby had had personal and marital problems, but his healing powers seemed to be developing, as Corean had predicted, and if he could convincingly demonstrate them to the residential programme participants at Brunel this would be a great step towards getting him more widely known.

When Bobby was in deep trance and Corean was speaking through him, that first night at Mill Hill, Andrija asked: 'Would you give Bobby and us the maximum support as you did in that burn case? You see, because this is Bobby's first introduction to the world of medicine and science, and what happens here will be carried all over the world in terms of the reputation it establishes. Can we count on your really intense, massive support in this period?'

'We will give our entire support,' Corean answered. 'We want you to know that there is no problem there. The only problem that exists right now is Bobby and his free will. He is fighting to be Bobby and no more. Can you understand?'

'I understand what an enormous burden has been placed upon Bobby,' Andrija said, 'and I know he has to make up his own mind. But may I ask just this: suppose Bobby in his own free will decides he'd rather be a cook than a healer, what will happen then?'

'We cannot change a free will,' Corean answered. 'We do not interfere. We try to help.' Bobby sometimes felt like running away, Corean continued, because he felt that everyone was trying to make him perfect and he was aware that he was not perfect. They shouldn't be overprotective with him. He should be allowed to act independently and even make some mistakes. 'Then he'll feel better,' Corean said, adding the helpful suggestion: 'Let him break a glass.'

On the subject of the proposed demonstration healing, they were given precise instructions. There should be no metal on or near Bobby. Everyone should keep well out of his reach. There would be a great deal of energy channelled and it was important that no one should touch Bobby or be alarmed by his reaction.

'We understand. I think we can cope with it,' Andrija said.

The instruction that there should be no metal on Bobby was particularly interesting in the light of an extraordinary thing Phyllis had told them some time before. Bobby had had

74

some metal fillings in his teeth and during the month they had been in Florida these had been paranormally replaced with compound ones. Bobby had a horror of dentists and certainly hadn't been near one at that time, and the only explanation of the strange transformation was that Corean had dematerialised the old fillings and materialised the new. Andrija, who professed to have experienced many materialisation phenomena in his work with Uri, seemed quite happy with this explanation, but it stretched John's credulity to its limits and he felt he would get on better with the work if he wasn't asked to believe in such outlandish miracles.

Corean confirmed the claim of one of the conference participants, Marcel Vogel, who had given a talk challengingly titled 'Inter personal Communication Between Man and Plant,' that a plant can function as a kind of transmitter of energy when psychic healing is attempted at a distance, so the preparation of the demonstration experiment was entrusted to Marcel. Distance, he said, was no object, so he made arrangements by telephone for a glaucoma patient in California to be the recipient of the healing energy and to be in a state of receptive meditation at the time the attempt was made in London.

All the residential programme participants, some fifty or sixty people in all, crowded into the room at Brunel University on the morning of 22 May to witness the experiment. Marcel brought in a tall, healthy-looking plant and carefully attached two steel electrodes to one of its leaves. The wires from the electrodes passed through a transformer and other pieces of equipment to a strip chart recorder, and when the electrodes were attached to the plant some wild oscillations were registered on the moving graph paper. Then a steady read-out was registered, and Marcel announced that the experiment could begin. Bobby wasn't ready, however. He was palpably nervous and wanted to smoke another cigarette before taking his place facing the plant. Phyllis, too, was nervous, though she tried not to show it and to give Bobby confidence. She was apprehensive about Marcel Vogel, whose showman qualities made him an excellent lecturer but were inappropriate in the present situation.

At last Bobby composed himself. This was a big moment for him, being the centre of attention of all these scientists and doctors. He stood before the plant and held the open palms of his hands out towards it. Marcel announced to the assembly that his consciousness was now 'locked into the plant' and that the transmission of his healing energy to the patient in California had begun.

For about fifteen minutes everyone sat around in silence. Marcel monitored the strip chart and described in a loud whisper the oscillations it recorded. Bobby stood and tried to pour out energy towards the plant. Then he began shaking. First his hands shook, then his shoulders and head. Phyllis knew that this was normal when he was attempting a healing, and she was dismayed when Marcel, apparently alarmed by Bobby's increasingly violent movement, suddenly went over to him and grabbed him by the shoulders. As soon as he was touched, Bobby convulsed and moaned as if a great electric shock had jolted through him, and at the same time many people in the room experienced a kind of shock. Also, they discovered afterwards, at this moment the step-down transformer in the power supply blew out. As Phyllis recalled later: 'Everyone in the room had a reaction. Some people had very good reactions. Others were frightened because they could feel the energy going through them. People who had never had a psychic experience had something happen to them in that room. When it blew, the energy just went in all directions.'

Phyllis's main concern was for Bobby. She went over to him and talked him softly out of his shocked state. 'His etheric body was shattered,' she said, and in an attempt to restore it she proceeded to give him what she calls an 'aura sweep'. I have seen her do this with another psychic, who said that he felt much better for it, though to the onlooker it looked like an exercise in mumbo-jumbo. Starting at the feet, with her palms turned upwards, she slowly raises her hands and arms, keeping them at a distance of about twelve inches from the body on either side, then brings her hands together above the subject's head, draws away from him and then shakes her hands as far away as possible from her own body as if to get rid of a cloying substance. She did this two or three times with Bobby, and eventually he became calmer. There was still pandemonium in the room, and a lot of people were crowded around Marcel examining his blown-out circuitry. Bobby said he felt sick and Phyllis quickly got him out of the room and found a toilet, where he vomited violently and repeatedly.

Later enquiries established that the glaucoma patient in California had not been cured, though she said she had felt that something was happening. A curious fact that emerged, which may or may not have had to do with the alleged energy transmission, was that one of a group of people sitting in meditation with the patient in California had suffered a heart attack at about the same time as Bobby's healing attempt had been abruptly halted in London.

Disastrous though the experiment was, obviously something paranormal had happened, and, in order to find out what, Andrija and Phyllis held a communication through Bobby that night at the house in Mill Hill. But before they could start interrogating Corean about the incident they were told: 'You do not realise what almost occurred today. You have taken a very big chance. Many have worked hard for this day. We had given special instructions concerning this. It could have been a complete healing if it had been done as we asked. We ask before any more discussion that you listen to our last meeting.'

Obediently, Andrija and Phyllis left Bobby in trance and went into another room to listen to the tape of the communication they had held two nights before. 'There were two points where perhaps we were wrong,' Phyllis admitted to Corean when they returned. First, she said, perhaps she had stood too far away from Bobby and had therefore not been able to give him enough psychic support; and secondly, of course, Marcel had touched Bobby. The second point, Corean said, was correct, but also the instruction that Bobby should have no metal on or near him had not been observed. He had worn a ring, there were coins in his pocket and his clothing had metal buttons. This, they later ascertained was true. Bobby had worn a new suit, which had a military-style jacket with metal buttons. Before the experiment, Phyllis had checked that the zipper in the trousers was plastic, but it hadn't occurred to her to examine the buttons. Also, just before the experiment, Bobby had bought a packet of cigarettes and put the change from a pound note in his pocket. 'We were sending very strong,' Corean explained. 'This is why we had asked of these special conditions . . . You did not understand the clothing. We stopped the machine, trying to show you to stop the man. We saw what was about to happen. We stopped the energy before it did damage to Bobby's physical.' And in answer to Andrija's question why other people in the room had experienced a strong reaction at the time, Corean said, 'Because of the metal, energy was being reflected in many directions.'

For the patient's sake, Andrija asked, shouldn't they repeat the experiment, try again perhaps without Marcel Vogel working with them? Corean deferred to Phyllis's opinion, and Phyllis said she felt that Bobby was not in a fit condition to make another attempt at present. He was generally in a low state of health and suffering from a cold.

'Could you do something to clear that up?' Andrija asked, and received the reply:

'This illness he has caused. He holds on to. He is punishing himself.' Phyllis asked if there was anything she could do to help. 'It is only within him,' was Corean's answer, and with this reminder of Bobby's autonomy for better or worse the session ended.

Andrija's question of two days before, as to what would happen if Bobby decided he would rather be a cook than a healer, expressed a profound concern which Phyllis and John also shared. It seemed at this stage as if their commitment would be meaningless and further work impossible if Bobby opted out. Awareness of this, and worry that he might not be able to acquit himself adequately in so crucial and responsible a role, were probably reasons for the nervousness he had shown all week, and possibly also for his illness. It was ironical that during this week when everyone was talking about man's neglected powers of self-healing the one person suffering ill-health should be Bobby, the healer. That he had succumbed in order to have an excuse for failure, or to minimise the responsibility laid upon him, was a thought that they had discussed, but if Corean was right and he was punishing himself with his illness this was more ominous, for it suggested that he had already acquiesced in a sense of failure. Andrija had asked, 'Do you have other people who can do the same thing which Bobby has been prepared for?' But instead of answering his question Corean had said, 'Bobby feels he's in a cage,' and reiterated that at any time he could exercise his free will to break out and run and there would be nothing they could do or anyone on earth could do to prevent him. What then, they all wondered, would become of the mission they had pledged themselves to? Would the cosmic connection be severed for good? And why should such supposedly important work as they were engaged on be so utterly dependent on someone so deficient in the qualities of character to perform it?

During the week of the May Lectures, John was tied down by his commitments to the guest speakers and was not able to get up to Mill Hill to participate in the communications held there. Transporting the lecturers from the States had been the major item of expense, and John was determined to make the most of the opportunities afforded by having these people simultaneously together in one place, despite the indifference of the press and the establishment. All week he was busy introducing people to each other, discussing projects, attending meetings. PR work was something he didn't find particularly congenial and had to put a lot of effort into, and at the end of these days he was immensely grateful for the repose he found with Diana, an intimate friend for three years (who is now his wife) with whom he was staying in London.

The scheduled programme finished on Friday night, but in order to keep some of the key people together for further discussions John had arranged for about fifteen of them to be house guests for the weekend at Orsett Hall in Essex. Orsett Hall was the ancient Whitmore family seat, and although no longer owned by John it still boasted portraits of generations of Whitmores, all endowed with the prominent nose that still distinguishes their renegade descendant and which, to judge

79

from the portraits, many of them used most effectively for looking down. John had been fortunate in finding as a purchaser for Orsett Hall a close friend, Tony Morgan, with whom he was on such terms that he could still regard the place as his home in England. Tony had helped with the funding of the May Lectures, and he and his wife Val had generously offered to host the weekend house party to conclude the event.

When John got down to Orsett on the Saturday morning most of the guests were already there. Andrija and his party had not arrived, however, and the first thing Tony told him was that there was a message for him to phone Mill Hill as soon as he arrived. He did so, and learnt that events there had taken a dramatic turn. The previous evening Andrija and Phyllis had worked with Bobby and a curious thing had happened. They had just begun when Corean had asked them to leave the room but keep the tape recorder going because there was a message for Bobby alone. About half an hour later Andrija had returned and taken Bobby out of trance. He had tested the recording and found that there was a message on it in Bobby's trance voice. Bobby had then listened to this alone, and afterwards all that he would say was that he wanted some time alone and would return to the States soon. In view of this, Andrija said, he thought that they ought to get together and have a communication as soon as possible, either at Mill Hill or Orsett. John agreed, and suggested that Andrija and the others should come down to Orsett, where they would be able to work in privacy at his mother's house as the Morgan home was now such a hive of activity.

Andrija, Phyllis and Bobby arrived about two hours later, and John allowed them little time for cordialities before hustling them off to his mother's house on the other side of the village. Lyall Watson joined them, because in a previous communication Corean had said that he should be given an opportunity to participate in the work, and had specifically instructed that he should listen to the tape of that communication. They settled in a bedroom and Andrija put Bobby through the trance-induction preliminaries. Corean came through and began by drawing their attention to the fact that

Lyall had not yet listened to the tape, so they interrupted the session for an hour to enable him to do so, leaving Bobby in trance. When they returned, Andrija asked Corean to take the initiative in the discussion, and Corean said, 'We only ask this at this time: there's much to be done, but it's not important that we discuss things until after Bobby's thirty . . . We ask until 5 June. We ask all of you to release him to us until this time.' They agreed, and Corean confirmed that Bobby had been given directions as to what he should do in the private message of the previous day, adding that after his thirtieth birthday they would all understand and know what was to be done with him.

Was this a case of Bobby's subconscious securing for him by subterfuge release from a situation that had become intolerable? The thought occurred to John, but on reflection he couldn't see that Corean could be just a function of Bobby's unconscious. There was too much in the communications that was inconsistent with such a theory, and besides the theory could not explain the undoubtedly paranormal energy effects produced in the abortive distant healing experiment.

There had been another, and even weirder, paranormal event recently involving Lyall. Lyall had received a letter from his parents in South Africa some days before thanking him for sending them a copy of his will. This was odd because he had not made a will and hadn't sent any communication to his parents for some time. They had suggested several times that he should prepare a will, probably because he tended to live a dangerous life as a lone explorer and sailor, but Lyall had not got round to doing so. In the earlier communication that they had just listened to, Andrija had asked whether Corean had had anything to do with the mysterious appearance of the will. 'This is a question you can ask after all that has happened?' Corean had answered, and in reply to Phyllis's question, 'Is Lyall one of us?' had said, 'Yes. He is ready but he is unsure of what he may do.'

'I have the feeling that things have been arranged for me to be free at this time,' Lyall now said. 'I have to choose a direction before 18 June, probably. Is there something I can do, or should be doing?'

'We only ask for a commitment at this time,' Corean answered. 'It will be clear by his thirty, to all of you. We do not ask anything else until then.'

So everything was still dependent upon Bobby, and further work was to be held in abeyance until after the birthday that he still irrationally feared. That night Bobby returned to London on the first stage of his journey back to Daytona Beach. Phyllis, too, would return to Florida in a few days' time, where she would be available if Bobby needed her but would observe Corean's request to leave him alone until after 5 June. Little did any of them know at this time that 5 June was to pass, and 18 June – Bobby's birthday – to approach before any of them heard from him again.

Between them, John, Andrija, Phyllis, Lyall and Norman Shealy, a neurosurgeon who had contributed to the May Lectures a talk on the use of psychics in medical diagnosis, travelled some 12,000 miles to get together at Miami airport on 17 June. When the expected sixth member of the party, Bobby, didn't turn up to join them for the onward flight to Georgetown in the Bahamas, they could hardly but wonder what they were doing incurring such expense and making such efforts for his sake. John certainly wondered, for he was paying the travel expenses. The idea had been that they should all be with Bobby on his birthday in order to give him all the moral and emotional support he might need to get through it, and that the ideal place for the purpose would be John's house in the Bahamas. Bobby had agreed to the proposal and said he would meet them at Miami airport, but it was over a week since Phyllis had made this arrangement with him and she hadn't been able to contact him since. She had spoken to his wife that morning and she had been in a panic because the last time she saw Bobby was three days ago, when he had told her that he was going into the Everglades to work things out for himself. Phyllis had left messages for him all over the place confirming the time of the meeting at the airport, and she kept hoping until the last minute that he would turn up. His failure to do so made the whole operation seem rather pointless and absurd, but they were too deeply committed to the arrangements to change them, so they took their scheduled flight to Georgetown without Bobby, who for all they knew was still in the Everglades, the treacherous and infested swamp region of inland Florida.

Stocking Island is a small island about a mile offshore from the larger Bahamian island of Great Exuma. Some years before, John had bought an unusual Spanish-style house perched on the rocky shore facing Georgetown on the main island. A young couple occupied and maintained the house when he was not there, which was most of the time, and they had prepared guest rooms and laid in supplies for the present visit. It was an idyllic place, with palm trees and colourful bougainvillea growing in the courtyard, and the guests expressed appropriate delight and admiration, but the unspoken question, 'What are we doing here?' was in all their minds. John reflected that, except for Lyall, none of his guests was a person that in normal circumstances he would make a friend of, and wondered how he was going to occupy them.

In the evening, they had a barbecue dinner in the courtyard during which, by tacit agreement, they talked about other things than the problem that preoccupied them all. After dinner they went into the house and assembled in the living-room to discuss what they should do. Corean, Andrija recalled, had promised that everything would be made clear to them after Bobby's birthday, which was tomorrow, so perhaps they should just wait and see what happened. Bobby might turn up on another flight. Phyllis said she wouldn't be surprised if he did, because the last time she had spoken to him he had really wanted to be with them all at this time. It was unfortunate there wasn't a telephone on the island so that she could phone his wife again and give her a number for Bobby to phone and leave a message if he wanted to.

John suddenly had an idea. Phyllis was a medium, wasn't she? She could communicate with other dimensions. Why not see if one of her spirit controls could give them any information about Bobby's whereabouts and well-being?

It was worth trying, Andrija said; and Phyllis agreed to co-operate. She would have to wait an hour or so, though, she said. She never did trance work so soon after a meal.

When an hour had passed and Phyllis said she was ready, Andrija set up equipment to record whatever transpired and John doused the lights. Phyllis slowly counted down into deep trance, her body slumped, remained so for about two minutes, then gradually straightened as the control took over. 'We are here,' she said in a firm voice. 'I am Ryr.'

This was an unexpected turn-up. Ryr was the name of the entity that had communicated through Phyllis during one of her classes the message about the three of them coming together and forming a core around Bobby. During one of the sessions at Ossining in April they had ascertained that Ryr and Corean worked in co-operation, so Ryr was presumably not a spirit but an extra-terrestrial.

Andrija asked about Bobby, and promptly received the answer: 'He is defying. He is being defiant. We understand why it is the nature of his thinking, but we are all gathered and you are all gathered, and we will be and pray with you. We are attempting to stop this testing. We are attempting to ease his burden. He will test us in the car tomorrow at three. A decision has been made among us that we must not interfere in the mechanics of the car because then he will do something of a more desperate nature. It is this nature that defies and dares that is also strong in releasing the energy that flows through.'

'I have a feeling that he actually will put himself in a situation where he can be killed,' Andrija said. 'And his reasoning is that if he is really wanted, by the powers you represent, he will then be spared, and that for him will be proof positive.'

'That is right,' Ryr confirmed. But there was another aspect to the situation that Andrija's analysis omitted. 'Besides the test that he is desiring of, in his mind he is positive that he has no value. He is positive that he will only disturb, harm and destroy you. That has been his pattern in his past. He is not aware that this destructive nature can be utilised for your world. When the testing he does is finished, and we pray it goes well, then he will have a glimpse of hope.'

The only way the assembled group could help at this time,

Ryr said, was by holding sessions of meditation, seated in a circle, and sending him love. 'Our love, your love, can penetrate the iron he has bound himself in,' Ryr said. They agreed to meditate that night and the following day at the crucial hour of three, but the feeling of frustration at being able to do no more than this, and at being so dependent as they were on Bobby for the continuation of their work, caused Andrija to ask some questions that they had all entertained. Why was a person with so many weaknesses and instabilities as Bobby had, chosen for such work? Why wasn't the opportunity to serve given to some other member of the group, any one of whom would be happy to take it on?

'We did not choose,' Ryr answered. 'He chose . . . We give each and every one of you a chance to perform your service . . . All of you are here for service, but for some of you that service is necessary. He is one of those . . . He is also one of us. When we return to your physical world, we oftentimes forget the spiritual side of our makeup. You have all been in this position at one time or another. All so evolved through processing. The work is not just our work. It is the work of the universe . . . All of you have served, all of you have evolved. It is now his chance, but if he should fail there will be two of you that can carry on, and then there will be more, because there are those that are waiting.'

This answer, which put Bobby's crisis in a universal context and gave it a relevance beyond the merely personal, and which also assured them that whatever happened the work would go on, at the same time considerably alleviated their feelings of frustration and impotence and strengthened their resolve to continue to give Bobby all possible support. But what would happen, Norman Shealy asked, if Bobby survived his crisis and decided no longer to participate in the work? Would the changes that had been effected in him be reversed?

'We do not take back what we give,' Ryr said. John asked if that meant that Bobby would retain some of his healing ability, and was given the answer, 'That is right. But it is tragic if that is so.'

'In your experience with this type of opportunity,' Andrija

said, 'do you often run into this kind of testing with the tinge of destructiveness in it? Is this more the case than not?'

'You are right,' Ryr answered, but went on to make an interesting assertion: 'We are coming to a time when that will not be a factor. We are on the fringe . . . In the past and until this time, that type of energy which is compatible with this planet has only evolved to this point. You have new people that will not be so.'

'Does this refer to some of these youngsters who have appeared all over the world recently with unusual powers?' Andrija asked.

'This is what we speak of,' said Ryr. This was the first mention in the communications of a subject that was to recur frequently in later ones. A number of other questions on various topics were put by members of the group and answered by Ryr before the session concluded with a moving assurance and exhortation:

'The one thing that we know is that the work and the service will go on, and we have the nucleus here. Know that, and have joy within you. This is a heavy time, a troubled time, because we are as responsible as you. Only love, unselfish, non-possessive, pure, will bring this into being, from our side as well as yours. You must always share and love and be open with each other. This then creates an energy with which we can work.'

'Well, it looks as if the cosmic connection is re-established,' Andrija said when Phyllis came out of trance, and he summarised for her the content of the communication. There followed an animated discussion in which they shared their hopes and fears, their beliefs and doubts about the communications, and speculated about what Ryr had meant about there being two among them who would be able to carry on if Bobby should fail. Presumably it meant that Phyllis would be able to serve as a channel, but Bobby was both a channel and a healer, so did it mean that healing powers would be developed in one of them? That was an intriguing question, but one that was impossible to answer, and anyway, Phyllis said, they shouldn't dwell too much on it at this stage but should concentrate all their efforts and thought energy on helping Bobby through his ordeal tomorrow.

At three o'clock in the afternoon of 18 June, Bobby's birthday, they all assembled in the courtyard and sat together in meditation for fifteen minutes as they had been instructed to do, trying to send Bobby psychic support and love in his hour of supreme crisis. Anxious to have news of what had happened to Bobby, they reassembled in the early evening for a communication.

'There are many of us here,' was the first thing that Ryr said when Phyllis was in trance. Apparently there was a conference in progress in the other dimension attended by Corean and other concerned parties, and several times during the ensuing conversation Ryr had to apologise for delays in responding, saying 'I am sorry, I was in another conference.'

Bobby, they learnt, was alive. Since ten o'clock that morning he had been going through a crisis in which 'in his mind he tried every way to eliminate without eliminating . . . his physical'. This presumably meant that he had contemplated ways of suicide but had not actually performed the act. With regard to his involvement in the work, however, he had made a decision, and it was in the negative. 'The decision of No was not what Bobby wanted,' Ryr explained, 'but he did what in his confused mind he considered the best for all parties involved.' The Corean group thought that there was a possibility that they might be able to work upon Bobby to get him to reverse his decision, and to this end they were requesting, Ryr reported from the other conference, that they should be given a two-week extension. They seemed to attach a great deal of importance to being granted this extension by Andrija, John and the others, which so far as the latter were concerned presented no problem, but they discussed the question with a seriousness consonant with its alleged importance while Ryr stood by waiting for their decision, which they then announced was in the affirmative. Corean's petition, however, was apparently a more contentious matter in the other conference, for Ryr reported that their request for two weeks had been disallowed and they had been granted only ten days. Who by? they all wondered, and

Andrija said, 'We'll go along with whatever decision is made. It is more important for us to help the soul than to be concerned about these arbitrary units of time.'

They could help, Ryr said, by sending Bobby a message assuring him of their support and that there would be a place for him in the work if ever he changed his mind. His function would not be the same as in the original plan after an alternative plan had been put in motion, but it was important for him to understand that the door was always open for him to return. Andrija promised that they would compose such a message and send it to Bobby as soon as possible, and Ryr said that it should be signed by the four of them.

This reference to the four was interesting, for it seemed to indicate that Ryr was aware of the commitment Lyall had entered into some weeks before in the communication with Corean held at Orsett, and to include him in the nuclear group. It did not, however, include Norman Shealy, whom John had invited to come to the Bahamas to learn more about their work and possibly play a role in it. It was clear from the conversations that they had had that Norman was intrigued but highly sceptical, and was concerned for his professional reputation should he get more deeply involved. As a medical practitioner, he had already gone out on a limb by recommending the use of psychics as diagnosticians, and obviously if he went back to his peers and said he had been talking with space beings he would put himself well beyond the pale.

'We have reviewed the outline of this new doctor,' Ryr said when Andrija introduced Norman into the discussion. 'It is of a practical purpose, we understand, in your world.'

Probably relieved at not being asked to make a commitment, Norman put a question about the purpose of Bobby's work as a healer.

'We explained that last evening,' Ryr said. 'The decision was made a long time ago.'

'I'm thinking more in terms of the purpose in the world, not for Bobby's soul,' Norman said. 'The purpose of your civilisation with its influence upon humanity.'

'This is why Corean is being given special allowance,' Ryr

said, and Andrija elaborated, explaining to Norman about the work of preparing mankind for the landing.

'Well, if this is true,' Norman said, 'then the main goal is to achieve as generalised a raising of consciousness as possible, is it not?'

'You used the statement, "if this is true",' Ryr admonished.

'If this is the purpose, is what I mean,' Norman corrected.

'That is better,' Ryr said. 'Doctor, will you explain?'

Andrija explained that the general idea was that Bobby was to be used gradually to win over the medical profession as part of an overall plan to prepare for the landing, then Ryr drew the session to a close:

'You will bear with me, but I have been conversing in two spheres. We send you love, we send you blessings, we send you peace. We are pleased that you have decided to continue with us. We know of your problems, we know of your concerns. We do not have the density that you must deal with. We do not know, given the same conditions, if we could do what you must do in the world of denseness. We go in peace.'

When Phyllis came out of trance she was disoriented and felt that something was wrong. She had been, she said, on a sort of big platform suspended in space where there were a lot of beings assembled, and she had acted as an interpreter, receiving and transmitting messages that were conveyed telepathically. John assured her that what she said made sense in relation to the communication they had just had, and that there was nothing wrong, but Phyllis remained disquieted and said, 'It was a strange place. I don't remember ever being in a place like that before when I do this stuff.'

'Something I don't understand is why they think this is so heavy for us,' Lyall said. 'Why do they think this is such a big thing we're doing for them?' This led to a discussion of the characteristics of the communicators and the impressions they had each formed of them.

'They seem to be concerned that we want instant action,' Norman said, 'and that if we don't get it we will be disappointed.'

'Yes,' John said, 'I think that they may think that our

capacity to change is considerably less than it is, or our capacity to adapt to a plan. Perhaps it is, in a sense, that their computers have limitations in adaptability and we have a greater degree of adaptability than they thought, which would explain their suprise.'

'I feel that they are learning a lesson,' said Phyllis. 'Is it possible for their souls to grow more?'

'Of course, for all souls,' said Andrija. 'We tend to think of them as being godlike. But they're not, right? They insist on being equals. Yet, as John says, their computers were programmed in a certain way to read us out, and they are surprised that we can actually operate as we are doing.'

It was a novel idea, that they might have something to teach as well as much to learn from their extra-terrestrial contacts. And the news about Bobby was a relief, if not exactly encouraging. They composed and signed a letter to him to mail the next day and retired for the night looking forward to their next communication, which Ryr had said could be at their convenience the following evening.

They spent the next day, for the first time since they had come to the island, swimming, sailing, and enjoying the sun and the sea. In the afternoon John and Phyllis went to Georgetown, and on an impulse of Phyllis's they went to the airport to meet the afternoon flight from Miami, but Bobby wasn't on it. They returned to the house for dinner, and when enough time had elapsed after the meal to enable Phyllis to work they assembled in the living-room. John put out the lights and lit a candle and a mosquito coil. Mosquitoes were a problem, for the breeze had dropped and the air was still and heavy. There was scarcely a sound from the water, which could usually be heard rhythmically slapping the coral a few feet from the house, and in the still air the sound of calypso music carried across the bay from the hotel on the main island.

Phyllis went into trance and the communication began with Ryr fussing about some technical problems, saying, 'We are attempting a new connection . . . We may need to adjust for fine tuning as we proceed . . . The energy field is strong. This being is now sensitive . . . We must turn down the volume.

We – every control operating, but the heart is very rapid.'

'Can you slow that down by just pressing the left carotid sinus?' Andrija put in helpfully.

'We correct that and the force field becomes again over-sensitive,' said Ryr. But eventually the technical problems were overcome. The channel, they were given to understand, was 'wired with nine sonars' or 'direct lines', and when the bio-engineering was completed Ryr announced, 'We are prepared to work as long as necessary.'

Reporting on Bobby's state of mind, Ryr informed them that 'He is in his heart with you. A decision in his heart has been made, but he is on the surface being deceptive. He must face and be honest with that condition. He is bright because of decision, but surrounds himself with dark because of still looking for the easy path.' Bobby should be left alone for ten days, and then would be the time to approach him and to decide whether he could still play his part in the plan. The plan had been that 'Bobby would have been a catalyst, the switch that would throw a light into your world, that would have been the master switch.' But, Ryr said, any good programme or organisation must have alternative courses of action in readiness, and proceeded to expound a concept that was completely new to everyone.

Future healing work, they were told, would be done by pairs or even groups of healers working together, and there were two people in the present group who could form such a team. The energy principle involved in channelled healing was difficult to explain in present circumstances, because 'This brain [Phyllis's] has not the words', but, Ryr urged, 'You will be patient as we attempt.' A thing they had learned, through working in the physical world, was the necessity of balancing the polarities of male and female energies, for 'When a subject is not balanced, the energy can be turned inward and it can then create a problem. But with the balancing of polarity, the flow stays, and strengthens in a positive manner.' In the past, many healing channels had been burned out because the importance of this balancing of polarised energies had not been fully appreciated. There were in every individual both types of energy, the male and female or positive and negative, but always one was predominant and 'In order for the flow to function, the energy flow we speak of, in order for it not to destroy, blow out, or burn out the channel, you must blend the female and male energies.' This did not imply, Ryr was careful to point out, apparently on instructions from above ('They say I must be clear'), a male-female physical relationship, but only a relationship between types of energy. 'I must clarify: we speak not of the physical . . . We speak of the etheric, we speak of the energy that flows through each of you . . . There is an envelope of energy around you . . . If, for example, a female is used to transmit the energy that we send in healing, without a balance we would not be able to continue using that vehicle for a great length of time. But if we work and blend in pairs . . . if one male is used and the energy is transmitted through the female, if they work in conjunction, it is purified . . . It operates similar to a cheesecloth. It filters out and clarifies and creates a pure energy.'

Such a conjunction, Ryr further explained, was not always necessary. Many human beings had the capacity to generate a certain amount of healing energy within themselves. But it was necessary for major healing work in which an external source was tapped. In such work, what was required was a balance and blending of male and female energies, or, more specifically, of two etheric bodies, one male and the other female, in order to form a kind of lens through which the healing energy would be channelled from its extra-terrestrial or other-dimensional source. Or, to use another metaphor, 'The female would work as a plug, and the male as a switch, or it could be reversed.' Of the people in the room, the two who were attuned to work together as a team were Phyllis and Lyall. The plan for the next stage of the work was to 'go on with the opening of many people', and this would be the task of Phyllis and Lyall working in conjunction, if they agreed to undertake it. 'The primary reason for Bobby,' Ryr said, 'was to make your professional people aware.' But the longer-term programme was to open many people, particularly among the young, as channels. 'The young can be trained, but they must be opened by using a male and female polarity.' The blended and balanced energies of Lyall's and Phyllis's etheric bodies could 'open and blend the energies of others, so that we can then use those beings to transmit healing through.'

The above paragraphs condense information that was elicited by questioning in the course of an unusually long communication. This was a key communication, not only because it divulged new information and plans but also because it brought into focus certain biases of attitude towards the work which were later to become both more prominent and more disruptive. Andrija's bias was towards obtaining the maximum possible information about the science, the technology, the way healing and channelling worked, whereas John and Lyall were more interested in the overall programme and purpose. 'We're trying to find out what the nature of the energy is,' said Andrija. 'Is there any way of giving us a hint? . . . Is there a true science of polarities? . . . Could you give us an elementary exposition of that science? . . . What would opening up mean to the person who was opened? What would they experience? What would they feel? What would their motivations be?' Ryr tried to cope with his barrage of questions, but said, 'I have difficulty with this brain,' and Lyall, becoming impatient, said 'Andrija, I think we can get bogged down in details.' John agreed and suggested they should proceed with the general overall plan and get back to the necessary details later. 'The doctor is unhappy, yes?' Ryr observed, and Andrija replied, 'Well, I would like to know what the science behind this is.' This conflict of priorities, between concern for knowing on the one hand and for being and doing on the other, was to become more acute in their later work.

When Ryr finally got round to outlining the tentative future programme, Lyall was disconcerted rather than pleased by the offer of so prominent a role in it. Up to the present, he had been quite comfortable in his position as an objective observer. He had said that he was willing to participate in the work, but he had had in mind that his contribution should be as an interpreter or a reporter, and the invitation to take on a more involved role caught him off guard. I can well understand how he felt, having had a similar experience myself.

The communication ended abruptly, with Ryr saying, 'We have created, because of the force, a problem. We must completely disconnect,' and suggesting that they might resume after about half an hour's rest. Phyllis came out of trance moaning and showing symptoms of intense physical pain, and when she regained normal consciousness her expression was fearful. Her eyes darted about as if she was following the movements of objects or entities invisible to the others. It was some time before she spoke, but eventually she turned to Andrija and asked him, 'Are you sure that we are dealing with the right people?' She had felt threatened, she said, on coming out of trance, by some creatures with black masks. John felt that Andrija was less reassuring than he might have been, and he told Phyllis he was certain she had nothing to fear, but when the half hour had elapsed Phyllis was reluctant to go into trance again, and she was only prevailed upon to do so some time later, after she had smoked several cigarettes.

Contact with Ryr was not re-established, however, so the communication that ensued was not a continuation but a new beginning. It was the beginning, in fact, of a new stage in Phyllis's channelling, for it was now that 'Tom' took over from Ryr as her control. 'I have worked with this being before. We have been in contact many years,' said Tom on his first appearance. John noticed that Phyllis's trance voice was changed. It was softer, more flowing, less mechanical and staccato. 'Would you please announce so all present here can hear your name?' Andrija said, and the reply came: 'My name is not important. But I am known as Tom.' The being, Tom said, believed that he was a spirit, and had been allowed to think over the many years that he had worked with her.

'Tom, where do you come from in this vast universe?' Andrija asked.

'We come from beyond your knowledge of light,' Tom answered. 'We come from the zone that you would call cold.' He was linked with Corean, as was Ryr, but Ryr was a computer and the difference between himself and the beings he represented and Ryr was that 'We are with soul'. Explaining, at Andrija's request, what had happened in the last session, Tom said that Phyllis had feared that she perhaps was working with a computer and that she had had a negative reaction to the new system that was being tried out. 'We were in error,' he admitted. But the fault had also been with them, the participants. 'There were many negative vibrations, that were then able to pull in other negative forces. It takes but one negative force to create the energy with which the negative can work. There were many negatives in this room. We had in this room the negativity of Dr Shealy, who in his own fears of his past was creating a negative storm. We had with you, Doctor, the frustrations of trying to have clarification, which created another negative storm. We had with Dr Watson, the feeling that he was being threatened. This too created another negative storm . . . When negativity breeds, it creates a force like a hurricane or a tornado in your world . . . We terminated.'

This analysis of the underlying tensions and conflicts of the last session showed impressive insight, particularly with regard to Lyall, who had not at that time confessed to anyone his feelings of being threatened by the new role he had been invited to play. Tom went on to reassure him that he was not being put under any duress but was simply being offered an opportunity to serve in a particular way. There would be other opportunities, other ways, if he chose not to accept the offered role; and Phyllis would find another working partner for she was 'a catalyst in conjunction with many different male polarities'. Lyall could take his time to reach a decision.

Probably feeling rather left out, and possibly a little piqued by the reference to 'the negativity of Dr Shealy', Norman asked if he would have a part to play in the work. 'It depends on where your commitment lies, sir,' Tom told him. Norman said that his commitment was 'to open up the channels within medicine', but that he had to keep busy and make a living. Tom said that he could be involved in the work in a small way in that case, but his commitment should be to his work in medicine, for 'When this project is put into motion, there must be a total commitment, because there will be no energies for anything else.'

In the rest of the communication, and one held the following day, Tom went on to give fuller details of the nature of the project referred to, and the information he gave corresponded with and elaborated on that which they had already received from Corean through Bobby's channelling. The main purpose of all the work being done on Earth at the present time by various extra-terrestrial groups in conjunction with human individuals and groups was to prepare mankind for the landing. It was their hope that by the time of their appearance seventy-five per cent of the people would have been prepared for the event. 'We speak only of what you call your civilised countries,' Tom said. 'The primitives will already know.' Andrija, Phyllis and John were the nucleus of a group which would be given the fullest and most detailed information, for they had in Phyllis a unique channel for information transfer, and one of their functions would be to disseminate that information. At the extra-terrestrial level, there were different units at work with different skills and special interests, and the work of these units was gradually being correlated. There was one unit, for instance, that was now working on the technology of interfering with television transmissions and projecting their own material onto television screens, as this was considered a good way of demonstrating their existence to a large number of people at once. The present group would continue to be involved in the area of healing, but it was important that they should always remember that they were 'the primary hub' of a world-wide plan and organisation established for the purpose of making the world aware of the existence of extra-terrestrial civilisations and of their benevolent concern for the world so that they should not be opposed when the time came for the landing. 'We have the technology to help your people,' Tom said. 'It is very difficult for us to help them, when we are being denied that we exist. And it's going to need our technology in order for them to survive. Need I say more?'

The process of expanding human awareness had in fact already begun. On 16 October 1971, a new situation and a new era in earth history had begun. Since then, Tom said,

'People – and you are aware of this Dr Watson, yourself included – have become more aware.' Lyall replied that the date of 16 October 1971, was very relevant to him, for it was on that day that he had sat down to write his book, *Supernature*. It was also John's thirty-fourth birthday, and about a month after this date Andrija had begun his research with Uri Geller. Work had been steadily progressing on several fronts since 1971, Tom said, but now the time had come for it to be accelerated. The world-wide emergence, in the wake of Geller, of children with paranormal powers was a sign of this acceleration. And there would be more such children, whose powers would become manifest in various ways, for instance in an ability to put animals into a sleep-like, calm condition just by touching them. 'Your world is becoming more open to the work that has been – that we have worked many thousands of years, many aeons, to bring into focus.' The 'we' in this context included present human company. 'You have worked on many planets doing what you are doing now,' Tom told them. Moreover, Bobby had been a part of their group in other incarnations, and there had been a time when he had been instrumental in pulling the rest of the group through circumstances of crisis caused by their own errors. This time it was their turn to bring Bobby through, and they should continue to try, but should not be too distressed if they failed. In his past five lives on the planet Earth, Bobby had failed to accomplish what he needed to do, and if he failed again he would have other opportunities. There was always a high failure rate with beings who had chosen to be in service while incarnated on the planet Earth, because of the physical nature of the planet and its seductions, and in fact only two per cent of people who returned to serve actually entered upon a commitment. That had been the problem with the Earth for thousands of years. There was reason to hope, though, that with the New Age consciousness developing there would be many more who would commit themselves to the work that was necessary for survival, as the doctor, the 'Being' (as Phyllis is referred to throughout the communications) and Sir John had committed themselves and as Dr Watson was now invited to do.

It was clear that the session was drawing to a close, so John asked about future communications. The group would be leaving the Bahamas the following day and dispersing to various parts of the world, and he wondered whether it was possible for them to communicate individually, perhaps by using other channels. His question elicited another piece of unexpected information:

'You can make contact with us by going into a meditative state, being aware of your left ear, and being aware of a force around it and an inspirational thought around it. At times we try to inspire you and to help you, and at many times I speak to all of you. You are confused and do not understand that it is our thought that we are transferring to you. Any time you need reassurance, or you feel depressed, or feel you need contact, go into a meditative state and ask for us to come. We will impress through your left ear the answers you need to know. Every one of you has been wired in your left ear.'

'I hope you speak in English, not in morse code or something,' Andrija quipped.

'We go in peace. We send you love. We surround you with protection. We wish you to know we are always with you,' said Tom when he finally took his leave.

It had been, they all agreed when they were talking after Phyllis emerged from trance, a very impressive and fascinating communication. Indeed, the entire Bahamian trip, which had begun so unpromisingly, had turned into an experience none of them would easily forget.

The following morning they flew to Miami together and then dispersed, Phyllis and Andrija to return to their homes in Orlando and Ossining, Norman to his clinic in Wisconsin, John to join Diana in Italy, and Lyall to take back with him to London certainly the strangest and possibly the most important dilemma he had ever been confronted with in his life. Except for Norman, they all agreed to get together again in a month's time at Ossining, unless the Management – as Phyllis now jokingly named their communicators – summoned them to a meeting earlier.

A publisher friend, in a letter declining the present book, wrote to me: 'If the Ossining experience turns out to be illusory or a hoax, then the tone of earnest enquiry in which it is described will be entirely inappropriate, it seems to me.' I see his point, and I have chosen to take the risk of adopting in relation to the material an attitude of serious (I would not say earnest, which suggests humourless) enquiry precisely because I am satisfied that it is neither illusory nor a hoax. I have participated in enough communications now, and have got to know the people involved well enough, to be satisfied on this point. I am not saying that John and Andrija may not be wrong in believing that they are conversing with extra-terrestrials, but to be wrong is not necessarily to be deluded, and I am satisfied that these are sane and serious men whose claims deserve to be taken seriously instead of being peremptorily derided. Derision is too often the recourse of mediocre minds when they are confronted with novelty. Such minds seek comfort and safety by huddling together, and it seems to me that an uncritically derisive huddle is not more admirable, though it may be safer, than an uncritically credulous one. So I make no apology for taking the communications seriously and trying to assess them intelligently.

In the period covered by the narrative so far there are three things that are particularly impressive: (1) the thematic consistency of the communications, (2) evidence of supernormal cognition, and (3) paranormal physical phenomena. Let us consider these in turn.

*Thematic consistency.* In the communications held between March and June 1974 there were two distinct channels, Bobby and Phyllis, and three different communicators identified themselves: Corean, Ryr and Tom. Yet the information channelled contains no contradictions or anomalies, but on the contrary in respect of a number of themes it follows a process of development with internal consistency though coming through different channels and allegedly from different sources. We are given to understand that Corean, Ryr and Tom are in communication among themselves, and the consistency of the information they give supports this proposition. For instance:

The theme of *the landing* was introduced by Corean in the first communication held. Corean also stated that the function of Bobby and of the group around him was to make mankind aware of the existence of other civilisations in order to prepare for the landing, and that there were other groups working on this project in other ways. These points were reiterated by Ryr and Tom, who added the information that one of the purposes of the landing was to give mankind advanced technologies that would help ensure the survival of the planet, and also that a New Age consciousness that was better adapted to the planned future scenario had been spontaneously developing among a minority of human beings.

The theme of *previous incarnations* of John, Andrija, Phyllis and Bobby was mentioned by all three communicators. 'He was with you before,' said Corean of Bobby on 14 March, and in the communication of 22 June Tom said, 'You have worked on many planets doing what you are doing now,' and explained how Bobby had helped the rest of them through a crisis on a previous occasion.

*Healing* and the energies involved in healing were subjects on which each of the communicators had information to contribute. 'We were sending very strong,' said Corean after the abortive demonstration to the May Lectures assembly, and Ryr later explained how the 'sending' takes place, through the blending of male and female energies in the etheric creating a kind of lens. From the start, Corean had said that Bobby and Phyllis should work together as a healing team, and Ryr gave the rationale behind this recommendation, expounding the theme of the balancing of polarities and the need for a process of filtering and refinement.

*Bio-engineering* is another recurrent theme. I suppose we have to accept that beings capable of intergalactic travel might possess other kinds of technological expertise incomprehensible to us, but all the talk in the communications – a lot of which I have omitted in my précis – about sonars, implants and wiring, is the bit I find most difficult to take. But if consistency argues for plausibility I suppose we have to suppress our natural repugnance for the idea of being messed about with biologically and concede bio-engineering as much credence as we choose to give to the other recurrent themes, for all three communicators talk about it. In the final session held in the Bahamas, Andrija asked Tom how they reconciled their bio-engineering work with their repeated statement that they never interfere with free will, referring particularly to the implants that were supposed to confer paranormal powers on certain children. Tom replied: 'It does not impinge on their free will as it was their decision at the time of birth.' Which is a clever answer, and one consistent with the claim that such children are incarnated souls from other civilisations.

Thematic consistency and the fact that themes are enlarged upon coherently with different channels and different alleged communicators certainly constitutes *prima facie* evidence that the information is not generated by any individual intelligence (human, spirit or extra-terrestrial) but exists independently of any such intelligence and under certain circumstances becomes accessible. I shall discuss this point at greater length later, but now let's go on to the second impressive characteristic of the communications reviewed up to now.

*Evidence of supernormal cognition.* A century of psychical research has established to the satisfaction of all but the most inveterate sceptics that telepathy, clairvoyance and precognition occur. As these are proven human faculties, evidence for their occurrence in the present context does not necessarily imply that the communications come from an external source, though the circumstances of their occurrence in some cases do seem more consistent with this hypothesis than with the alternative one that the information was obtained psychically by the medium. For instance:

In the Ossining communication of 8 April Corean reproached Phyllis and Andrija for not giving a message to Bobby, as they had been asked to do the previous night. The fact that Corean knew that the message had not been delivered is significant, for it is unlikely that the knowledge could come from Bobby, who was in trance and supposed to be the recipient of the message, or from the sitters, Andrija or Phyllis, for they were being admonished for forgetting it.

Corean's explanation of the cause of the failure of the demonstration healing is a similar case to the above. After listening again to the instructions for the demonstration given in an earlier communication, Phyllis and Andrija suggested two reasons for the failure but omitted the main one, which was that Bobby had metal in his pockets and on his clothing: a fact which neither of them knew. Bobby presumably knew that he had had coins in his pocket, but he was in trance, and the very fact that he had the coins implies that in his normal state of consciousness he had no recall of his trance utterances.

Ryr's reports on Bobby's actions and state of mind throughout the time the group were at John's house on Stocking Island were later found to be quite correct. Bobby had contemplated various means of suicide, including an automobile accident on his birthday, he had resolved to withdraw from the work, but at depth he was still undecided and struggling with his problem of confidence. Of course Phyllis, knowing Bobby well by now, might have been able to make an intelligent guess as to how he would feel and act, or she may be capable, like the seer Edgar Cayce, of trance clairvoyance of a distant person's physical and mental condition, so the fact that Ryr's reports were true does not prove Ryr's existence as an independent mind, though it does strongly suggest the operation of paranormal cognition.

Finally, Tom's insight into the causes of the negativity that disrupted the last session with Ryr, and particularly into Lyall's feeling of being threatened by the role it was proposed he should play, is impressive evidence, for no one had anticipated that Lyall would be offered such a role and he had had no time to tell anyone how he felt about it.

*Paranormal physical phenomena.* The most incredible part of Andrija's account of his work with Uri is his record of numerous materialisation, dematerialisation, psychokinetic and teleportation events, and I'm sure many readers of his book felt, 'If he wants me to take him seriously, I wish he wouldn't ask me to believe all this stuff.' The present narrative raises the same problem. What are we to make of the story of the miraculous burn healing or of the blow out of the transformer that terminated the attempted demonstration in London? Witnesses to both events (about sixty to the second of them) vouch that they happened, and although for most of us human mendacity is a commoner experience than physical paranormality this is a poor reason for dismissing them as lies. The attitude, 'Reality must be such-and-such because I've never experienced it otherwise than such-and-such' is not only unphilosophical but fundamentally unintelligent, the cry not of the truth-seeker but of the man who seeks the fixation of belief. In later chapters I shall be reporting other incredible physical phenomena, and I confess that this is the part of the story that causes me most unease, although in connection with the work I have now experienced one or two things myself that have rather eroded my scepticism. With our Western scientific-rationalist cultural background, which has been dominated for the last three centuries by the principles and methods of physical science, we find paranormal mental phenomena easier to deal with than paranormal physical phenomena. We are readier to concede that telepathy or clairvoyance might occur than that materialisation or levitation might. This is a cultural bias, and we ought to recognise it as such even if we can't or don't want to transcend it. Western science has been so stupendously successful in fathoming the laws and harnessing the powers of the physical world that it cannot give credence to anything that apparently subverts known laws or manifests a power that it has not harnessed.

Such considerations may help us come to terms with paranormal physical events, but they do not help us understand what such events may signify. In point of fact, some contemporary theoretical physicists find physical paranormality easier to accept than does the man in the street, for the events resemble quantum events on a macroscopic scale. It is interesting and perhaps relevant to note that physicists working in the field of superconductors and superfluids (the physics of very low temperatures) have observed quantum events occur on a macroscopic scale, and to remember that Tom's answer to Andrija's question, 'Where do you come from in this vast universe?' was: We come from beyond your knowledge of light. We come from the zone that you would call cold.'

But this is to embark upon a subject that could have a chapter to itself, and which I shall return to later when we have more data to discuss. For the present, I just want to leave the reader with the question whether the internal thematic consistency of the communications, the evidence for supernormal cognition within them and for the occurrence of paranormal physical events in connection with them, constitute convincing or even *prima facie* evidence that the communications are what they purport to be. It is not necessary, however, to come to a decision about this at the present stage, for there is a great deal more of the story to tell.

# CHAPTER FOUR

## *Exits*

In 1973 John and his then girlfriend and future wife Diana Becchetti had attended a six-week course together at the California Institute of Psychosynthesis, and it was here that Diana had discovered her vocation. She had gone on to take advanced training in the techniques of psychosynthesis, and after the May Lectures she had gone to Italy to spend some time working with Roberto Assagioli. The founder of psychosynthesis was now eighty-six and very frail. Although Diana went to him as a student, they soon struck up a close relationship in which she figured as a kind of combination of daughter figure and beloved disciple. 'I realised when he died,' Diana later said, 'that I had been sent to serve Roberto in the last months of his life, to bring him joy and contact and humanness for his last months on earth.'

John joined Diana in Italy after the gathering in the Bahamas and spent three weeks with her there. He was eager to have Roberto's opinion of the communications, and he wrote a long report of events and information received up to that time for him to read. Fortunately, he recorded the remarks Assagioli made after he had read the report. Assagioli spoke English well, but jerkily and in a high-pitched voice with pronounced Italian inflections, which makes the tape difficult to transcribe, but after listening to it several times phrase by phrase I have been able to decipher the following interesting comments: '. . . Very pleased with the report because of the agreement between the communications and my intuition is really remarkable. The main points should be a basis for our co-operation . . . Mediums are not always reliable because they are open to different influences and they cannot discriminate . . . The point which I really doubt is that of a landing, a physical landing of these beings . . . As regards the New Wave from 1975 on, and the coming of higher beings: I think it will be a gradual thing, but the main point is the realisation by humanity that there are higher beings, which they are strangely reluctant to admit. I think that to help them to recognise that is good. And this is one of the main esoteric teachings. The time has come for the recognition of that, of the hierarchy that is there . . . The only point of caution is that there are dark forces that try to prevent all this happening, and one of their ways is to insinuate false teachings in the communications. It is not so difficult for them for they are sly and under the guise of something fine they can be misleading. So we must always be on guard . . .'

Assagioli was well versed in the esoteric traditions and teachings, and he could speak of the hierarchy of higher beings, and of the dark forces that opposed them with complete naturalness, as if he had long ago accepted the reality of such entities. What is most interesting, of course, is that Assagioli found nothing intrinsically preposterous in the idea of communications emanating from an extra-terrestrial intelligence. What he said about the unreliability of mediums and the possibility of false teachings being insinuated into communications must always be borne in mind when we attempt to assess this material. But it was a possibility that both Phyllis and Andrija were aware of, for Phyllis said to Andrija when she came out of trance at the conclusion of the Ryr channelling, 'Are you sure that we are dealing with the right people?'

To a non-psychic who falls in with people involved in the psychic scene it is impressive to find that they have a consensus reality. Intensely subjective though psychic and spiritual experiences are, they belong to an area of human experience that has been well mapped, and knowledge of the topography of this strange area is shared by psychics and psychologists. Freudian psychologists tend to lump psychic experiences together as products of morbid or pathological mental states, and Jung and Assagioli were pioneers in taking psychism seriously and studying the varieties of its manifestations.

In conversation with me, Diana said of Assagioli: 'He believed that certain things were lower psychism and certain things were higher, in the sense that lower psychism was astral projection, telepathy, clairvoyance, mediumship, whereas higher psychism was intuition, illumination, inspiration, and he felt very much that if we tune into and focus all our attention on the lower aspects of psychism we won't allow the higher development to occur.' What worried Diana about the communications and John's involvement was that she felt that there was a good deal of lower psychism involved in them.

John promised Assagioli that when he returned to Ossining in July he would bring back to Italy a further report on what transpired in the next series of communications. He also promised to consult the Management on the question whether it would be in order for a healing to be attempted on Roberto. Assagioli had agreed to this on the condition that no attempt should be made to cure his deafness, for he said he had lived with that condition long enough to have learnt that it had certain advantages.

Phyllis was already at Ossining when John arrived on 18 July. Lyall was due to come on the 20th, but, Andrija said, they had already learnt from the Management that he had decided against getting more deeply involved in the work. Andrija had held a communication alone with Phyllis the night before, in which Tom had said, 'Dr Watson was given an opportunity and declined. If he had said yes he would not necessarily have had to do that project. We were asking for faith. He knew for the last three years that he would be involved in healing. Within his heart this pleased him, but he asked for more and we were willing to give this, but he was not willing to test us.'

Phyllis, Andrija and John were all disappointed by this news, but in the same communication there had been more encouraging news about Bobby. 'He has made a commitment, but under certain conditions,' Tom said. 'In his heart his commitment is made, but he is now trying to make us make a commitment to him. Things will be resolved and all your systems in motion by the middle of August.' That was unexpected news, for when Phyllis had last seen Bobby in Orlando he had not intimated that he was now willing to make his commitment to work with the group again. He had, however, tried to exercise his healing powers on Phyllis herself.

On 8 July, Phyllis had had a heart attack. She had been in her office with two close friends when she had suddenly collapsed. They had driven her round to her doctor, who had immediately sent her to hospital, where she was in intensive care for four days. When the worst of the crisis was over and she was convalescing she had had an argument with the doctor about smoking, and by threatening to discharge herself from the hospital and convincing him that the stress she underwent without cigarettes was likely to cause a relapse, she managed to prevail upon him to allow her four or five cigarettes a day. The doctor therefore arranged for her to be moved to another room, immediately next to the intensive care unit, where although she was alone she was still under continual observation for she was wired to electronic monitoring equipment. She was supposed to remain in bed all the time and call a nurse if she needed anything, but on the second day she got bored and wondered what would happen if she detached the belts that connected her to the electronic devices. She did so and nobody came to investigate, so she took the opportunity to go to the toilet. The next day she became more adventurous and left the room for about twenty minutes to take a shower, and still nobody seemed to have noticed her absence. She thought it extraordinarily inefficient, for a nurse was supposed to be keeping an eye on the monitoring equipment in the next room, but she wasn't disposed to complain and she continued to enjoy her surreptitious daily excursions throughout the rest of her convalescence. She soon felt fully recovered. Among the tests she was put through before being finally discharged was one on a running machine. Her heartbeat was monitored while she ran, and the doctor was amazed at the steadiness of the beat and at the length of time that she kept up the running. He told her she seemed to have more than recovered, and that she had the heart of a girl of twenty. He was obviously very puzzled.

The doctor and the hospital staff were even more puzzled on the day she left. Phyllis only heard the story three days later from the superintendent of nurses, who was an acquaintance of hers. Apparently after she had left the hospital the electrocardiogram had continued giving a read-out of her heartbeat, as if she was still wired to the machine. Technicians were called to check the machine for faults. They dismantled it and put it together again, and it still went on recording Phyllis's heartbeat. It continued to do so, in fact, for eight hours after she had left the hospital.

Twice while she was in hospital Bobby had tried to get in to see her and had managed to do so briefly on one occasion, masquerading as a relative who had come a long way to pay the visit. He had attempted to do a healing but had been allowed little time and it was doubtful that Phyllis's recovery was due to his efforts. There were so many unusual elements in the case that Andrija had asked for an explanation during the communication he held alone with Phyllis on 17 July. 'We are sorry that we had to inconvenience her,' Tom had said, 'but we decided this was the best way. We had much work to do.' Phyllis had been getting too little rest and had been generating too much energy inward, which had weakened the heart. 'So we decided that this Being needed to be brought down so that we could repair and fix the heart at the same time.' Her heart was now as good as when she was a child, Tom went on, and also its function and composition had been changed. 'It is a method not known in your world,' he said, and tried to explain that the heart now had nine sorts of antennae which functioned both as sensors and transducers. 'What it will do is filter the energy. Part of it will filter the energy, part of it will be used as a satellite for us, and it filters and purifies the blood. Energy can then be dissipated into the ether without a blowout.' Andrija asked whether the abnormal reactions on the hospital equipment were due to this energy, and Tom replied: 'This is correct. The energy that we use radiates out from this Being. We have talked to you before about the sonars [heart implants, mentioned by Ryr in the communications held on Stocking Island on 21 June]. This sonar continues to radiate after it is activated. It is also the same principle as is used in healing. When we use these beings for healings, after the healing or the actual physical contact has taken place, then the healing continues. The sonars continue to radiate out for approximately eight to twenty-four of your hours.'

'Nobody in the world seems to have known this,' Andrija said wonderingly.

'Nobody before has hooked one of our beings into one of these machines,' Tom said.

In the same communication, Tom had spoken at some length about the relation between sexual and spiritual energies. Being involved in the type of work they were all involved in, he had said, tended to activate sexual energy and desire to a high degree.

'It's obvious that we need tremendous help in this area,' Andrija said, 'for it seems to be the main obstacle to our carrying out the commitments that we make.'

'You must realise that I do not understand that emotion,' Tom said. But he apparently managed to get some help from colleagues better acquainted with the problems of physical beings, for after a long pause he went on: 'They are explaining to me that there is nothing wrong with this emotion, but if the being is not able to transmute the vibration it becomes like a furnace that is stoked. And the furnace must have a safety valve. The refined way of doing this would be to elevate the energy or to walk off the steam. Within all of you there is a pipeline, and if the energy is not funnelled upward so that the steam can be released properly, it then becomes a heart-burning furnace. If you let off too much steam from the furnace it dissipates the energy of that furnace and it no longer is functional as it should be. This is the problem in your physical world. There is too much involvement in releasing the energy instead of refining the energy.'

What this amounted to, of course, was an advocacy of sublimation instead of satiation of sexual desires, and although it was not particularly original it was apparently particularly relevant to Andrija, for the following day he made a decision to terminate a liaison which he knew had been jeopardising his work.

John also made a decision on the same morning, 20 July. Here is how he describes it: 'Early in the morning while in bed I got to thinking about my frustration with the wealthy people I know who claim to be committed yet still do not give money even though they know it is urgently needed. I realised that whilst I had given a lot of money I had not in so doing endangered my own financial security, so in real terms I had given nothing. I felt that that indicated some lack of faith in myself and in God, and that if I overcame that my frustration would go away, for it is of course frustration with myself and not with others. I also believed that money would only begin to flow from others when I had dealt with my hang-up about it. When I honestly faced my problem in this way it simply melted away and I was overwhelmed with a sense of relief, joy and peace.'

The Management seemingly understood and appreciated that Andrija and John had both resolved personal problems that had been affecting their work for on the night of 20 July they held a party to celebrate the reaffirmation of their commitment. Early in this session, which was to be the weirdest they had had to date and one of the longest, Tom said, 'This room is filled with our people this evening. We have come to surround you with protection and with light.' Because of the large number of extra-terrestrials present, they were given to understand, questions on a wide variety of topics would be able to be dealt with promptly, and they proceeded to take advantage of this situation. Among the points of information that their questions elicited in the course of the next hour were the following:

- that a certain chemical element taken in very minute doses has the property of heightening psychic powers; both the element and its organic source were identified by name, but as it is a poison and has to be handled with great care I have judged it advisable to withhold these details from the present narrative;

- that the structure of Christianity is in decline and will continue to decline, but there are groups within Christianity who disagree with the dogmatic aspects of the religion and will preserve its essential core;
- that the Management have people 'attempting to do the work that is necessary' placed in all the governments of the major countries of the world except the Chinese;
- that the US and Russian governments had had a secret agreement for many years to suppress information about UFO sightings and contacts, but they were now going to be put under increasing pressure by people demanding release of official information;
- that the telephone lines of the Ossining house were tapped by government agencies, but there was no need to worry because 'we know how to erase';
- that the most reliable esoteric writings were those of 'the Tibetan' channelled through Mrs Alice Bailey;
- that the group working with Uri was still optimistic about getting him to come back into service, but 'we cannot make him change his decision, we can only try to inspire, and if his ego is not tempered there is not much we can do'.

Some other minor bits of information were conveyed, then Tom said, 'All of our people are now smiling. We are all around you. This room is filled, this house is filled, and the top of your house is filled. We are very happy to be with you. You must understand that this is a party in your world.'

'Perhaps John and I should address ourselves to this marvellous multitude, and tell them how we feel,' Andrija said.

'They would like to address themselves to you,' Tom said, and after a short pause he delivered a celebratory speech:

'All this array of people and beings – because we are people as you are people – is a gathering of all that have worked for many hundreds and thousands of your years in order to help you. Whether you realise this or not, we have come the farthest that we have ever come in order to help mankind. We are all very excited and exhilarated with being close to the completion of our project. In your time it is short, but in our time it has been very long and we realise how short it has now become. As I look around this group that has gathered in your home, on top of your home and outside your home, I see nothing but joy and peace and love that is being generated to all of you, and with all of this power that we bring to you, and this love, we cannot fail in this mission. There will be no way that we can fail in this mission because at this time we have also on the planet Earth new physical beings that will help to see that we do not fail. This we have never had before. We have never had the communication system that you now have, the awareness that you now have, and the openness that you now have. We are sad that some of you fail, but remember, in the past everything failed, so we expect a casualty rate. We do not like it, but we know that this is so. We would like you to keep in your hearts the understanding that this is an honest and sincere effort and a pure love that we have for you beings.'

Profoundly moved, Andrija asked the reason for the celebration at this particular time and was told, 'The cosmic event that is going on is because of the final acceptance by our Council that our project will be completed. This came about due to the work of you three. We are having a party of joy. You would use the expression, "dancing in the streets".' Moreover, the immediate cause of the celebration was the fact that the decisions Andrija and John had individually made that morning would enable the work to be accelerated and ensure its eventual success.

'We would like to have your permission to introduce the Being to many that have come,' Tom said at the conclusion of the session. They agreed, and there was a pause of a couple of minutes before Tom said that the session should now be ended and Phyllis brought back. Andrija slowly brought her out of trance, and when she was fully conscious Phyllis spoke with undisguised excitement and awe about the experience she had just been through. She kept saying there weren't the words to describe it, but she managed to convey something of her vision in a series of exclamations.

'My God, Andrija! They were outside this place. It was

beautiful. It was absolutely glowing. And there were ledges, and there were all kinds of people, but they weren't physical. And they had this glow. I was on the top of your house and all these people were surrounding this whole house, and they were smiling, beaming. The ledges were all round your house.'

'What did they look like?' Andrija said. 'Were they like people?'

'No, not like people, not really,' Phyllis said. She struggled to find words. 'They had different forms, as if they came from different planets or galaxies or something. But they all had this smile. They were laughing and giggling and they were like kids that were bubbling over and that had just got too much of something or other. But there were some with long robes. And one took me by the hand, and they said, "We want you to know how many are working with you." And there are thousands and thousands and thousands. The ones in the robes were looking on like fathers or grandfathers looking at their children and saying with great pride, "You've done it!" The higher ones had such pride in their people.'

Andrija explained what had happened in the communication, and about the party and the reason for it, and how at the end Tom had asked permission to take Phyllis to meet their people. 'What blasts my mind out,' he said, 'is that here we are, just three ordinary little schmos, and the Council of the supergalaxy chooses to drop in!'

They all laughed. It was just too incredible and beautiful, utterly preposterous but totally believable because at the time none of them had expected anything like this, and as Phyllis in trance was always quite oblivious to what she channelled the correspondences between her experiences and what Tom had said were sufficient proof for Andrija and John that there really had been this intergalactic gathering of beings around them. There seemed no other way of expressing their mixed feelings of delight and amazement than by laughter.

Lyall had arrived that morning as arranged, but because of his decision not to get more involved in the work of the group he had not participated in this session. He had spent the past month in London and at his home in Bermuda and had devoted a lot of thought to the work of the Ossining group and the question of his own commitment and future work. Basically, he explained to me some time later, he felt that he had to remain a loner and could not work as a member of a group. His training and expertise were as a naturalist and biologist, and he felt that the Earth had marvels and mysteries enough to engage him, and despite all the evidence he could never be quite comfortable with the idea of intelligent super-beings from eslewhere intervening in Earth's affairs. Nor could he see how he could ever be entirely satisfied that the communications came from an external source and not from the unconscious of one or more of the people involved. His respect for Andrija as a scientist was immense, but he was convinced that he was also a shaman, a 'magic man' as he said, and was the key figure in the story.

I took the opportunity to ask Lyall about the puzzling appearance of the will. That really was a mystery, but he was not prepared to take it as proof positive of the existence of the Management. He had investigated the incident. The will had been drawn up by solicitors in Johannesburg who said they had received instructions from him by telephone. They had then posted the will to his home in Bermuda and it had come back with his signature on it, whereupon they had for-warded it to his parents. But, Lyall said, he had not made the phone call, had not signed the document, and had not even been in Bermuda at the time when he was supposed to have returned it from there. He didn't see how anyone could have contrived such an elaborate hoax, or who could have done so, and he admitted that it looked like a materialisation event con-ceived and executed by some intelligence, but even so it didn't prove anything and he was content to shelve it as an unsolved and probably insoluble mystery. His work in the Philippines and in Indonesia had accustomed him to living with the in-soluble and the imponderable.

So Lyall was no longer a participant in the communications, though he remained for several days at Ossining as a guest. On the day following the 'party' John and Andrija retired in the evening with Phyllis to Andrija's room to conduct another session which revolved around two questions that Andrija put to Tom at the start: What had been going on elsewhere on the planet the night before to cause the celebration? and, What precisely was meant by preparing mankind for the landing?

The first question, Tom indicated, showed that they still did not fully appreciate the importance of their role. They had to understand, difficult though it was to accept, that together the three of them constituted the energy core for the work of transformation that was going to be done on the planet. Their function was that of a trigger or a catalyst, and the previous night 'there was not so much a global awareness as there was in the three of you a true commitment made'. They had to remember, too, that they were really beings from other levels who had chosen to come to Earth to do this work.

John asked about his specific role. He well understood that Andrija and Phyllis had special abilities and experience to equip them for the work, but he didn't really understand what his contribution could be. 'Your balance and support for these two will be your main role,' Tom said, 'your love, your logic, and your balance.' Andrija and Phyllis, because of their past work and experience, were in the habit of questioning, checking and looking for proofs, which was right and good up to a point but could be overdone, and John would 'serve the purpose of being more open and helping them to see that there are other things besides their constant striving for positive proof, so that they will not be trapped'.

Andrija should not be so concerned as he was about the immensity of the task or feel that he alone was responsible for its accomplishment. 'We have set many things in motion on your planet . . . There will be many that will come to you. Doors will be opened. The advancement of knowledge will be very rapid. We will put these things into motion. We are helping you, Doctor. You have had knowledge and you have had faith in us for many years. Now have a little more faith and understand that this will not have to be done by you alone as it has in the past.'

In answer to Andrija's question about the meaning of preparing mankind for the landing, Tom now gave a detailed description of the nature and purpose of the event.

The landing would be a physical, visible event that would take place all over the planet over a period of nine days. Many different types of craft would land and beings would descend from them and be among men. Some would remain on Earth as teachers and some would go on after a while to work in other areas, for then the planet Earth would have begun to evolve in its truest sense.

Thinking of the landing as the Second Coming, John asked, 'Will the beings that remain collectively represent the Christ or will the Christ be among them?'

'You must remember that all of you and all of us have the Christ within us,' Tom said. 'It will be a collective consciousness . . . Man is now coming out of the true dark ages of the planet and becoming aware of the existence of other life forms in other parts of the universe. Men have always assumed that there was someone sitting up there taking care of their problems, but they also assumed through their ego that they were the only existents and that this being called God was only concerned with them. Man now has to understand that there are other forms of life and that the universe does not revolve, or evolve, just around man.'

The beings that were going to come to Earth would bring technologies that would help man deal with some of the problems he was faced with, but their main purpose would be what we would call a spiritual one. It would be 'to raise the vibration of the souls, to bring them out of darkness – and when we say darkness we do not mean negativity but true darkness, for they do not see and do not understand the cosmic, and they also do not understand that when they hate and when they are angry this creates a problem for the universe. Only by raising the level of the consciousness of this planet, and perfecting the love and the core that is inside each human being, can we go on then to perfect other planets in the galaxies. This planet is one of the lowest that the soul comes to to learn a lesson. The tragedy of this planet is its density. It is like a mire, it is sticky, and these beings get trapped in this stickiness. With your help we are going to raise the level of this planet, make it a lighter planet. The energy then coming from it will be sent into the universe and will help raise the levels of consciousness and the levels of other planets . . . We have spoken to you before of this Being and young Bobby and their relationship in the etheric: your planet will be raised to that type of vibration.'

To prepare man for the landing, Tom now explained in specific answer to Andrija's question, meant to nullify his fear of other beings and bring him to awareness of their existence. The group must use their own initiative and knowledge of the world to work towards this end, but they would be helped in some ways. For instance, there was the project to interfere with the electronics of mass communications. This would make people ask questions, and at the time of the landing the most stubborn non-believers would remember the interferences and thus be prepared to begin to understand what was going on.

John and Andrija thanked Tom for this elucidation of the cosmic plan and their role in it. Tom then asked if they had any further questions, and Andrija took the opportunity to raise the question of the proposed healing of Roberto Assagioli. Tom said that the healing could and should be done. It would require a number of sessions and the combined energies of three couples: Bobby and Phyllis, John and Diana, and Andrija and another female. But a distant healing would take a long time, and it would be best if they could work on Assagioli at his home in Italy. Andrija said this was no problem, and they would arrange to make the trip in the near future. Tom stressed that the most essential preliminary would be to secure Bobby's co-operation.

It was partly on account of this that John and Phyllis went down to Daytona Beach the following day. Also, in an earlier communication, Tom had said that John should go and talk to Bobby and it was not necessary for Andrija to be present. So he did so, and was delighted to find Tom's information confirmed. Bobby was willing to work with the group again and to join them on the trip to Italy to work on Assagioli. Meanwhile he and Phyllis would work together in Orlando for two or three weeks and then go up to Ossining, where it was proposed that they should all gather to hold further communications the second week in August.

On his previous trip to Italy John had chanced to meet in a Florence hotel a film-maker he had known in California, and they had discussed the possibility of making a film about Assagioli's life and work. So John now returned to Italy to discuss the project with Roberto, as well as to be with Diana.

He had been away only two weeks, but in that time Roberto seemed to have become much older and frailer. He was suffering from severe arthritis and pulmonary trouble, and was in pain nearly all the time, but in spite of this he engaged in the work of planning the film with much vigour and enthusiasm. John told him all about the most recent communications and that the Management had said that he could and should be healed, and Assagioli said he would welcome the healers and co-operate with them in any way possible just as soon as it could be arranged. When John returned to New York he had prepared, with Assagioli's help, a rough shooting script for the film, and had made all arrangements for filming to start at the beginning of September.

In the communications held at Ossining daily throughout the week 9–16 August some new themes were introduced and old ones were elaborated upon. This was a series that was prolific in its information content, but it began with a session, on 9 August, devoted almost entirely to discussion of the problems of channelling through Phyllis and further elucidation of the theme of bio-engineering. It was a particularly interesting communication from an overall evidential point of view because it purported to explain events in Phyllis's life eleven years before, events which neither Andrija nor John knew about at this time.

In 1967 Phyllis had been almost totally blind. The condition was attributed by a specialist to glaucoma, and her sight had been steadily deteriorating for four years and not responding to treatment, so that by 1967 she could neither drive nor read. She went to a different specialist, who diagnosed a brain tumour and sent her to hospital. But before any treatment was attempted she acted on an impulse and signed herself out of the hospital, demanding that the specialist should give her six weeks to see if she could heal herself. She went to a remote spot in Pennsylvania, near where she had been brought up, and 'sat on a mountain for five weeks'. At the end of that period her sight was completely restored. She attributed the self-healing to meditation and self-analysis. She had always believed, she says, 'that if you cannot hear it's because you refuse to listen, and if you go blind it's because you refuse to see'. So she 'looked inside very closely and realised that what I was refusing to look at, what I was blind to was the fact that I was using my psychic abilities to control people and make them dependent on me'. This, she says, 'is what my analysation of it was'.

Tom's version of the story was different. Her blindness, he said, 'was our fault . . . In 1963, when an implant was put in this brain, because of the sensitivity of this being and us not realising that this sensitivity had been carried from our zone to this physical planet, this created a problem in the physical body and this was the reason for the loss of eyes. We were also responsible for removing her from the hospital because we knew at that time that this implant which was a physical implant would be found. We then had to work on overcoming the mechanics of the physical implant. At the time that we did this we also in error erased part of her memory. This is why it has been difficult for her to find the proper words . . . We also did another thing which was in error, and which she does not understand and has never questioned. At one time this Being played concert piano, but she no longer can remember a note.'

This is an interesting explanation of facts that were known only to Phyllis at the time of this communication, namely, that she had gone blind and had apparently miraculously recovered her sight, and that she had once been able to play the piano but was no longer able to do so. Readers disposed to believe that her unconscious generates the information that she 'channels' might argue that the difference between her conscious explanation of the recovery of her sight and the explanation she gave in trance does not invalidate their theory because conflicting intelligent functions are a common phenomenon in psychopathology. But the sequel poses problems for this explanation.

Andrija asked what was the purpose of the device they had planted in Phyllis's brain in 1963, and Tom said it was 'to translate our language into your language'.

'May I just ask,' said Andrija, 'what kind of language is yours? Is it digital, numerical, tonal? What is the nature of your language?'

'It is not truly any of those,' Tom said, 'although perhaps we would say it would be more tonal than anything else you would understand.'

'And what is the frequency range you would operate in tonally?' Andrija asked.

'It would be 98.6 in your terms,' Tom said.

'We have different terms,' Andrija said. 'Does that mean cycles per second, hertz, kilohertz, megahertz or what?'

'I will verify this,' Tom said, and after a long pause continued: 'It is something beyond your knowledge, but they tell me it would be closer to megacycles.'

'Okay, I understand this,' Andrija said. 'So your implant was to step down your high frequency language to our very low audial frequency, to transpose your values to our values. Is this the means you are using right now to communicate with us?'

Tom confirmed that it was, that the implant was functioning, but that they had not been able fully to rectify their error of erasing part of Phyllis's memory, which was why they often had difficulty in finding the right words for their communications.

(Perhaps Phyllis's use of the word 'analysation' instead of 'analysis' in her explanation, quoted above, of how she recovered her sight may be an example of the kind of difficulty they encountered.)

That Andrija was at home discussing electronics with Tom came as no surprise, for in the past he had invented an electronic healing device about which I will have more to say later.

He now asked whether this instrument would be of any help in Phyllis's case.

'I must verify this,' Tom said, and after pausing to do so went on: 'They tell me it would be all right because it is similar to a charge.'

'Yes, this is what essentially happens,' Andrija said. 'The charge on the membranes of the cells is increased, and this increases the function.'

This dialogue is, as I have said, particularly interesting from an evidential point of view, for to maintain a parapsychological explanation of the communications it would be necessary in the light of this material to argue that *both* Andrija and Phyllis generate the information at an unconscious level. Andrija did not possess the knowledge about Phyllis's past to create Tom's explanation of her blindness and memory loss, and Phyllis did not possess the technical knowledge to supply the term 'megacycles' and particularly to specify the effect of Andrija's healing device. These facts create problems for the two most obvious parapsychological explanations of the communications: that Tom is a secondary personality of Phyllis's, or that Phyllis is functioning as a channel for information emanating from Andrija.

The communication that they held the next day was an unusual one. Tom began by putting a proposition: that they should take Phyllis right away to their dimension and hold a meeting with her present so that things could be explained to her directly and she could report back. 'When she arrives,' he said, 'we will turn her vocal over to you and you can ask her questions . . . She may or may not answer you. We are not sure. We have never attempted this before.'

Andrija agreed to the experiment and he and John waited patiently while the interdimensional journey took place. After about half a minute, Tom said, 'We have her now here before all of us to understand what is happening. The body is now split in two. We are going to be working in our world as well as yours.'

Andrija said, gently, 'I'm addressing the Phyllis who is here on Earth and asking her to reach the Phyllis who is out there in space. Is it possible for you to speak to me from where you are?'

Phyllis was silent for some time, then said in a low, hesitant voice, 'I'm in a big building. We're having a meeting.' For the next seven or eight minutes the silence was punctuated only by short incoherent phrases from Phyllis, presumably her responses to what was being said at the meeting. Her voice expressed by turns puzzlement and distress: 'No, I don't want to . . . No, it does not . . . Yes, I will tell him, but they don't understand . . . You understand, they don't understand . . . I'm in a place, and there are nine . . . They are my friends . . . I have to make you understand . . . But I can't do that . . . But he doesn't even remember . . . I'm in this big place and there are nine, and they are reminding me of the commitment . . . I know them . . . They are very very loving . . . They don't understand our emotions . . . They say they've made an error in me . . . It can be corrected . . . I'm working in two places. It's very difficult.'

Her distress increased, but when John assured her that her physical body was protected she became calmer. Then suddenly her speech became more fluent as she explained what she was being told about their commitment. 'We were here before. That was in the beginning. Then we incarnated for some reason or other, not in this particular position, but in order to get the feel of this planet. We lived here, each of us, maybe three or four times before, but it was to get the pulse, but at the same time we performed a service . . . I don't quite understand what is so important about this planet. It's, like, really bad. It's holding back the universe, that's what it's doing. This planet is holding back the universe. So then we made this commitment. This is something you're going to have to help me understand. We committed to be the beings here that would open up the consciousness of the physical beings that live here. We're physical beings, but at the same time we're not, none of us are . . .'

Andrija said, 'So we're committed to open up people's consciousness. For what purpose?' And Phyllis relayed the answer:

'Well, because this planet has lagged behind, it hasn't progressed like it's supposed to. They say that if this planet does not progress . . . You see, beneath this planet there are other different civilisations, and this planet is stuck.'

'Yes, it's a brake on the whole system,' Andrija said.

'So we are here to raise the level of consciousness of this planet, to explain to people that there are other beings, other civilisations, that there are other people with more technology that can help raise it, but this planet is so bogged down in pure ego, and without harmony and out of balance, that it's upsetting the master plan. Does that make sense to you?' Phyllis sounded as if it didn't make much sense to her.

'Yes, but what do we do about it?' Andrija said. 'How do we raise consciousness? So far we've done very little.'

'They say you are wrong,' Phyllis said. Then apparently her role in the 'master plan' was explained to her in more detail, and she learnt about the bio-engineering work that had been done on her and the mistake that had partially incapacitated her. Part of the original plan had been that she would be able to relate information about physics and mathematical formulae, but they had found that this didn't work. However, they could use Uri for this purpose.

Yes, Andrija said, Geller had transmitted complex mathematical formulae flawlessly when he had worked with him. He asked Phyllis to ask whether Uri was part of the same mission that they were involved in. She reported back that he was, and that 'he would be a perfect being if they could add humility and softness', but that when he had been prepared for earthly existence with implants when he was young they had programmed in an excess of ego consciousness 'because they thought he needed ego in order to function because this entire world was all ego'. His testing time, Phyllis learnt, would come in the following January/February period, and after that he might come back into service.

'Wait a minute now, I have to go somewhere,' Phyllis suddenly said, and after some time she said in her trance voice, 'This is Tom. We have taken the Being away to explain things to her.'

'Welcome back, Tom,' Andrija said, and there followed about fifteen minutes of normal communication on a variety of topics. In the course of this there occurred a brief and amusing exchange which nicely illustrates the difficulties the communicators have in finding appropriate terminology in Phyllis's brain.

Andrija said, 'May I be so bold as to ask for some characterisation of the nine beings that Phyllis went and talked to? Who are they, in our simple language?' He was particularly interested in this information because of his previous communications with 'The Nine' through Dr Vinod.

'In your world, to use one of your phrases,' Tom answered, 'they would be nine bananas.'

Andrija laughed. 'We don't quite understand the meaning of that phrase. Is it a mafioso expression or something.'

'They are tops,' Tom said.

'Oh, I see, they're the top bananas!' Andrija said. 'Are they the same nine that appeared years ago through Dr Vinod?'

'Yes.'

When Phyllis returned to her physical body and came out of trance she was exuberant and eager to express the new understanding she had acquired through her conference with the nine beings who, she thought, were a kind of cosmic governing Council. She recounted what she had learnt with her own kind of eloquence: 'This universe is so big, you wouldn't believe! They showed me this chain of all the galaxies and planets and things, and, you know, this planet is doing such, dumb, stupid things! Inside each galaxy there are solar systems, is that right?'

'Yes,' Andrija said.

'Well, I guess I learnt something about astronomy. And each solar system inside the galaxies, each one has to do its thing in order to clean up the galaxy, and that galaxy in turn becomes a part of the universe. What has happened is we've done something to screw up our solar system, our solar system in turn has screwed up our galaxy, our galaxy in turn because of us has screwed up the master plan of the universe. Because there are other solar systems and galaxies that we're holding back. The problem is that in this entire universe there is no other planet like this one. One thing that came through very strong is that every being that lives in the universe must exist at one time or another on this planet, and if this planet goes all those souls that haven't had a chance to be here will go with it, they won't have had this necessary part of the growth process.'

'Yes, I can understand that,' Andrija said. 'We're a sort of bottleneck in a huge production line.'

'So part of our work must be to get across this idea that we are part of a larger whole,' John said. 'I mean, that is the expansion of consciousness, isn't it?'

Gradually, the project they were engaged in was becoming more and more grandiose. At first they had understood that the purpose was to demonstrate to the world, through Bobby, the reality of paranormal healing abilities. Then they had learnt that this was part of an overall programme to prepare mankind for the landing, and that the purpose of the landing was to rescue the planet from the consequences of the dire spiritual and ecological crisis that, as millions of people had begun to realise in recent years, put the very survival of humanity in jeopardy. But now it appeared that this rescue operation was not for the Earth's sake alone, but was part of a cosmic plan, as the Earth and its life forms were part of a cosmic order, and that much more was in jeopardy than the continuation of physical life on the planet Earth. It was indeed a grandiose conception, and the way it had been revealed by degrees suggested that there was an intelligence at work behind the communications, measuring out the amount of novelty they could assimilate at any one time and gradually building up the general picture.

It was as if, too, some intelligence had been guiding their lives. Tom said, in one communication. 'The things you three have done over the past years were not by coincidence.' And they all felt this, were aware that events in their separate lives over several years, the manner of their coming together when they did, and the fact that their different endowments and connections neatly complemented each other, were all factors in a coherent pattern. John regarded his meeting Roberto

Assagioli at this time as part of the pattern too, for things that the old psychologist had said, particularly on his last trip to Italy, had in a way prepared him to comprehend the cosmic relevance of the project. For instance, speaking as an esotericist rather than a psychologist, Assagioli had said to John in one of their conversations: 'Communications from higher sources depend upon humanity, and its readiness and ability to respond positively. Mankind is at varying stages of comprehension and understanding. This is part of our work towards preparing mankind for the externalisation of the Hierarchy.'

John had ascertained in an earlier communication that Roberto was known to the Management, and at the conclusion of the 10 August session Tom said that they should immediately afterwards hold a distant healing meditation in order to send him strength. On 12 August John asked, 'Can you tell us anything about Assagioli's condition at this moment?' Tom replied, 'He had a moment of severe weakness yesterday, and we tried to generate energy. There is an improvement. Do not forget your healing this evening.' The next day there was a phone call from Diana, who said that Roberto had become much weaker in the last few days and she feared that he was going to die. John gently reproached her for adopting a negative attitude, and said he was sure Roberto would be healed and that he would consult the others and see if they could make the trip to Italy earlier.

As it happened, Bobby was due to come up to Ossining that same day, 13 August, and soon after his arrival in the afternoon they assembled to hold a communication with Phyllis as channel. Tom began by welcoming Bobby: 'We come in peace and love and we are grateful that our brother is here . . . We were with you through your trial and we surrounded you with love. We had faith in you, and we know at times that you doubted and we sympathised with this. There will be times in the future when you will doubt but remember always that our love is with you and we will try to give you peace and surround you with harmony. Because of you and these three beings we know that our project will be completed. We are grateful for your commitment.'

Invited to ask questions to start the discussion, Andrija formulated a complex and searching one: 'Since this is the first time that John, Bobby and I have met with you together, it might help us all if you could tell us something which has been a great puzzle, in my mind certainly, and which might give us all a common starting point. We've accepted your existence on faith, as you know, and what we would like to know is something of your natural history. We would like to know what you look like, how you reproduce, what you do for nourishment, what your role is in the universe, how you relate to the Nine, what your interest is in the Earth, etcetera, etcetera. It would help us all immensely if you could give us some idea of who you are in a descriptive sense.'

This bold and challenging formulation initiated one of the most informative communications they had held to date. Tom began his explanation with a clear answer to the main point of Andrija's question:

'We don't have a physical body, although we may put on a mantle of a physical body when it is necessary. It would be difficult to explain to you what we appear like. We appear in many forms. We may appear as a human. We may appear as an energy bar. We may appear as a very bright light. We have evolved beyond the point of needing a physical-type body.'

Andrija recalled that a week or two ago two members of the household had entered the house at 8.30 p.m. and had both seen what they believed was a lightning ball in the living-room. 'Is that one of your appearances?' he asked.

'We were here,' Tom said. 'At times we use your electrical impulses and your lightning in order to come into your atmosphere and to generate.'

'I see,' Andrija said. 'So you could manifest now assuming that you had certain physical energies to draw upon, for instance, as you suggested, the plasma from lightning, or perhaps water vapour, or even the energy we could give? You could mould this energy into something that would manifest in our world. Is that the idea?'

'It would be similar to that,' Tom said, 'but our technology you would not understand. For instance, in the manifestation that took place in this Being's office: we have a unit that was placed over the office, and through this we were able to manifest a being that appeared in a physical body to her.'

This clearly referred to an incident Phyllis had spoken about and which had occurred some years before. It was such an extraordinary incident, and so curiously linked to the events of this narrative, that I must digress briefly to report Phyllis's account of it.

She had been in the office of her school in Orlando one afternoon waiting for a client who had an appointment for a reading at three o'clock. At ten minutes to three she went out into the reception area to find out from her secretary who the expected client was, and learnt that it was a woman named Mary, who was a regular and who had always been reliable and punctual with her appointments. Seated in the reception area was a stranger, a dark man wearing a dark suit who stood about five feet six inches in height. He looked Italian or Jewish, Phyllis said, except that he had almond-shaped eyes. The stranger said to her, 'I want to see you at three.' Phyllis explained that he couldn't because she had a client at that time, and he said, 'She won't be here.' Phyllis returned to her office and waited. Mary hadn't arrived by ten past three, which was unlike her. Thinking about the stranger, Phyllis wondered how he had known that the client was a woman. She went back to the reception area where he was still sitting, and asked him how he had known this and also that she wouldn't come. He answered, 'Her car stalled on the Parkway.' Intrigued, Phyllis invited him into her office and asked what he wanted. 'I want you to give me a reading,' he said. She touched his hand and in an instant, she said, she knew that he wasn't from Earth. She told him her impression. He said, 'That's right. Give me a reading anyway.' Phyllis said, 'This isn't why you came, is it? Why did you?' He said, 'You've been asking for signs since 1953.' Phyllis thought she would test him and said, 'If you are who you say, then bring in one of your people.' She had scarcely spoken the words when the being materialised before her eyes. He was about six feet four inches high, well-built, with blond hair and blue eyes, and was wearing a silver-blue jump suit. He didn't speak but communicated to her telepathically that his name was Ultima, that he and others were coming to help the planet, and that in future she would be able to call on him in any emergency. He remained in the office for less than five minutes, then dematerialised. The dark man left and Phyllis watched from her window as he got into a white Cadillac with Miami number plates and drove away. One Friday afternoon about two months later, just as Phyllis was about to leave the office to go home, he suddenly reappeared, put his head round the door and said, 'Hi, Phyllis. Everything okay? Just checking on you.'

As a preposterous tale, this ranks equal to the one Andrija and Uri tell about Uri being teleported from New York to Ossining, but to this day Phyllis remembers the incident vividly and swears this is precisely what happened.

To return to the communication. Andrija asked about 'Ultima' and Tom said that it was the name of the unit working in co-operation with them on their present project.

Andrija now asked about UFOs, and whether they were also created manifestations. Tom answered: 'Many of these flying things that you call UFOs come from our place, but they come from other places also, and they do come in physical form. But many of them are not physical. They are like your movie screen.'

When they had been staying at Mill Hill in London at the time of the May Lectures, Andrija and several other people had seen a number of aerial objects. They had counted forty-three in all, and Andrija had taken some photographs. 'On the photographs,' he now said, 'there was a strange, spirally, vaporous kind of figure that was quite large. Now what would that be?'

'That would be one of us,' Tom said. 'We are energy.'

Would it have been a form taken for the occasion, Andrija asked, or what they really looked like as their natural selves.

'It is difficult to explain to you, Doctor, that we do not really have a natural self,' Tom said. 'We are what we think we are at that time . . . We exist in the zone that you call cold. Because

130

of this we have no problem in manifesting in any manner we desire.'

'Yes,' Andrija said, 'on Earth we are just beginning to understand very feebly the zone of cold or superconductivity, and we know that there's no resistance there, no friction, in other words that it's the area of perpetual motion. Is that not essentially true?'

'It is true, and this is perfection,' Tom said.

'So from all this,' Andrija went on, 'we gather that you are pure light beings in a sense that we don't even understand because you exist at a velocity beyond light, beyond photons, beyond tachyons. And secondly, I would assume that you are more of the nature of what we would call soul than any other thing we can imagine.'

'We are soul.'

'Are the Nine of the same nature as you are?'

'We are one and the same.'

'Can you explain the profound mystery of why there are nine manifestations of . . . I guess we have to use the word God for lack of a better one.'

'I will consult with the Council to see if we may relate this,' Tom said. 'Will you bide with us?' After a pause he went on: 'Nine is complete. Everything is nine. In your world you have said seven many times, when everything is truly nine. There are nine chakras which are the nine principles and elements of God. There are nine bands round this planet Earth. There are nine etheric bodies, and going through your transitions is to attain the nine bodies. Nine is a complete number. It is whole. This becomes one. Over nine it cancels, and nine is complete.'

Andrija mentioned his communications with the Nine of many years ago through Dr Vinod and asked if this material was still valid.

'This does not change,' Tom said. 'But remember this: we are not God. All of you and all of us make God . . . Many of your physical beings deify other physical beings, when it is truly them.'

'I think that's the best way I've ever heard it put,' Andrija said, then he changed the subject and asked Tom why he and his like were concerned about the insignificant speck of dust in the universe called the planet Earth.

'We have explained this to you before,' Tom said. 'Sometimes you seem to understand and then you ask the same question again.' There was a suggestion of exasperation in the voice. Andrija explained, however, that he was asking the question for Bobby's benefit, and Tom said contritely, 'We are sorry,' and proceeded to outline the scenario that had been given to Phyllis on her intergalactic trip a few days before and that had been confirmed in two subsequent communications (which have been omitted from this narrative because their essential content is most concisely summarised in the following explanation that Tom gave for Bobby's benefit).

'In order for the universe to evolve, it is important for this planet to evolve. The souls that have come to this planet have become irresponsible in their physical bodies. The density of this planet is so heavy and thick and is . . . we know not the word to explain to you what this planet does to the soul. This planet is a planet of desire. The souls that are here act as if they are in quicksand, and are being gobbled up and swallowed in this desire. It is important for this planet to evolve or other planets in the universe that are under this planet or surrounding this planet are not able to go forward. It has stopped the growth of the universe. It has contaminated and polluted the universe. It is important for the level of consciousness of this planet to be raised. It is the love from this planet that generates the energy that becomes God . . . Many souls when they die are trapped in the atmosphere and are evolved over and over on this planet, and seem to be going nowhere. This planet was originally created to teach a being balance between the spiritual and the physical world, but in this physical world they got involved in a material world, and so these beings never evolve beyond the belt of this planet. Their desires hold them to this planet, and so you have a multiplication that is going on until this planet will sink . . . They can't get beyond it because of desire, because of hate, because of greed, because of enjoying their physical pleasures.

We have no objections to the physical, you understand, but it is when this becomes their primary concern and they are not concerned with the evolving of the planet, and with their fellow men, and with trying to find the true God. You explained this, Doctor, when we listened to your conversation the other day and you called it a bottleneck. We consulted and decided that if we looked in a bottle and there was a plug and we couldn't get it out: this is exactly what this planet is. Your description was correct.'

'Could you explain once more,' Andrija said, ' – though I think I understand – how a few humble beings like us, who are very simple beings, can really help to unplug this bottleneck?'

Tom answered: 'The energy that surrounds you and which comes from us, because you are our channels, creates a vortex that then radiates out and then can raise the consciousness of this planet. Even though you feel it is an impossible task, it is not so. You chose this situation. You willingly gave of yourselves to come back to this dense, heavy Earth. You have reincarnated on this planet several times, not because it was necessary but because you needed to understand and to get the feel of this planet in order to raise its level of consciousness. This energy, as I explained, creates a vortex of love and peace and harmony. Everything needs an energy base. We are energy, and we need you to channel our energy.'

This detailed explanation had been chiefly for Bobby's benefit, and Tom now concluded the session by addressing Bobby directly on the subject of his role, asking him first whether he was aware that he had chosen this existence. Bobby said that he was, and Tom continued:

'And we know that you must ask within yourself at times why. First we will explain about Uri. Uri also chose to come to this planet, and we worked with him and we thought that in Uri being able to manifest in a scientific world this perhaps would be the way to get the people on your physical planet to understand the existence of other beings and intelligences; not just us, for remember, there are those who are much superior to you in other civilisations. But also we realised that the area to reach more physical beings would be in the area of health. Bobby chose this role, and he has come here five times before to help raise the consciousness of this planet, but he was not able to complete the work. Perhaps it was both our error and your error, because your world was not ready; although there was a time two thousand years ago when it was. And so we are here again, and through your communications systems we will be able to reach the masses. The time has come for the people of the Earth to demand from their governments, to demand from their religious leaders, to demand from their teachers, knowledge and understanding of what is truly happening. It is now the time of the people. Whereas before, your religions and your governments and your society kept your masses in ignorance and kept mankind tied down, it is now coming to the time when man is demanding answers. It is now the time for us to come through on communications. As Uri comes through on television and opens up and makes people aware that there are others besides him who can do these things, particularly the children, this will cause those in your world to demand answers from their scientific community. But the way to reach men, we have finally decided, is through their own physical bodies in healing, and through Bobby many people will be healed and many will be opened to healing. Are you aware of this, Bobby?'

'Yes,' Bobby said.

'And are you with us?'

'Yes,' he repeated.

A month before, Tom had said, *a propos* Bobby, 'Things will be resolved and all your systems in motion by the middle of August.' It seemed now that the prediction had been precisely fulfilled, and the group were joyful in their new-found cohesion and clearer sense of purpose, but though they didn't know it, events were looming that were to give them cause to doubt Tom's prophetic abilities.

On 16 August John flew to London and Phyllis and Bobby to Florida, but before separating they made arrangements to meet the following week in Rome and drive to Capalona and carry out the proposed series of healing sessions on Assagioli.

Daily throughout the week they were together at Ossining they had held the distant healing meditations, and on 14 August Diana had telephoned and said that Roberto was much better. This was confirmed the following day by Tom, who said, 'Assagioli's improvement continues. Only loss of hope in him would cause a problem. He has not lost hope. He will be well.' So it was arranged that Phyllis and Bobby should join Andrija at Kennedy Airport in the evening of 21 August to catch a night flight to Rome, where they would meet John the following morning.

In Andrija's home at Ossining, at noon on 21 August, just a few hours before he was due to leave for the airport, the phone rang. Andrija picked it up and a voice said, 'We have a message. We will stand by for it to be recorded.' The voice was Bobby's, but it was not his normal voice, it was more like his trance voice, but exaggeratedly mechanical and halting. Andrija quickly attached his recording apparatus to the phone and then listened to the voice, which said: 'We tried to reach Phyllis last night but could not, and therefore we are contacting you as the director and you must take the initiative and responsibility to do the following. Cancel your plans for travel immediately. We will contact you again later. You must all stay exactly where you are until you get further instructions. We ask you to carry out these instructions.'

Two things disposed Andrija to believe that this was a genuine message from Corean and not a hoax perpetrated by Bobby. The first thing was the reference to him as the director, for Bobby had not heard the tapes of the early communications with Corean and therefore could not know that Andrija had been nominated director. Secondly, the tape was blank when he played it back, though when he checked the apparatus by dialling the local time signal he found that it was working perfectly. In his work with Uri, Andrija had had many experiences of tapes being paranormally erased, and also he had known people receive phone calls from Uri when Uri was asleep, so the idea of Corean using Bobby's trance voice without Bobby being aware of the fact was not so unfamiliar and absurd as it will be to most readers of this narrative.

Andrija had to act quickly. He phoned Phyllis's home and learnt from her daughter that she had left for the airport some time ago. He rang Orlando Airport and managed to get Phyllis on the phone just as she was due to get on the plane for New York. He told her about the message and the reasons for his belief in its genuineness and asked her to return home and wait for him to call her again. Phyllis said that Bobby hadn't turned up at the airport, though when she had spoken to him at eight o'clock that morning he had said he would join her there for the New York flight that was now about to leave.

Andrija's next problem was to get in touch with John. He phoned his London number, only to learn that he too had already left for the airport, so he called Alitalia at London Airport and left a message for John to contact him as soon as possible.

Some time later, Phyllis phoned back. She said that she had been to Bobby's house and what she had seen there and what he had said convinced her that he had never had any intention of going to Italy and that he had faked the Corean call. She had noticed a tape recorder beside his phone and accused him of using it to produce the mechanical-sounding voice of the message. 'And my God, Andrija,' she said, 'when I faced him with that – his aura! The fear that came into it!' They had had a bitter argument. Bobby accused Phyllis in turn of lying to him, and said he didn't believe any of them. Phyllis retaliated: 'Don't do this to people's souls. If you don't want to work with us, just say so.' He hadn't even packed for the trip, she said, so it was obvious he'd never intended to go to Italy. Bobby denied that but said anyway that he wasn't even sure that he could heal, and Phyllis said, 'Don't give me that bullshit. You've proved it.'

Bobby phoned soon after Phyllis had hung up and told Andrija his side of the story. He said Phyllis was upset with him and accused him of faking some message, but swore he didn't know anything about a message and that he had meant to go with them to Italy, and had in fact been driving to Orlando Airport to meet Phyllis as arranged when his car had broken down. Andrija was conciliatory and told Bobby that he personally believed that the Corean message was genuine, and that he was now waiting for the promised second message before deciding what to do next and would let Bobby know when he received it. Bobby said that whatever happened he must see Andrija soon to talk things over and would come up to Ossining in the next few days.

The next caller was John, from London Airport. An Alitalia official had given him Andrija's message. When he heard the news, John said that he would postpone his flight to Rome until the following morning but would certainly go then whatever happened because he felt that Diana would need him. He checked into a hotel near the airport and phoned Andrija again to give him the number so that he could contact him immediately if there was a second message from Corean.

There was. It came at one o'clock in the morning, New York time, and this time Andrija's equipment recorded it. After all that had happened and all that had been said – for Andrija had had another long heart-to-heart conversation with Bobby in the evening – it would have been an act of supreme duplicity and contempt on Bobby's part to have faked this second message. In a later communication Tom explained that Bobby hadn't faked it, but he had fallen into involuntary trance and his voice had been used by Corean. Presumably his wife had seen what was happening and had recorded the message on instructions that had also asked for it to be played over the phone to Andrija, which was done. For some reason neither Bobby nor his wife had revealed this. Here is my transcription of it direct from the tape:

'This is a message for Andrija. Thank you for stopping the trip. We feel at this time things among your group are unsettled. It appears that it has been left up to you to take the responsibility. We have asked in the past that the group rely on Phyllis's judgment. We feel at this time the group can no longer do this. We feel you are aware of the person, of the ego as you call it, which has become involved in the work. There would have been much damage to the group if this trip had been made under these conditions. We cannot answer your questions at this time. There is a lapse, a time gap, in communications from us to you. We will explain this at another time. We would like to ask that you follow your impressions concerning Uri. We should ask that possibly Bobby could speak with him, and you know Phyllis was against this. We feel the responsibility is yours as the director to use the knowledge that you possess to straighten these matters out. There will be more communications. We will not be able to explain completely to-night. We feel you must sort things out and decide. We do not fully understand all of your emotions, therefore we ask you to be the one. We must leave at this time.'

There were three statements in this message which were consistent with earlier communications. First, there was the repeated reference to Andrija as the director; second, the statement, 'We have asked in the past that the group rely on Phyllis's judgment'; and third, 'we do not fully understand all of your emotions'. The latter statement was one that had come into the communications very recently, and Bobby had had no contact with the group since he left London in May, and though the two former statements referred to communications of the earlier period when he had been closely involved he had never, so far as anyone knew, had an opportunity to listen to the tapes. On the other hand, the anti-Phyllis attitude and the recommendation to arrange a meeting between Bobby and Uri were consistent with Bobby's personal feelings and wishes at this time. It was a puzzle, but on the whole Andrija found the internal evidence for the authenticity of the message the more weighty, and he phoned John at his hotel in London to report what had happened, catching him just before he left to catch the flight to Rome.

Diana had no idea of the dramatic events of the last twenty-four hours, and she had kept reassuring the dying Roberto that the healers were coming from America. When John arrived alone she was dismayed, incredulous and angry. He arrived at Capalona at ten o'clock in the morning, and Assagioli died at five-thirty the following morning. Diana had spent all the intervening hours at Roberto's bedside, and when at last she returned to her own home, where John was awaiting her, she lay in his arms and cried for six hours.

Two days after Assagioli's death, while Diana was still grief-stricken and John was doing his best but feeling powerless to comfort her, Bobby went up to Ossining. He agreed, at Andrija's request, to be put into deep trance in order to serve as a channel for Corean, so that Andrija could ask for some explanation of the events of the last few days. 'We feel you are aware of what took place,' Corean began when contact was established. 'We have asked for this group to come together. You have done much in this direction. We feel at this time there is much disturbance among your group. You followed what we asked, the remaining ones of the group still are not sure. Each one brought his own personality into this. We would like to ask these things be settled. There has been much work done, much time spent. We ask it not be wasted. We ask things be settled among the group as quickly as possible so the work may continue.'

Andrija said he was certain personality conflict problems could be settled, and asked, 'How did this disturbance look to you from your side at the moment when we were about to embark for Italy? What did you see that we didn't see?'

'There would have been a setback if this trip had been made,' Corean answered. 'Things that are coming to light now would have come out in this trip. We do not feel this would have been the best way to settle these things. We thank you for handling what could have been a bad situation in the way you did. Many will learn in future from this group. This would have been starting things on the wrong foot.'

Andrija asked about Assagioli, and whether it in fact would have been possible for them to prolong his life if they had gone to Italy. Corean answered: 'This man of whom you speak was aware of his death. This man played a very important part. There is much about him that you are not aware of at this time. We will not discuss this now.'

'I would like to ask another question,' Andrija said. 'With reference to your use of the telephone to reach me. Could you tell me how you do that process, since it is Bobby's voice that I hear, even though it is your inflections and personality. To me it is a vastly mysterious process, and I would like to know a little more about it.'

Corean answered: 'First, we would like to say this is the voice of Corean. The voice you hear is travelling through this being. You are aware of the difference in the voice. We have tried to make arrangements for direct tape, as you have asked for the statement. Do you understand of what we speak?'

'Oh, perfectly,' Andrija said.

'Because part of the trouble was in the group we were unable to do so. We have tried more than once to make these communications. There is outside interference of sound, and electrical, that breaks the connections down. We will bring information that you may understand how your electrical systems are used. We feel, though, this is not as important at this time as the work we have asked and the work you have done. These will be things that come only for your self-satisfaction. They will be of no importance concerning the healings and the other work.'

A fortnight before the session, before Bobby went up to Ossining, there had been a lot of talk in the communications about the Management preparing a statement of purpose and a programme and communicating it by means of direct imprinting on magnetic tape. The mention of the statement in the above-quoted Corean communication is interesting, for no reference had been made to it in the sessions in which Bobby participated in the period 13–16 August, though there had been some mention of the problems of channelling energy for direct tape imprinting. It is of course possible that Andrija, Phyllis or John mentioned the statement in conversation with Bobby, so the reference to it in the Corean communication does not prove Corean's independence of Bobby's conscious or unconscious mind, but as correspondences between the material channelled independently by Phyllis and by Bobby constitute one of the most convincing arguments for the probability that the communications as a whole emanate from a source independent of both of them I think it is worth drawing the reader's attention to this mention of the statement by Corean.

\*

Is it a memory or a longing, the myth of the marvellous stranger possessed of omnipotence and omniscience who appears suddenly out of the blue and changes the world? Certainly there is in man a deeply rooted tendency to relinquish judgment and independence to such a being, to make a God of him, which suggests that the world-wide myth is the projection of a longing.

One might imagine the Ossining communications a product of the mythopoeic imagination, but on closer acquaintance we find they don't conform to this pattern. The marvellous stranger is not omniscient or omnipotent. He insists, 'We are not your gods,' and insists, too, that man has free will and must bear the burden of it, and that the meaning of service is not obedience but co-operation. The events of July and August certainly brought these points home to Andrija, John and Phyllis. They also brought the Bobby Horne story to a climax and, as it turned out, to a conclusion, at least so far as the work was concerned. But for the others there was much more yet to learn, and there were new and even more amazing perspectives to be opened up.

## CHAPTER FIVE

# Encounters with the Opposition

Dr Neil Hitchen is a pseudonym we will use for an acquaintance of Andrija's who had had an interest in his work for many years. Formerly a leading political figure, Dr Hitchen had more recently spent several years in education. He had begun his career, however, in the ministry, so when he and his wife Alice paid a visit to Ossining and participated in some communications, it was natural that the subject of Christianity and the Church should come up.

Recalling that in a recent communication Tom had said that there was a time, two thousand years ago, when the Earth was ready to make the evolutionary change now being attempted, Andrija asked if the time referred to was the period of Jesus Christ.

'This is correct,' Tom answered. 'But we do not call him Jesus Christ. We call him the Nazarene. He was one of us. His inspirational work and healings were inspired by us and his energy was supplied by us. We had great hopes at that time, but then you made a god of him as you have made a god of many. This will not happen this time. There will not be one but there will be a collection of beings who will raise the consciousness of this planet.'

'There are many on Earth who expect the return of the Nazarene,' Andrija said, 'but I gather from what you say that this is not possible.'

'A single individual will not return,' Tom said. 'There are many of you on this planet that are similar to the Nazarene. It is very important that you do not defy us. It is important that you understand that God is in each and every one of you, that God is love and it is love that creates the one God.'

Neil Hitchen said that he would be willing to help in any appropriate way, and was wondering whether he should go back into the religious sphere, for instance by accepting an offer of the presidency of a university with religious affiliations. Tom said emphatically, 'No. With them you can only go so far, because of the indoctrination they have had over two thousand years.' Neil then asked if his political connections could be of any use to the project. For instance, he could speak to people in the new President's entourage and possibly to President Ford himself. In response to this suggestion Tom said, 'We have found in the past that when you tell people the truth they feel threatened or feel that it cannot be so. But if it is their thought and they come to you, they readily accept . . . We are grateful for your offer to help this project. You are in a position, more than any of these beings, to help with contacts and credibility. You must walk softly and with patience, and you must drop the seeds.'

At the beginning of the next extended series of communications held at Ossining after Assagioli's death, Tom volunteered some information which will be as challenging for the reader as it was for John, Andrija and Phyllis, and no doubt will cause some to conclude that the communications must be contaminated by the unconscious of one or other of the participants. Recalling the 20 July celebration and what they had learnt about their roles at that time, Tom said he would now like to take the explanation one step further. It was very important that they should now understand their special relationship to the Nine. 'The Nine of us are in the area that you call the zone of cold. The three of you are here on the planet Earth. Now visualise as we are speaking to you of what is transpiring. Around each of you beings there are three other beings which are three beings of the Nine. This makes you then the centre as three of the Nine surround each of you . . . This then feeds and nourishes and sustains you, who in turn sustain us because without you three beings we cannot accomplish what is needed on this mission. You cannot be replaced. Do you understand?'

'We are honoured,' Andrija said, 'but it is difficult to understand.'

Tom said that there were also problems of understanding on their side. 'The difficulty we have is in understanding the problems you have in this gross, heavy, density world that as physical beings you must exist upon. This is creating problems for our project, but the project must continue, and its completion cannot be delayed.'

It would greatly help the project, Andrija said, if the Management would provide them, as promised some time ago, with the clear statement of purpose and programme imprinted on magnetic tape so that in future there should be no ambiguities arising out of their personal interpretations of the communications and understanding of the work. The statement had not yet been received, and Andrija now asked when they might expect it.

This brought from Tom a rapidly-spoken reproach: 'We have observed the great anxiety generating around all three of you beings waiting for this statement and programme. We have actually at times given you part of the programme before you asked, and at times after you asked, and you seem to be delayed by waiting for this programme, as if you cannot go forward without it. We do not understand its importance, or why you are waiting, when you already know why you are here, why we are coming and why we are doing this work with you. We understand that you would like to relay this statement to the rest of the world, and that you feel that this would be something that could be given to the people and they would believe. But there are those that still would not believe. Do you understand?'

Andrija answered that they understood that, but the point was that each of them had a partial and personal understanding of the programme and the philosophy, and they wanted a definitive statement in order to give their group internal coherence. 'I'm sorry if we're transmitting anxiety,' he said, 'but it is not a lack of faith or concern that leads to our anxiety. It is an anxiety to get ahead with the work. I hope you understand that.'

'I understand it because I am the one that works most closely with all of you,' said Tom, 'but the other members do not understand it.'

Andrija asked John to put his point of view to the Council, and John said that he too was concerned that their understanding of the message and the programme might be distorted in their individual interpretations, or even that the communications themselves might be distorted by the consciousness of the channel. Tom assured him that there were no distortions in the channelling. Then Andrija asked if the Council now understood their anxiety, saying, 'It is a kind of healthy anticipatory anxiety. I hope it has no negative connotations for you.'

Tom absented himself for about half a minute to consult with the Council, then returned and said, 'Let me explain to you their feeling. It is now the consensus among our group that the delay that was brought about in giving this statement has now caused us to take a new look at why you want this statement. I know why you want it, but when we observe you it is as if you have put down your plough and are no longer ploughing the ground to plant the seeds because you are waiting for the horse to pull the plough. We are disturbed, the entire Council is disturbed, because of your anxieties, and because you are waiting only for a statement. You must understand that I am their spokesman as I am your spokesman, and I understand why you do what you do. I am only relating to you the Council's feelings.'

Andrija said that for his part he didn't see the justice of the reproach that the work had stopped. He, John and Phyllis had all been working consistently for the cause in their different ways.

'We did not say the work had stopped,' Tom said. 'We were speaking of within your minds. All three of you have thought that you could not really go forward until this statement had been completed. This is what we speak of.'

John conceded that this was true of himself, but Andrija continued to rebut the reproach. 'I think what may have been interpreted as a kind of stoppage is really prudence on our part,' he said. 'Our interest is largely in economy of effort. We want to do the right thing. So it's in this spirit that we're asking for guidance.'

Tom replied to this, after a long pause of consultation, with a strong speech and the introduction of a shift of perspective on the problem, which virtually disposed of the question of the need for a statement and programme.

'You know this physical world better than we know it,' he said. 'We need your minds, and we need your energies. We suggest that you know better than we in which direction you are to go. If we feel that anything you are doing will jeopardise the programme, you will be made aware of that. We cannot lay out a complete formula for you, and a direction. There are things that we try to help you with, and there are things that we try to institute. In the past we have made many errors with this, because from where we sit it looks as if this may be possible or feasible, but then we find in your physical world it is not always so. We do not understand your material world, so therefore we have decided that only when we feel the programme could be contaminated or disrupted will we then step in. We will guide and direct you as much as we can. You can ask us if we feel you are going in the right direction or the wrong direction, but at the same time you must realise that we do not understand this material world and physical thing that you exist with. You understand that this is the error we made with Uri. We did not understand about the material part.'

Andrija and John never did get their definitive statement, but after this explanation the lack of it ceased to be a matter of concern, for they tended to regard themselves more as responsible partners in a project than as servants of a cause.

On 14 September, Tom brought up for the first time the subject of the opposition. Hitherto, Andrija and John had understood that the Management's effectiveness was limited only by lack of human understanding and the necessity to maintain the principle of individual free will. But now it emerged that the problem was more complex and more sinister than that, for there were strong and intelligent opposition forces at work whose aim was to frustrate and undermine the project, and one of the ways they would operate would be by availing themselves of any opportunity to attack any member of the group. So it was particularly important, Tom said, for them to keep in good physical condition and have proper rest and nourishment, for 'when the physical body is in a weakened condition and is lacking your physical rest or sleep, your energy levels are then down, and at these times other beings, other forces, other vibrations may interfere. And without your physical bodies, without your energies and without your minds we cannot do the work. Do you understand?'

Andrija said they understood the general idea, but were not clear about what was meant by other forces, other beings, other energies taking over. Tom elaborated: 'We have negative and we have positive, and as we have explained to you many times, we must reach a balance between the two. To be all positive is not right, and to be all negative is not right, but in this universe we have those that are all positive or all negative, and this causes an imbalance. The mission of the three of you is to bring this planet into balance. This planet is weighted and it is heavy and it is what you would call a negative vibration. We discovered this many of your years ago, and this is why you chose, as we explained to you before, to be the funnel . . . Because of the unbalance in your planet the negative forces have taken on power, and this has created the problem.'

Furthermore, Tom went on to explain, the forces of the opposition were going to be particularly active and dangerous, and 'until we pass the twenty-second of your month of October our project will not be removed from danger'. It was imperative that the three should remain together for the next month until the crisis period was over. The Nine would give all the protection they could, but, Tom said, 'there are technical problems at this time and there will be difficulties'. The powers of the opposition should not be underestimated. 'Be careful in your movements. Be careful of your electricity. Be careful with what is around you. If they remove this physical being, then they have nullified all our work. And if they removed one of you it would be the same.'

This reminded Andrija of a harrowing journey he had had some days before, when he had driven to the airport to pick up Phyllis and John and through no fault of his own he had nearly been involved in an automobile accident on four separate occasions, one of them on the return journey when they were all three in the car. He asked if the experience was relevant to the situation under discussion. 'It was a warning,' Tom said. 'This is going to be a very difficult time, for us and for you . . . Part of the problem is the earthly imbalances of the three of you . . . We are sorry that we must bring these things to your attention, but we are at a critical time. When one of you becomes out of balance, then the negative feeds on your energies, they deplete and take from you.'

Tom now proceeded to point out the characteristic faults of each of them which rendered them particularly vulnerable. To John he said, 'You can be out of balance by not listening at times. You can be out of balance by presenting a problem in anger before it starts . . . Then when you are out of balance and you become angry or fearful, the more angry or fearful you become the more they feed on you.'

John said he understood this, and Tom next addressed Andrija: 'Be very careful, Doctor, that you do not miss some points. We know that you have a tendency to check and check and check. This we appreciate and are grateful for. But at times also you believe too readily. You are very trusting . . . You have now had antennae added to you, and you should use your antennae to feel the vibration.'

This reference to bio-engineering performed upon him interested Andrija, because for approximately the past two months he had been troubled by general itching and spots and rashes on his skin and he had difficulty sleeping on account of excessive energy. He mentioned this and Tom confirmed that it was because of the implants, which when functioning properly would serve to balance the physical body and at the same time act as sensors. 'This is a new implant in you and we are adjusting,' he explained. 'It should be neutralised in a period of your four weeks. Remember that the civilisations are technical and are not perfect.'

Tom now spoke about Phyllis. 'This Being's problem is doubt and not believing. This is good at times, but to constantly doubt everything creates an imbalance. Her problem is that she does not listen to what is being said inside because of the doubts and the fears that what is being received will not be correct. That is ego. You will talk to her about this ego.'

Andrija took this up and asked about Phyllis's channelling. 'You know the degree of trance dissociation she has, and how accurately your thoughts get through,' he said. 'Could you give us an idea how accurate the transmission is?'

'It is the most accurate and refined that has been transmitted,' Tom replied.

'But tell us how inaccurate it gets when her ego gets in the way and she starts doubting and fighting etcetera,' Andrija said.

'It creates a problem and a frustration within the physical body, and then we in turn get short-circuited. But what we would like to talk to you about more than about the transmissions – because we are mostly in control of the transmissions – is the impressions received during the day. There are things that arise in your world that we must get through. This Being is also being used for that. She refuses to bring to attention some of the things that she feels because she fears there will be an error and then her ego would be bruised, or that she would interpret it wrong. The ego must be removed.'

Andrija suggested that a way of dealing with this problem would be to have Phyllis keep notes of her impressions and then check them against future events. To discover correspondences between her impressions and the events would give her confidence.

John contributed the suggestion that Phyllis should find more time to listen to the tapes of the communications, for she had in fact heard very few of them.

Both suggestions might help to an extent, Tom said, but neither would solve the main problem, which was that Phyllis could not always correctly analyse her impressions. John and

Andrija could help by discussing them with her, for 'energy then would generate so that it can become clarified'. What they had to understand was that Phyllis's difficulty was not wanting to talk for fear of error and then the ego being hurt.

'We'll try and get round that by notes and giving her a sense of confidence about what things to share and what not to share, just to avoid bruising the ego,' Andrija said.

'You are misunderstanding,' Tom said. 'You are concerned about bruising the ego. That is the problem at this time.'

'Well, I understand that eventually she has to get rid of the ego,' Andrija said, 'but in the interim I think we should be careful about her ego, so long as she understands that some time she must conquer that sense of "I" and "me" and "self".'

'You are misunderstanding what we say,' Tom said in a tone of rather weary patience. John said that he thought he understood and would explain to Andrija afterwards, and Tom accepted this, saying, 'We are reading you and we are sure that you are aware.'

John took the opportunity to put in a question about the bio-engineering that had been carried out on himself, but Tom asked him if this was something he really needed to know at the moment because if not there were 'more cosmic things' to talk about. John said that in that case they should certainly defer answering his personal questions, and Tom went on: 'As you know, our project is at a critical time. We know that as long as we can keep the energy balance between you – and we know that this will be done, and we have not lost hope, and we have not lost faith, as we know that you have not, and we are still joyous because of your commitment – but as you become more aware of what is transpiring there are also those who will tempt you, create problems for you, cause danger for you, in order for you to give up the project. This is not a test of faith but is a test of stamina. What may happen between now and your October twenty-second, besides the danger that the Being is in, is that the three of you become so tired and so weary that you wonder if you can continue. It is not a test you are going through – there is no test – but it is your opponents that would like to see you fail.'

'It's clear to me that we have to address ourselves to two classes of opponents,' Andrija said, 'those that we have on Earth, who I think we can recognise, and on the other hand the negative cosmic forces. Could you say something about each of these forces that we have to contend with?'

'They are one and the same,' Tom said. 'Those that oppose you here are emissaries of those that oppose you in the cosmos. The cosmic civilisations that are in opposition feed on the negativity of this planet and of other planets: they are the civilisations that instil in the physical beings of your planet their greeds, their hates, their desires and their love of possessions. By doing this they are able to generate more power. If you understand what we have explained to you before, that the energy which is created then creates God, because the energy is love, then you also understand that the energy of greed, the energy of jealousy, the energy of desire, also creates an opposing force. The opposing force is very powerful, it is very strong physically because it has no morals, no ethic, because of what is fed to it. We know your question, "How can we then bring it into balance?" And the positive forces also can create a problem by being too naïve, but the positive forces also believe that acting on the principle of love they can then bring into balance the negative forces. This is a great cosmic battle. This may sound very strange to you, but if the forces of dark win over the forces of light, then the soul of the individual will no longer be the individual soul because it will then feed a gigantic power but will have no free will.'

We are getting into deep waters, and I feel that a few comments might be relevant here. There are readers who will have no trouble with the idea of the great cosmic battle between the forces of light and those of darkness, and there are others for whom it will be all too reminiscent of a Jehovah's Witnesses' doorstep sermon. Again, some will find the idea of reincarnation easily acceptable, while others will regard it as baseless superstition or wishful thinking. And probably a majority of readers will find the idea of the existence of 'pure light beings' endowed with intelligence, wisdom and insight, and of an intelligent and cunning 'opposition' difficult to entertain. It may be pertinent, therefore, to draw the reader's attention to a few facts and arguments that may dispose him to regard these concepts – of the cosmic battle, reincarnation and the existence of discarnate intelligences of both benevolent and malevolent disposition – in a new light, and to see some relation between them.

The key concept which helps elucidate and interrelate not only the three ideas mentioned above, but also a great deal else in the communications, is that *thought is a field phenomenon*. This is a concept familiar to any modern physicist, and by now virtually accepted as axiomatic by the *avant-garde* of that profession, but it has not yet been very widely publicised or understood in our culture. I know of only one book written for the general reader in which the implications of the idea have been explored at all thoroughly: Edward W. Russell's *Design for Destiny*. The terms 'L-fields' ('fields of life') and 'T-fields' ('fields of thought') used in the following paragraphs are Russell's coinage, though his book is inspired by the work of Professor Harold Saxton Burr of Yale University, whose own book, *The Fields of Life – Our Links with the Universe*, is also recommended to the reader who is finding the credibility difficulties of the present material insuperable.

Any schoolboy who has played about with a magnet and iron filings is familiar with the phenomenon of an electromagnetic field. A 'field' in the scientific sense may be defined as an invisible and intangible force which has the property of being able to organise matter. A fundamental principle of modern science is that everything, from cells, seeds and atoms to suns and astronomical 'black holes' and 'white dwarves', possesses field properties, electromagnetic or gravitational. Another fundamental principle is that it is not substance but *organisation* that is the basis of reality. The traditional scientific, the naïve realist and the common-sense views of reality tend to consider *things* more real and concrete than the *relationships* between them, whereas modern physics has demonstrated that what distinguishes from each other the basic elements which are the components of all matter is their atomic *structure*, the number and organisation of electrons in sub-atomic space. And what distinguishes the different kinds of electromagnetic energy is the frequency per second of wave cycles, in other words, organisation in time. The substratum of reality, then, is an invisible and intangible thing: organisation. Wherever there is life or substance, there is an organising field.

Physics tends to lead the way among the sciences, and the adaptation of field theory to biology has been slow although the thirty years of research work that Professor Burr and his colleagues have put in has demonstrated its relevance. The biologist Sir Charles Dobbs once pointed out that 'the whole of the protein in the human body is replaced in roughly 160 days', and wrote that, 'When one contrasts the great complexity of the protein molecule with the fact that millions of these substances are constantly being built up and disintegrated in the human body, and moreover rebuilt to precisely the same structure, one cannot help but speculate about the controlling mechanism.' The 'controlling mechanism', we now know, is the L-field. The L-field carries all the relevant information to enable the living organism to maintain its individual identity despite numerous changes in the material of which it is constituted. L-fields are non-material but they organise and control living forms. And, as Russell points out, being non-material, L-fields 'cannot possibly be the result of physical evolution' and therefore 'it is not necessary to assume that they must have been designed or developed in association with the matter of this planet, any more than an architect's plans have to be drawn on the site'. Furthemore, since 'any thing that can organise has to exist before what it organises', human L-fields must exist before the bodies that they organise and 'there is no reason to suppose that they cease to exist when the bodies they have organised die and decompose, any more than a magnet's field ceases to exist when the iron filings it has formed into a pattern are thrown away'.

So field-theory biology lends support to the concept of reincarnation. In a sense we are reincarnated many times in the course of our normal life-spans, so we shouldn't have any difficulty with the idea that the L-field that controls and organises the several physical bodies we inhabit during our 'allotted span' might occupy other bodies in other times or places. Moreover, as fields can travel immense distances at the speed of light, the other places need not be the planet Earth. L-fields may be, to use Professor Burr's term, 'our links with the universe', the basis of our cosmic connection. In this context, we might recall Roberto Assagioli's enigmatic statement that there are 60,000 million souls in the universe and only 4,000 million of them are incarnated at the present time. The rest, we may surmise, exist as unattached L-fields or in association with some other form of organisation of matter, and when we recall, too, that according to relativity theory mass is convertible to energy and vice versa, the idea of the existence of what Andrija called 'pure light beings' becomes plausible.

Let's now consider the evidence for the existence of the T-field. That minds can interact with each other independently of the channels of sense, and that mind can interact with matter independently of the laws of mechanical cause and effect, are facts established by psychical researchers and parapsychologists over the past century to the satisfaction of all but a minority of diehard orthodox scientists. The evidence for telepathy, clairvoyance and psychokinesis has demonstrated clearly the fact that thought is a field phenomenon. More recently, biofeedback research has enabled interactions between the T-field and the L-field to be measured and observed. The work of Elmer Green (which he reported at the May Lectures) has shown that people can generate a T-field that will slow their heartbeat or stop a wound bleeding if they are fed back through electronic circuitry information about these physiological states. Modern studies of memory, too, point to its being a field phenomenon. Brain physiologists today speak of 'memory molecules' and envisage these as analogous to holographic plates on which an immense amount of information can be stored in a minute space. The information remains constant, but the memory molecule itself does not. Like all the other protein molecules in the body, it is unstable and subject to decay. Both neurosurgical experiments and observations of people suffering brain damage have shown that one part of the brain can take over the memory contents of another. So these contents must exist independently of the container, the brain cell. Experiment and observation, too, have established that memories are tremendously enduring (old people recall in detail sometimes events of infancy). To be enduring and to exist independently of substance or spatial location are properties of field phenomena, so memory functions afford us convincing evidence of the existence of the T-field.

That T-fields can travel great distances instantaneously is proved by both anecdotal and experimental evidence for telepathy, or thought transmission. That they can attach themselves to material objects is suggested by the phenomenon of psychometry, or object-reading. Psychics can pick up from material objects impressions and information about people or events formerly connected with them, and many people who are not particularly psychically gifted are sensitive to the atmospheres or moods of places or people, especially when these are charged with violence or negativity. In religious, magical and occult lore the world over, there are prescribed rituals for putting blessings or curses upon people or objects, i.e. for influencing them with a positive or a negative T-field.

In the light of these considerations, some of the things Tom said in response to Andrija's questions about the Nine's mode of existence are interesting. The statements, 'We are what we think we are at the time', 'we are soul' and 'we are energy', are all consistent with the idea that the basic mode of existence of the communicators is as T-fields. As we have seen T-fields can interact with L-fields, which makes sense of the claim that extra-terrestrials can manifest in various forms including a human form although they 'have evolved beyond the point of needing a physical body.'

The same rationale would explain the existence of the 'opposition', the negative T-field. As the human body is an aggregate of millions of fields of varying sizes and functions, all of which may come under the control of a dominant field force giving the body as a whole a disposition towards health or disease, so a powerful cosmic negative field force might mobilise a body of sub-fields to work together negatively and thus constitute an opposition to the positive, evolutionary force. That a cosmic situation of such a kind and of such proportions exists is attested not only by the Ossining communications but by some of the oldest of the world's mythologies, for instance the ancient Zoroastrian myth of the cosmic contest between Ahura Mazda, the principle of light, and Angra Mainyu, the principle of darkness. Of course, the problem with correspondence is always that one doesn't know whether to regard them as mutually corroborative or to consider one derivative from the other. The Zoroastrian myth influenced, or was repeated in, Judaism and Christianity, and as we get deeper into the mythic-cosmological aspects of the communications the correspondences with Judaic-Christian traditions and beliefs become more prominent. Some will see the correspondences as evidence of truth and others will regard them as evidence that the conscious or unconscious minds of the participants have contributed to the material allegedly channelled, and I do not propose to attempt to arbitrate between these two basically subjective views of the matter here. The purpose of this digression has been to suggest ways of regarding the situation that was developing and some of the ideas that were emerging in the communications during these crucial weeks of September and October 1974. I have tried to show that neither the situation nor the ideas were inherently implausible. The thing I can't help the reader with is the implausibility that this particular trio of human beings were involved in this cosmic situation, the suspicion that there is a touch of megalomania in the idea of their unique destiny or of paranoia in the idea that they should be subject to the attentions of the cosmic opposition. These things worry me too. But let's get back to the story.

In point of fact, it was Diana who first fell foul of the opposition. It happened in the evening of 15 September, the day after the subject of the opposition had been raised by Tom and he had given the specific instruction, 'Be careful of your electricity.' Recalling the circumstances and the event in a recent conversation with me, Diana said:

Soon after Assagioli's death, I went to Ossining and my own psychic awakening started. I suddenly started seeing auras, thought forms, beings, energies: all that stuff. I'd never seen anything like it before. The attacks started coming with my awakening. I wasn't very experienced or discriminating in this area, and I suppose some of them weren't strictly attacks. I tended to freak out whenever I saw anything. But there was no doubt about the big one.

'The Management had apparently said that the opposition might try to get at the three of them by attacking their loved ones, and had also made a point of telling them to be careful of electricity and using electrical appliances. But at that time the Management was shit so far as I was concerned, because it was such a short time after Roberto's death. So I ignored the advice and used the electric iron. After about twenty minutes I had to stop because there was this crackling in the air and a queer sensation of current running up my arm. I began to feel really strange. I told Phyllis and she made me lie down and put cold towels on my neck. Then all of a sudden the attack started. There are no words to describe it. It was as if something was trying to suck my consciousness out of my being. I knew very clearly that that was what was happening, that they were trying to possess me, to take me over, and I knew that if I would sit still I would feel my consciousness being drawn back and down and out of me. It was a very strange feeling. But if I kept making erratic movements I could pull out of it.

'Well, John came into the room to see what all the noise was about, and Phyllis told him to stay away from me, not to touch me, or else, she said, "they might get you". Phyllis knew what to do. She wanted to get me outside and wrap me round a tree, which was what eventually happened. But at first when she tried to drag me out I fought. Then I experienced this click inside my head, this sudden realisation that nothing could ever take my consciousness. I was suddenly stronger than whatever it was attacking me. I kept saying, "It's okay". There I'd been, raging and hysterical a few seconds before, and now suddenly I felt calm and everybody around me was freaked out. I said, "It's okay, just get me outside". So they took me outside and wrapped me round a tree, and I had to stay there for about an hour. All that time I could feel the negative forces being withdrawn from me by that tree, and this incredible vibration that was in my body very gradually subsided.'

Later the same day they held a communication session, which John opened by asking for some explanation of what had happened to Diana. Tom answered: 'This had been building since the 22nd of your August. In her weakened condition, the negative forces were able to get through . . . When a being, whether it be one of you or one of yours, generates a fear or an anger, it then permits an energy wave, and as we had explained to you before, it was important to be careful with electricity, for this again creates another type of energy which we and also other forces may generate on.'

Moreover, Tom went on to say, it was still a dangerous day and they might have to leave suddenly, 'not because there is danger for us, but because there is danger for you'. But for the present they were holding, and John and Andrija could ask questions.

Andrija was anxious to follow up a new topic which Tom had introduced in a communication the previous day. He had led up to it in a roundabout way, and the conclusion came as a surprise to both Andrija and John:

'We know that there is a concern in your minds about the relation between you and the Nine. As you know, I am the spokesman for the Nine. But I also have another position, which I have with you in the project. I will try to give you names so you can then understand in what you work and who we are. I may not pronounce who I am in a manner which you would understand because of the problem in the Being's brain, but I will explain so that the Doctor perhaps will understand. I am Tom, but I am also Harmarkus, I am also Harenkar, I am also known as Tum and I am known as Atum.'

'Yes, we know something of these names historically, of course,' Andrija said.

'If you understand that,' Tom went on, 'you may understand what my position is in this situation and this project. Before there was light there was dark, and dark lasted longer than light. It is now time for it to be balanced. And this was attempted five thousand of your years ago and more, and now it is again the time, and this time it must be accomplished because the planet that you exist on cannot exist many more of your years otherwise.'

The references to ancient Egyptian civilisation were quite new in the communications, and Andrija was anxious to follow up the topic, so when he was invited to put questions the following day he said: 'I'd like to go on with the identifications that you were giving for yourself, Tom, and the other names by which you have been known. I was particularly impressed by Harmarkus. Could you tell us . . .'

Tom didn't let him complete the question, but said enigmatically, 'I am the day, I am the evening, and I am the midnoon.'

Andrija wasn't in a mood to be sidetracked by enigmas however. There was something he wanted to know: 'How did the Egyptians come to build the sphinx and name it after you?'

There was a long pause before Tom said, 'You have found the secret.' He then said he would have to verify whether this information could be disclosed, and after a pause for consultation he said, 'The true knowledge of that will be related to you another time. But I will say briefly to you concerning the sphinx: I am the beginning. I am the end. I am the emissary.'

Another enigma. Though the word 'emissary' was interesting. Emissary from where? From the Nine presumably. Support for the view that ancient Egyptian lore and symbology were so strange that they must have come from another world.

Tom now said: 'Today is a day of danger and we must be very cautious. There are electric impulses in your atmospheric air conditions. We are having interference. You are being probed. We must speak guardedly.'

Andrija had been experiencing a chest irritation for some minutes, and he now started coughing convulsively. Tom explained that it was because of the probes. John asked if it would be advisable to terminate the communication and Tom confirmed that it would be the best thing for all concerned, and that they should send energy to Phyllis as she came out of trance.

On her way out, Phyllis said later, she had seen 'wires like spider webs that were sparking like crazy', and also she had seen something that made her urge Andrija to rest. 'Every time we sit they're doing something to you,' she said. 'They're draining you, Andrija, they're wiping you out. And they're doing something to John, too. He thinks he feels great, but it's a false thing.'

Looking back on this time some two years later, John wondered how much of what happened was due to suggestion. It was a strange time, with the three of them shut away together at Ossining for several weeks – for Diana only stayed a few days – and of course there were interpersonal tensions, and as they had been told that things were going to be bad until 22 October he wondered whether anticipation might not have played some part in how bad they actually turned out to be. They all suffered depletion of energy, though he did so less than the other two, and Phyllis underwent regular psychic attacks going into and coming out of trance, at least until they got the Faraday cage. But in retrospect John sees these weeks as a period when they were drawn inward upon themselves in order to learn and in order to be strengthened for the work that was to come. He is dubious about the extent to which any cosmic opposition might have been responsible, and for him the concept of the opposition is most meaningful when it is regarded as the negative side of oneself, for so to regard it, he has found, is to have something specific to contend with.

It was different for Phyllis, for she was the one of them that was most vulnerable, and in her experience lower psychic manifestations taking physical form and producing physical effects were a reality. The day following the occasion when the communication had been abruptly terminated she had a curious experience. She was counting down through the levels into deep trance and when she reached the number thirty-six she stopped abruptly, fascinated by what she was seeing. 'I'm getting all sorts of Egyptian pictures and scarabs and everything,' she said. 'What's a scarab represent?'

'It's a symbol of the rising sun and of creation and of rebirth,' Andrija said.

'Such a lot of energy around. Those beings are here, and they're trying to put darts in me. But wait a minute, they had something to do with the Egyptians also.'

'Yes,' Andrija said, 'they were the opponents, the enemies of Horus. They were collectively known as Set.'

'Were they from the sea?'

'We don't really know, but they're symbolised to a great extent by hippopotami and crocodiles, so that may be a clue. They did come up from the river, as I remember the legend.'

'I seem to be in a place in the desert,' Phyllis went on, 'and I feel I'm going down underneath a pyramid . . . But these fish men . . . I'm sorry, that's not right. I'm not supposed to call them that. These men that are wearing rubber suits. They came up out of the sea. And what have they to do with doing experiments? They tried to do experiments in order to control.' Phyllis felt that there was some elusive but important truth to be gleaned and said she must go further in. She was just going to count down further when suddenly the Egyptian scenario was eclipsed and she cried out: 'Oh, Christ! Now they're working on my left hand on the side. Can you see what's happening? Oh, the pain!'

Andrija examined her left hand. It was appreciably swollen.

'They're doing something to me,' Phyllis said.

'Yes, the veins are very distended,' Andrija said.

'They've got a big needle in,' Phyllis said, and she cried out with pain.

Andrija said, 'I want you to come out of it right away,' and very firmly he brought her back, counting with her through the levels from thirty-six back to forty-five. When she was out, Phyllis said she felt as if she had been drugged.

She wanted to go back immediately, though, and get an explanation of what had happened from Tom. This time she counted down, urged on by Andrija, without pausing. Eventually Tom announced his presence, and in answer to Andrija's request for an explanation of what had just happened said, 'What was actually done was an implant was placed at the very last moment in this Being. It was not of our doing. And in coming out, the sensitivity of this channel was aware of those that work with us attempting to remove. It has now been removed. Will you explain to this Being that those she said were of fish were workers of ours.'

With a touch of exasperation, Andrija asked if there weren't some way to give warning of potential harassment by the opposition so that Phyllis wouldn't have to go through doubt and agony each time she went into trance.

'This will pass, as we told you,' Tom said. 'We are in a game of war. We had thought, and you had thought also, that we would have adequate protective devices, but this time they came fast and swift. Remember what we told you, though: that we will never permit any of you three to be taken. We have those that work with us that arrange antidotes, and problems will be removed. Be assured of this.'

The occurrence of Egyptian imagery at the beginning of this session, and the fact that Andrija had the recondite knowledge necessary to answer Phyllis's questions, might cause us to think that Andrija generated the whole Egyptian scenario that Phyllis experienced in light trance. But if that were the case we would not expect his and Tom's explanations of the 'fish men' to differ. Andrija thought they were the opposition, but Tom said they were 'workers of ours'. Also, the pain and swelling in Phyllis's hand were unanticipated and quite unconnected with the mental imagery she was experiencing, and only Tom could explain how the two were linked. Which would appear to confront us with a choice between accepting Tom's explanation of the pain and swelling, which were undoubtedly genuine, or attributing them to some other cause and regarding Tom as an opportunist improviser skilled at accommodating any occurrence within his own crazy scheme of things.

Crazy or not, Tom's scheme of things has to be given high marks for consistency. In the same communication as the above, Andrija referred back to the very first communication with Tom and asked if they might now take up again the subject of early Earth history. Tom showed an impressive capacity for recall, saying, 'We spoke, at that particular time, of a massacre.' Andrija hadn't prompted him with this fact. He ignored Andrija's request for information about early history, and went on: 'And you are very much aware that this is what is happening. The massacre will not be in the cosmic but on the physical planet and because of the problems which the people of this planet have created. We are here to prevent this. This is our third time with you in preventing this. This is the third in a series, and this time because of the three being together, as we told you in our celebration, we know that this will be accomplished.'

If it will be accomplished, then presumably there will be no 'massacre'. Tom frequently appears to be making definite predictions when in fact he is talking about possibilities, about what is likely to happen unless something is done to prevent it. This is the case with references to the coming 'ice age' which came up several times in the communications in this period, and which are in fact a variation on the theme of the 'massacre'.

'Within a two hundred of your year period,' Tom said, 'there will be an ice age on this planet if something is not done, and then the souls who have been trapped on this planet will for ever be trapped. They will not be able to evolve or understand because they will be involved constantly in the desires of the physical.'

The theme was developed in a later communication: 'We spoke to you of an ice age that is coming, and this is something that is occurring because of the illnesses of the human race, and when we say illnesses we mean of your technology, which has not been refined. This is not something that is being brought to you from outside your planet or by other forces. It is coming about because of the greed and because of the desires of the beings of this planet . . . because of the pollution in your atmosphere, and in your waters which in turn pollute your atmosphere, so that the sun can then no longer penetrate. With our technology we will be able to help rid the earth of

163

the problems that your pollution and your technology have created.'

Human greed, desire, jealousy and emotional imbalance are responsible both for the dire situation the planet is in ecologically and for the general cosmic crisis, and as it would require a fundamental change in human consciousness and orientation to overcome these failings it is important both for the Earth and for the universe that such a change be effected. This message, embellished with the warnings about the cunning and power of the opposition forces bent upon preventing the change, is not remarkably original in the context of traditional ideas of apocalypse and the literature of moral exhortation. But there is one rather original aspect to it, which kept coming up in the communications of October: the stress on the fact that the primary need was for balance, and the cosmology related to this idea. The prescription for success and for continuing growth, both in the individual and in the cosmos, is not to beat the devil in a dramatic final contest and thus usher in a new age of sweetness and light, but through unremitting effort to hold in balance conflicting but complementary forces.

In answer to a question of Andrija's as to what the opposition forces were like, how they operated and where they came from, Tom said: 'You ask from where they come, and we know that in your mind you wonder if they are the counterpart of us. Is this not correct?'

'Yes,' Andrija said.

'No, they are not the counterpart of us,' Tom went on. 'Remember this: that we are in the centre; and we don't wish to sound as if we are perfect or as if we are egotistical, but on either side of us there is the positive and there is the negative, and when I say this I mean there is the positive which is not balanced and there is the negative which is not balanced. We are in the centre, and we are balanced. We are trying to bring those other forces into balance. Do you understand? They are not the counterpart of us.'

Andrija confessed that he was still puzzled. 'We don't understand the nature of these two forces that you are in the centre of,' he said.

Tom said patiently that he would try to explain in terms that they would understand, though he stressed that the explanation was really inadequate and only a rough analogy: 'You are a physical being, and you have a left and a right, and without your left you would be unbalanced with your right, and without your right you would be unbalanced with your left. This is the situation. They are part, but they are not all, and they are not complete.'

This wasn't profoundly enlightening, but they let the question rest for the time being. Andrija took it up a few days later, asking how the forces that Tom called positive and negative related to what people on Earth considered good and bad. This elicited a long and interesting statement.

'It is difficult for you in your physical world to truly understand the importance of both,' Tom began. 'I will try to explain. Visualise the universe as a giant scale. We are the pivot of this scale. Visualise that on one side of the universe all would be negative and that all on the other side would be positive, and as you see this you know that there is a complete out-of-balance situation. The universe actually has four sides, and within each of the sides there are many galaxies and solar systems. Now on the other two sides of the universe from this side it is in perfect balance. But on this side . . . How may I explain? If you would take a stone for each of the galaxies and they would be in perfect weight and perfect proportion to those on the other three sides, then this would also be in balance. But if one of those stones was a porous substance and you placed it in oil and it absorbed the oil and became weighted with it, then it would upset the balance and pull this scale out of calibre and would upset the other side of the universe. Your planet Earth is accomplishing that. The negative is the heavy oil. Remember, the other sides are balanced, but this imbalance that we have can in turn topple the rest.'

That seemed fairly lucid, but Tom wasn't entirely happy with his analogy, for he said, with a touch of the resigned weariness that anyone who has struggled to find words for abstruse concepts would recognise, 'That is not quite correct'. Then, apparently recalling Andrija's original question, he went on: 'In actuality, there is no good and there is no bad. It is only when one becomes sour or rotten that it contaminates the rest, whether it would be good or bad.'

'We understand that you are now working with us and what we consider the positive forces,' Andrija said. 'But have you ever in the past stepped in to actively aid the negative forces when the positive has been causing the imbalance?'

'When the positive has no understanding of the negative, it is out of balance,' Tom said. 'Without being aware of the negative and being aware that it must be balanced, then that is out of balance. And the answer to your question is yes.'

'That is very important for our understanding,' Andrija said.

Tom continued: 'Because of the ignorance of the peoples of your planet, and because of their religious leaders who have taught this ignorance, the negative forces, which are not truly as you see them, manifest in that way in order to instil fear. But what is truly negative, what has created the upset, besides the desires and the greed, is the complete denial of the existence of God. Do you understand?'

'Yes,' Andrija said, 'so this is the greatest thing that has to be redressed or righted?'

'This is correct,' Tom said. 'And you must explain also to people the necessity for earth people, and for the souls and spirits that surround your earth, to release themselves from greed and desire, because that is the trap. Your religious leaders do not understand this and do not teach the people.'

At the beginning of the communication that contained this discussion, which took place on 8 October, Tom said that there was a meeting of the Council in progress, and that while she was out of her physical body Phyllis would be taken before the Council again to have some things explained to her which she would report to the others when the communication was over. Towards the end of the session, Tom politely took leave of John and Andrija for a short time in order to 'go and meet with the Being', and when he returned he said that many things had been explained to her and they should have a conversation immediately on her return, for she would remember part of what she had experienced and learnt and other parts of it would be recalled in the conversation.

This is one of the most interesting of all Phyllis's reports of her out-of-the-body experiences, both in itself and because of the way some of its themes parallel and complement the themes of the communication that was taking place at the same time. This simultaneity of two corresponding but distinctly different and individually coherent experiences argues strongly, it seems to me, in favour of the view – which I'm sure some readers will still doubt – that Tom exists independently of Phyllis's unconscious.

'Oh, I went on a trip,' was the first thing Phyllis said when she came out of trance. 'I think I've been before the Nine. First of all they showed me how I go there and how they communicate. They come in on different beams. Like when I'm being removed from my body, they use a beam. They bounce it off things like satellites, and it depends on something in the atmosphere, the way they beam in. Anyway, so I got called up, and they said I was creating problems. I wish I could remember it all. They appeared in human form and I said, "You're not like that at all. Why do you look like that?" And then they were energy. They said that I'm causing problems, that I'm frustrating you and John, that you have faith and I haven't. I argued that point, because I do have faith. I have faith in God. They said what I was doing was creating problems by wanting "intricate revelations" – and I don't understand what they mean by that, but I got the essence of what they were saying. Then I asked them something, I said, "I'm quite upset about all the stuff you're telling John and Andrija, because I don't know if you're going to make all these things happen." They said I shouldn't doubt them. So I asked them to show me how things were going to happen, you know, with the radios and televisions. And it's Ultima that's going to do it, Ultima hooking up with Hoova.'

'Did they tell you how?' Andrija said.

'Yes, with these kind of beams, the same kind of beams they use with me. It's difficult to explain. I'm not scientific. But there's like a big spiral and they're in the centre, and out of

167

this centre in all directions come literally thousands of very thin wires. And they take one of these beams, or one of these wires, and this is how they come in. And they can move them around and bounce them off things.'

It was hardly a description to satisfy Andrija's longing for new and verifiable technological know-how, but he had to be content with it because Phyllis suddenly remembered something else. 'Oh yes, do you know who they had on their carpet? They had a Pope up there.'

'A Pope?' John laughed. 'They had him on the carpet?'

'Yes. They were bawling the Pope out. They said he was creating more problems . . .' The memories were crowding each other now. Phyllis changed the subject again. 'Oh yes, and then they explained evil and good. They showed me very ugly things and they said, "These, in your world, are very frightening to you." They weren't frightening to me there. They were just animals and insects and things that we're not accustomed to. They said, "These, to some people, are beautiful, and to other people they're ugly, and it depends on where you're at in your relationship to it," and they said that they weren't ugly or beautiful, they just were. Then they showed me other civilisations, I didn't like them. They weren't good – though that's not the right word now, we're not supposed to use that word.'

John was intrigued by the image of the Pope on the carpet and asked Phyllis if she could recall anything more about that.

'Well, John, I think he'd been there for a hell of a long time,' Phyllis said.

'You mean it may not have been the present Pope Paul?'

'What does he look like?' Andrija described him as thin, with a beaky nose and Phyllis said, with a cry of recognition, 'That's him!'

'Were they trying to straighten him out?' John asked.

'Yes.'

'And was he going along with it?'

'No,' Phyllis said. 'He felt that he was absolutely right in his rationale.'

Most of the time, she said, she had been in the presence of

just eight members of the Council, and then Tom had come along. Asked by Andrija to describe what they had looked like, she said that at first they had looked like venerable old men, but when she said, 'None of you are really like this, I want to see what you're really like,' they had turned into 'balls of light that were, like, pure energy, but with a soul'.

'Perhaps that's what a soul looks like,' Andrija said. 'Perhaps that's what they are, all soul and no body.

'Right,' Phyllis said. 'Anyway, they were very nice to me. They explained to me my responsibility and they were very very loving and they said I'd got to stop denying them. I said I wasn't denying them. Oh, and they showed me . . . now this was interesting. They took like the negative and positive forces or energy and they showed . . . Now, if you're so positive and you spin – they showed me this energy spinning, and it keeps spinning so fast it gets light and it disappears . . . And the negative also spins, but with its spinning it picks up other stuff and it gets dark. It's an energy that gets dark and then it falls. And they showed me that neither one of those was good because the way they were going that soul was out of line.'

'Or balance,' Andrija suggested.

'Out of balance, right,' Phyllis said.

'Hm,' Andrija said, 'that's interesting.' And he tried to make scientific sense of Phyllis's imagery in terms of spinning leading to increased velocity and eventually to disappearance into another dimension. After toying with this idea for a while, he asked her, 'Did they give you any special instructions when they sent you back?'

'Mainly, they wanted me to tell you that what they say will happen will happen,' Phyllis said.

'You mean there's no bullshit?' Andrija said.

'Right, no bullshit,' Phyllis said.

Some readers may be of contrary opinion, but from any point of view the correspondences between this post-session report of Phyllis's and the information content of the communication itself must stand out as a phenomenon that challenges explanation. Tom's explanation of how an excess of the positive is as undesirable as an excess of the negative, and of the need to keep the two in balance, is paralleled in Phyllis's imagery of the spinning energies. And his point that really 'there is no good and there is no bad' was vividly brought home to Phyllis when she was shown things that to her were very ugly and told that to others they were beautiful. Again, Tom deplores the ignorance and ineptitude of the world's religious leaders, and Phyllis sees the Pope 'on the carpet'. This phenomenon of Phyllis getting visual imagery corresponding to information that Tom expresses conceptually often occurs, and as human brains tend to have a bias towards conceptualisation or visualisation it seems highly unlikely that Phyllis herself at an unconscious level should be generating both the concepts and the images. According to Tom, she is generating neither, but is channelling the concepts and being shown the imagery; in other words, both concepts and images are emanating from an external source, indeed from an extra-terrestrial source. That may be difficult to believe, but it is equally difficult to find a plausible psychological explanation of the phenomenon, even in the light of all that is known about the psychology of the dissociation of personality, for it is a case of two mental functions, of a type that are totally different and usually mutually exclusive, going on at the same time. Though some of Phyllis's out-of-the-body-experience reports tend to sound like science-fiction scenarios, it seems to me that when, as in this case, they include imagery that parallels and complements the conceptual content of the communication, they must confound psychological explanation and constitute *prima facie* evidence that the communications as a whole emanate from an external source, which depending on your point of view and the height of your credulity threshold might be either a stunning revelation or a pretty obvious point no longer needing evidence. Of course, even if the existence of the external source be considered thus proved, this evidence says nothing for its reliability. But in this perplexing area you can't ask too much of any one piece of evidence. Detective work has to be painstaking, patient and piecemeal.

The opposition would have less chance of getting up to mischief, Tom indicated, if the communication sessions could be held under conditions of electromagnetic shielding. The day after he made this suggestion Andrija received a call from a company that was going bankrupt and wished to dispose of, cheaply and quickly, an unusual piece of equipment, namely a Faraday cage. He made arrangements to go and see the equipment in New York, and in the course of the next session with Tom mentioned that 'fortunately' he would be able to get a Faraday cage for them to work in in the near future.

'Things are not fortunate,' Tom said.

It is synchronistic happenings of this kind – and many such have occurred in the course of the work – that have convinced the group that they are not just spinning the entire web out of their own heads.

The conversation that followed is worth reporting, for it gets back to one of the recurrent themes of this period and one of the basic and more difficult themes of the communications as a whole.

Andrija chuckled at the thought that the opportune offer of the Faraday cage was not just chance coincidence. There was just a suggestion of admonition in Tom's 'Things are not fortunate', as if to say Andrija should have known this.

'Well, you have to remember that we're stuck in bodies on the physical plane,' Andrija said, 'so we haven't got the lofty perspective that you have.'

'You have, because you are one of us,* or you would not be where you are,' Tom said.

'Yes, I understand that we are one of you,' Andrija conceded, 'but I think we are like one of you who has chosen to come onto Earth and take on the body of an ant with all its limitations, and therefore what one thinks, feels and does has all the limitations of the ant. Is that not true?'

'This is true. And all of us have decided that if such a situa-

* 'One of us' means one of the spiritual hierarchy whe have returned to Earth to assist in the evolution of souls rather than a soul that is currently evolving here. This is consistent with the esoteric teachings about such a hierarchy and the 'new group of world servers' which I will elaborate upon in the final chapter.

tion arose again, if a planet should fall out of calibre again, rather than permitting a few of our people to return to help that planet all of us would return in order to understand, but that is not possible now for there is no longer enough time.'

'So then we came with a total memory wipe-out and just acted and lived like people on Earth. Right?' Andrija asked.

'The reason for the memory wipe-out is because of the atmosphere in which you live.'

'Well, I can understand that if we had had the slightest inkling of who we were we couldn't have tolerated the situation,' Andrija said. But Tom didn't agree.

'This is not necessarily so. Because you are who you are you can tolerate anything. You have had glimpses in your consciousness of who you are.'

'Yes, but those seem like wild imaginings, as you can surely conceive. Have you yourself ever been on this planet, Tom?'

'Yes, but you must remember that in my time there was not the confusion that there is now, and there was not the density that there is now – and I do not mean gravitational density but density of pollution and radiation, which also affects the physical body and the mind.'

'Yes, that's a very serious problem,' Andrija said. 'Is there anything that can be done in the next few years?'

'The reason for us will be that, will be one,' Tom said, then added after a pause: 'They say I am talking in riddles.'

'Yes, that was a bit of a riddle,' Andrija agreed.

'One of the reasons for the arrival of the civilisations that will help this planet is because of this problem,' Tom explained, getting it clearer this time.

In a number of communications over this period, Tom set out to make good their memory wipe-out by giving them details about their earliest associations with the planet Earth. The purpose was ostensibly to make them more clearly understand their roles in the present mission, and Tom repeatedly insists that the information is not given in order to flatter their egos.

'You were among the first arrivals of us, and that was over thirty-four thousand years ago,' Andrija was told. 'You were one of the founders of the first civilisation. Your story of Adam and Eve was from this time.'

'And where would that have been on Earth?' he asked.

'In Aksu.'

Andrija remembered the name. It was still on modern maps. They had come across it when they had checked the co-ordinates that Tom had given in his very first communication, at Count Pino Turolla's house in March. 'Ah, that's the place in the Tarim Basin?' he said.

'That is right.'

'And I gather that that civilisation didn't succeed?'

'It was not your fault. It was too soon. It was a high civilisation, but not adapted.'

'Can you tell us what elements of civilisation we tried to give at that time?' Andrija asked. 'What was it we were concerned with? Was it agriculture, medicine, astronomy, or what?'

'It was a language. It was to raise the beings from the level of near-animal. It was a way to communicate.'

A sophisticated idea this, that language is not so much the product as the basis of civilisation, the prerequisite of any evolutionary leap, as is stated in St John's Gospel, 'In the beginning was the Word'. Andrija asked if the language had survived and Tom said that it had, but not down to the present age. When the first civilisation had failed not all had been lost, for groups of people from it had moved into three other parts of the world, where civilisations had in due course developed, but these in turn were eventually eclipsed.

Andrija further learnt that he had spent 1,600 years on Earth at that time, and that during this period he helped give the civilisation of Aksu not only language but also knowledge of building, agriculture and healing. John had been incarnated as his son and had kept up the good work after his departure for a further 2,000 and some years. Then, 600 years after John's first earthly stint, some natural disaster had brought the civilisation of Aksu to an end. On a later mission to Earth, John and Andrija had been joined by Phyllis who had been involved with the civilisations of Ur, or Sumer. They had also all three worked together in Egypt, Tom said, 'in the time of 5,000 to 6,000' (if we take this to mean between five and six thousand years ago he is talking about the fourth millennium BC, when, according to the Egyptologist, J. Viau, 'the earliest representations of the Egyptian deities appeared').

Andrija and John were fascinated by this information and wanted Tom to tell them more, but he declined to do so at the present time because, he said, there were problems, opposition forces were building up and if the information about their heritage were known the opposition would become angrier and more dangerous. He too would be glad when the twenty-second of the month came, for after that the opposition's powers would be much diminished and they would not be capable of mounting a sustained attack. So he would resume the record of their earlier lives at a later date.

I wonder how many readers the last two pages have lost us. Even thinking of Andrija, John and Phyllis not as personalities in a specific space and time but as T-fields does not help put down the suspicion that all this previous lives stuff is one monumental ego-trip, though it is difficult to know whose ego-trip it is since they are all credited with important historical roles. I envisage two types of reader who might have stayed with this narrative so far: those who are interested in the message and those who are intrigued by the mystery. It is primarily to the latter that the following remarks are addressed.

Tom divulged more information about previous lives in the course of the following months. If we ask what kind of information it is and where it comes from, and discount for the present the possibility that it is literally true and comes from an extra-terrestrial intelligence, its consistency has to be taken into account in any answer we propose. The way that the information comes out also has to be taken into account. It is not given *en bloc* at any one time, but is elicited in bits over a long period of time, sometimes by Andrija or John asking questions and sometimes by Tom volunteering information when their discussion takes an appropriate turn. If somebody were making up the entire background as they went along, the problem of maintaining consistency with the increasing complexity would become more and more formidable, and we would surely expect to find some anomalies cropping up in the later stages. If, on the other hand, it is not a case of the picture being gradually built up, then presumably the information exists *in toto* somewhere at all times and bits of it become available from time to time. But then the question is, where does it exist? In the conscious or unconscious mind of a particular individual? In a disembodied mind or T-field? Whose mind? What T-field? The reader intrigued by mysteries will be greatly exercised by these questions as the full story unfolds.

Though Tom was unable to say more about their previous lives at this time, on 12 October he had a great deal to say about their present lives. Emphasising that it was important for the work that the trio, both individually and as a group, should be well integrated and balanced, he said: 'There are aspects of your personality that perhaps each of you do not recognise within yourself. We could tell you those aspects, but would you believe at this time?'

Andrija said he was sure they were all honest enough to acknowledge their weaknesses, and it would help if Tom would pinpoint the important ones. John agreed, saying it would be very valuable to have specific problem areas that they should work on pointed out to them. Tom said he would have to consult, and after a brief absence returned to report: 'They tell me it is important you should understand that we are not criticising.'

'Oh yes,' Andrija said, 'we understand that you are just trying to make sure the project doesn't fail.'

But there was more to it than that. 'Remember, besides the project, the world that will exist after the landing. Do you understand that every aspect of your personality must be balanced for the work after?'

To help them effect the balance, Tom now delivered a little speech addressed to each of them in turn, stressing different points than the ones he had brought up in a similar session the previous month. As before, John was the first to be put under scrutiny.

'Sir John, can you learn not to run from the world? Can you learn to be involved and not hurt? Can your frustrations be tempered? Can your frustrations be channelled and the energy used? Can your guilts be removed?'

John said he didn't understand the first statement, about his running from the world, and Tom explained: 'Remember that in the future it will be important for you to deal with the world. It is difficult for you to deal with the world. Can you remove your guilts? Can you love yourself? Can you not voice your needs? Remember, you are the balance, but also remember that you need those to balance you.'

To Andrija Tom said: 'It has been your need to share your work and to share your love that has created problems in your marriages. Is it possible in your life to have a separate life and not involve the work? It is easier the other way, but let us explain to you your own insecurities. You do not face your insecurities. You think that as a fellow human of all the fellow humans of the human race there is an element missing in you. May we say that as a human – which you are in your physical body – you have no need to have insecurities. You are complete. But in the vibration of your human life you have a need to prove yourself and a need to involve those in your personal life in your work, because your insecurity tells you that only through your work will they be with you, and that is not true.'

Andrija admitted that this was pertinent comment, and Tom went on to speak about Phyllis. She had over the past weeks largely overcome her problems of doubt and disbelief, but there was still the problem of ego. 'In this Being's vibration, because of past history in this life, there is the necessity to be in front, the necessity to be in motion, the necessity to be completely independent, and that is ego. Can this Being now be passive? Can she remove herself from the need to be in the centre with people and to have people? Can she remove herself completely and be placed in an area of no contact?'

Andrija asked for clarification of the last phrase, and Tom

said, 'She is now in an area of no contact. If you understand this Being's human life you will understand of what we speak.' Andrija said he assumed what was meant was no contact with friends, relatives and loved ones, and Tom had to correct him: 'We mean no contact with many people and with the public.' Which clarified the apparent ambiguity of maintaining that she needed to be independent and at the same time needed to have people, for if the term 'people' was understood to mean the public the two needs were not inconsistent.

From an evidential point of view, passages like this, of which there are several in the communications, are particularly interesting, for they do suggest that some intelligence independent of the trio under scrutiny is commenting from an objective viewpoint. Whatever the trio may have been in previous existences of elsewhere in the universe, they are now human beings with human limitations, and Tom has superior insight and knowledge and so can function as a kind of guru-figure to them. He frequently does, and is never at a loss for an answer even when he is called on to produce one spontaneously to the most abstruse questions. ('What is enlightenment?' was one that John brought up during one of the few sessions I have personally attended.) Following the above-quoted psychoanalytic session, there occurred in the same communication a discussion very reminiscent of the guru-disciple situation, which is worth quoting because of the general interest of the questions raised.

'We don't quite understand the way you use the terms "soul" and "spirit",' Andrija said. 'I wonder if you could clarify what the distinction is?'

'There are actually three,' Tom said, 'mind, soul and spirit, and when they blend completely then you are pure energy which is pure soul.'

'And what is spirit, as distinguished from the other two?' Andrija asked.

'Spirit is the soul in the physical world, or the soul that manifests in the atmosphere of your physical world. It is a vehicle.'

'Does it have any relation to the astral body?'

'Yes, it is the astral.'

'And what about mind? Is it connected with the brain, with the spirit, or with the soul?'

'The mind is connected with the soul.'

'And the etheric body . . .?'

'Is the soul cover.'

Andrija recapitulated: 'So these are distinct functions of the human personality: the mind, related to the soul; the spirit, related to the body; and the soul of course independent if it is not in a body, but if it is connected with a body then it is connected with the etheric.'

'This is right,' Tom confirmed.

'Well, that's very important, because world literature is in total confusion about these things,' Andrija said.

While they were onto definitions, John asked about humour. 'Most of our humour,' he said, 'is based on our physical existence. So I wonder if you understand our humour, and if you have humour in your world.'

'We have cosmic humour. God could not have survived without being able to laugh at himself.'

'What happens in the universe when God laughs?' Andrija asked. 'Does everything shake?'

'Everything shines.'


As the climacteric of 22 October drew closer, it seemed indeed that the opposition forces were redoubling their efforts. John, Andrija and Phyllis all suffered from insomnia, and Andrija and Phyllis particularly felt that their energies were low. Phyllis, out of trance, saw ugly or hostile presences around them, and though John and Andrija did not possess the dubious boon of psychic sight they were both aware of an eerie atmosphere around the house. At the end of one session Tom said, 'There is an energy being sent. You are protected and you will be protected, but the energy being sent is pacing outside of your home and it is of a wolf-like nature. It is a creation that may be given life if they attempt that.' John listened intently in the ensuing silence, and could swear that he heard something moving outside the house. None of them slept that night.

'There is being mobilised in the area around you the nature of a brute force, and an attempt is being made to use the lower forms,' Tom told them on another occasion. 'We ask you not to become alarmed or frightened, because we will be with you, but we may not be able to prevent the problem totally.'

And indeed they were not able to. Phyllis continued to suffer attacks of varying degrees of ferocity on her way into and out of trance, and on several occasions she couldn't get down to the necessary level because of the opposition. Once she counted down as far as thirty and then quickly brought herself out. She said she had seen a horrible thing and had known that if she didn't get out it would take her. It was a very primitive thing, a reptilian form, and it was lying dormant somewhere and had one eye that blinked now and then. 'That thing couldn't have taken me,' Phyllis said in disbelief, 'but I did have this strong sense of danger.' When eventually she tried again, successfully this time, Tom explained that the reptilian creature was a manifestation of the opposition.

'But couldn't she just ignore it, go on past it?' Andrija said. 'It doesn't have any power, does it?'

'There is power in all things,' Tom said, 'and in the in-tuition if it is followed there is protection.' He went on to explain, interestingly, 'What is happening in going into com-munication with us is the reviewing and seeing of all life, and of the beginning of all life . . . As we go to communicate, we go to what we were and through what we were. In order to communicate with us, this Being must go to the beginning and through . . . She goes through all levels of existence, and civilisations and times. And it is not always the experiences of the planet Earth. It is sometimes the experiences of the universe.' As she went through the levels, he explained on another occasion, she had protection up to a point, but beyond that point there was an area to be crossed which was crowded with beings and forms, an area 'similar to a no-man's land . . . and that should be a truce area, but those that oppose do not honour the truce'.

Several communications during this period ended abruptly, with Tom saying that they were experiencing difficulties, that the opposition forces were building, or simply that they had to leave. Sometimes the departure was so hurried that there wasn't time for the customary valediction, 'We go in love and peace,' and on these occasions Phyllis came out of trance very distressed and sometimes crying. Discussing this after one such session, Andrija said: 'It's very funny. It's as if Tom sees them coming, says, "Oops, sorry, but I've got to get out of here," and then bales out.'

'Yes, how come he doesn't take them on?' Phyllis said.

'That's what I was wondering,' Andrija said. 'Why doesn't he stay around and do battle with the dragon instead of leaving the fair lady stuck and having to fend for herself?'

'Why don't you ask him?' Phyllis suggested.

So at the beginning of their next communication, Andrija said: 'We're very happy that our channel, Phyllis, was able to run this gauntlet, but we're getting very concerned about these endless attacks. I say this with all due respect, but are you indeed powerless to prevent them?'

'We have explained to you many times that until the twenty-second of your October attempts will be made to prevent you from doing what is necessary,' Tom said patiently. 'The only way you would be stopped at this time would be if those opposing could frighten this Being, but they are operating a useless war and they realise that this Being is one that will not give in.'

Which amounted to saying that Phyllis could look after herself. That reminded Andrija of an odd thing that had occurred that afternoon. Immediately after the previous communication he and Phyllis had been in the kitchen and he had complimented her on her bravery in running the gauntlet and happened to add that neither Lyall nor Bobby would have had what it would take to do that. Ten minutes later Phyllis's daughter had called from Florida and said that some poltergeist-type phenomena had just occurred in the house, for instance, Lyall's book, *Supernature*, had jumped out of the bookcase and into the middle of the room. 'Can you explain this strange circumstance?' Andrija asked Tom, and he received the reply:

'Yes, it was the anger and the frustration of those that are opposing.'

Even during these fraught last days there were periods of calm, when the opposition was quiescent, which gave Tom an opportunity to expatiate freely and at depth on a theme. At the beginning of a communication held on 18 October, Tom said, 'All is in harmony and balance,' and proposed, if they were agreeable, to speak to them on the subject of knowledge. 'We would welcome such a discourse,' said Andrija, and Tom spoke at some length about knowledge and responsibility, stressing that as the former increased so did the latter. 'All the knowledge that we impart to you brings additional responsibility to you,' he said, and explained that the Council were concerned about this. They thought that because of the limitations of the physical world in which they lived it might be difficult for John, Andrija and Phyllis to maintain their balance as they gained in knowledge, and they wanted all three of them to consider, before they asked for further knowledge, whether it was needed for them to function, because, Tom concluded, 'additional knowledge that is not needed for you to function in the limited space of your world brings an additional responsibility.'

'Yes, we understand that,' Andrija said, and he went on to make a distinction that John did not agree with, though he withheld his protest until after the session in order not to disrupt it: 'I think there are two aspects of what you speak about. There is the knowledge that is for our own personal growth, which we do not need necessarily to function. There is a part of us that would like to know as much as you may know, as part of our spiritual development. As for the knowledge that is just functional, we agree that we only need to know as much as is necessary to carry out our tasks.'

'May we ask a question of you?' Tom said.

'Yes.'

'Do you in your hearts, all three of you, believe that by partaking of knowledge you consider necessary for your spiritual development, your soul will grow?

'I personally believe that,' Andrija said.

John said, 'I believe that knowledge is useful if it helps us understand the great responsibility that we have here. Some of the historical knowledge you have given us is helpful in this way. But I do understand that there is only a limited value for our functioning in that. On the other hand, both Andrija and I are very inquisitive and always like to acquire knowledge.'

'If you so desire, it will be transferred to you, but remember what we have said.'

'Yes, I think we are capable of handling that,' John said.

'Can you handle it in humility? Do you walk in humility? Do you walk without desire? Do you walk without vanity? We ask you to review these questions. Listen very carefully to what we say. You are now existing in a jungle in comparison with your true vibration. You are in a physical body, and we know that it is difficult, but you must remember that you must not permit your physical body to rule you. You must walk with the gods. And when we say this we do not mean that you may not have your human comforts and needs, but we ask that what you do you do with discretion, you do with knowledge, and that you never, as individuals or as a triangle, give reason for any of those in your physical world to throw stones at you.'

'Yes, that's very clear,' Andrija said. 'Talking about the gods, there's one question I'd very much like to ask. On Earth there are many ideals of God: the Buddhist, the Christian, the Mosaic, the Hindu, and so on. Could you indicate which of these ideals most closely matches the ideal of the Nine?'

'The ideal of the man called Christ, because he was the last of those of us,' Tom answered.

'And of those descriptions of Christ given in the Bible, which is the most accurate?'

'There are many misinterpretations in your Bible. It is true that the man you call Christ lived a normal, human existence, but he was a man of discretion, and he walked with discretion among the people.'

'Was he one of the Nine?'

'No, but he emulated their thoughts and their understanding. There are many things that are not told about him, for what he did he did in private and did not allow the world to see him in his human frailties.'

'That is a big problem for us,' Andrija said.

'Remember who you are, and remember it is important to master the areas of your life. If you can be discredited, for no matter what reason, then the jackals that are against you will find that reason.'

'It's very difficult for us to understand,' said Andrija, 'how so much could be at stake because of us. You've made it quite plain that if we remembered who we are these things would become clear, and we have tried to do that, but it's difficult.'

'We have told you who you are,' Tom said, 'and we understand that it is difficult for you to know who you are in your remembrance, but the most important thing for you now is to have faith in who you are.'

'We do have faith,' Andrija said. 'Our difficulty is articulating it, understanding it and rationalising it.'

'We wish to tell you that we realise that we have asked much of you and have promised you nothing,' said Tom in conclusion. 'And you have proceeded with faith, because within you you know. Within all three of you, you have the wisdom, the knowledge and the strength. Walk with humility, walk with love, and walk with the peace that is in you, for when you do this you generate peace around you. We leave you now. We go with peace and love.'

Phyllis came out of trance feeling good and without mishap, and the moving exhortations and assurances of this communication helped them all get through the trials and tensions of the final days. Another thing that helped was the diversion afforded by the delivery, erection and first use of the Faraday cage. It was delivered on the 18th, and they spent most of the next two days getting it set up and equipped. It was set up in the library, where it took up most of the floor space and left only a narrow book-lined passage around it. A heavy metal rectangular box of dimensions $8 \times 8 \times 12$ feet, it had a heavy door that shut tightly and quietly, and Andrija equipped the interior with three chairs, a desk and his recording apparatus.

'Oh, we have some friends in here,' said Phyllis when they

went into the cage to work for the first time, and she described some lights and colours and shapes that she could see and which she knew signified the presence of the space people. She was enthusiastic to work under the new conditions.

'Well, now we can control the heat, the light, and the electrical environment that we work in,' said Andrija to Tom at the beginning of this first session in the cage. 'Are there any further improvements we can make?'

Tom answered with instructions to line the interior of the cage with three layers of copper foil. They should also all obtain copper bracelets to wear during communications in future. The bracelets should be moulded so that they were as closely in contact with the skin as possible, and be worn just above the pulse on both wrists. Also, when they had obtained the bracelets they were to leave them in the cage for three days so that they could be worked on, for copper, after being submitted to certain processing, was a great aid to communication. If all these conditions were fulfilled, Tom said, they would be able to work at a higher rate of vibration. Although the opposition would not be entirely excluded from the cage, the cruder, elemental forms would be, and its manifestations would tend to be subtler and cleverer.

The opposition was not going to be totally inactive after the 22nd, but its attacks would be less consistent and sustained, and the time of cosmic crisis would be over. There was going to be, however, a situation of worsening crisis on earth which may require their intervention. Between 8 November and 12 December there would be increased potential of a war breaking out in the Middle East, Tom said, and it might be necessary for them to go to the area.

'When you have completed this period, there are very few things that cannot be accomplished,' Tom had told them on 16 October, and two days later he said that because of the energy they had generated the danger of war had temporarily receded. The danger had been that the United States and Britain would foment trouble in the Middle East in order to compromise Israel and protect their oil interests. The US President had met with the Security Council that day and there had been a swing away from a war-like posture, but their deliberations would not be completed until the following Monday, and each day until then the trio in Ossining should sit in meditation and send guidance and energy to the decision-makers in Washington. President Ford, Tom said, could create problems. Ford, he correctly prophesied, would be the target for an assassination attempt within two years 'made not by opposing forces but by people in your country who will think he is a fool.'

So before their period of trial was over, the trio received intimations that this period of intense subjectivity and introversion would be followed by one of extraversion, of their playing a significant role in the international political situation. Given the dates 8 November to 12 December as the time of political crisis, they must have been relieved that they were going to be able to have a couple of weeks off to relax and attend to their private affairs between rescuing the universe and rescuing the world from their respective crises.

'It is a joyous time for the universe because of you,' Tom told them at the beginning of the session they held on 23 October. 'We do not flatter you, we tell you a truth. We are overjoyed because this is a great day and a time of joy in the universe.' To celebrate the occasion he divulged some more of the information about past lives that had previously been withheld lest the opposition should overhear it. 'We understand that in your physical world it is difficult for you to relate to other than what you are,' he said, but it was important that they should learn to do so and today and in some future meetings they would be given information that they would have to subsequently review in their minds, work on and try to understand in relation to their present lives and work.

As this information about the previous incarnations of the three is not of particular interest to anybody else, and as it does rather overtax one's credulity, I will not report it in full here, but will give just one interesting example.

John was told that one of his incarnations was as Peter; 'not the Peter that was with Jesus,' Tom said, 'but the Peter that was alone.' That was a mystery to both John and Andrija, so John asked which period this Peter had lived in. Tom consulted, and returned with the information that the date was about AD 1090. John asked which country he had worked in. 'Near Jerusalem,' Tom said, but then he said he would check and after a pause corrected his statement: 'They tell me that a trip was made to Jerusalem.'

The further information threw no light on the identity of Peter, but Tom said, 'If you look you will find,' and left the subject at that.

They did look, after the session, and under the listings of Peter in an encyclopaedia they found one known as Peter the Hermit ('the Peter that was alone,' Tom had said), who had rallied the peasants of France with his emotional revivalist preaching to participate in the first ill-fated crusade during the 1090s, and had entered Jerusalem with the survivors in 1098.

At the conclusion of this 23 October communication, John asked: 'Now that this period is over, can you give us any general information about our future plans?'

'Yes,' Tom replied. 'The most important thing we must do is work towards the preservation of the planet Earth. As we have told you before, if something is not done to reverse the devastation that has been perpetrated on the planet Earth, within two hundred of your years there will be an ice age. The important thing at this time is to prepare for the landing which will bring the technology to help and save the planet.' The plan to alert mankind by interfering with television communications was still in effect and a unit was working on it. There was also now another extra-terrestrial civilisation working with them. Named Ashand its field was creativity, and it would work through many people. Matthew Manning, the young English psychic who had recently been astonishing scientists as much as Geller had done the year before, was from Ashand and, Tom said, one of his talents was that he 'could draw and paint us'. Uri himself was still struggling with his personality, but there was a possibility that he might come back to the work and be involved in healing. One of the things John and Andrija could do was to pursue a plan they had been discussing for some time, to convene a conference of all the scientists who had worked with Uri, for their collective testimony would convince themselves and others that what Uri did was genuine and make them ask how these things could occur. Another thing they should do was plan to make a film that would make ordinary people aware of what was going on in the universe and make them ask questions. But all these projects might have to be put aside, Tom intimated, if the situation in the Middle East deteriorated. The three were now going their separate ways for a short time, but, he stressed, they must be prepared to be recalled at short notice and to travel East.

# CHAPTER SIX

# *Ambassadors Extraordinary*

If any imagination invented the tale this chapter is going to tell, it was an imagination of extraordinary audacity and with a well-developed sense of melodrama. Melodramatic, yes, and apparently quixotic were the activities of Andrija, John and Phyllis in November–December 1974. To venture out into the world in order to set things right, to attempt to turn the tide of historical events, to move heroically through a world of hazard and adventure superimposed on the world of ordinary reality: it was by virtue of such actions that Cervantes' hero won immortality as an epithet in all the European languages. But poor Don Quixote was deluded, was a noble fantasist, and all the hazards that he faced and the heroism he manifested were of his own imagining. Whether the same was true of our trio when they embarked on their first mission to the Middle East at the behest of the Management is more of an open question than that of the Don's insanity.

It was on 2 November that John, Andrija and Phyllis re-assembled at Ossining. John came from London and Phyllis from Florida, and they came earlier than they had planned for Andrija had phoned them both to say that the Management required them to work again. He himself had been working with two other psychics in the interim, which was how he knew, for a message had come through one of them that the international situation was getting worse and the trio ought to be back in harness. Andrija had continued to work independently with other psychics throughout the period of the Tom communications, one of whom had channelled some highly complex and interesting scientific material, again allegedly from an extra-terrestrial source. In sessions held during the week John and Phyllis were away, information had been channelled that corresponded with that of recent communications with Tom, speaking of Ashand, the civilisation concerned with creativity, and also of the threatening war situation in the Middle East, which by the end of October had apparently become so serious as to warrant the funnelling of some positive, balancing energy into the area.

One didn't have to possess paranormal faculties or special sources of information to know that there was tension in the Middle East situation at this time, for during the last days of October the leaders of the Arab nations had held their summit conference at Rabat, Morocco, and European and American newspapers had carried reports of their decisions. The most controversial and provocative of these was a decision to recognise the PLO (Palestine Liberation Organisation) as official spokesman for the Palestinian Arabs. The Israeli government regarded the PLO as a bunch of bandits and murderers, and refused to consider ever negotiating with them, so the Arab decision was regarded, as one Israeli official put it, as 'counter-productive'. On 1 November, the London *Times* carried a headline: 'Israel Puts Troops on Exercise as Precaution', and reported ominous troop movements in the disputed Golan Heights territory, which had been annexed from Syria in the war of October 1973. The same report stated that 'American diplomats are concerned over the fatalistic talk of a new war in Israel in the wake of Rabat', and the Israeli Prime Minister, Mr Rabin, publicly stated that only the United States could act as an intermediary in the Middle East for the European countries were all pro-Arab on account of their oil interests. Arrangements were hurriedly made for the US Secretary of State, Henry Kissinger, to visit the Middle East in the course of the next week.

So the Middle East crisis was public knowledge by the beginning of November, and the information that brought John and Phyllis back to Ossining could just as well have been read in the newspapers as channelled from an extra-terrestrial source. But if there was nothing particularly remarkable about the recognition of a state of emergency at this time, the fact that it had been predicted by Tom nearly three weeks before was impressive, for there had been little about the Middle East in the news at that time. Moreover, his prediction that the worst crisis period was to begin on 8 November was, as we shall see, not far off the mark, though he would have been closer if he had made it a few days earlier.

'We explained to you before about the explosive situation in the Middle East,' Tom said at the beginning of the first communication they held at Ossining after their return. 'We thought that perhaps we could hold, but we cannot.' He went on to say that at present there were negotiations taking place which were not going well, and that on 4 November the decisions would be made in the US concerning oil which, if put into effect, would precipitate a war. 'And as we have told you before, your nation, with the Russian and the Chinese, will be drawn into it, and it will be a major war,' Tom warned. The ideological and border disputes of the Russians and the Chinese had direct bearing upon the Middle East situation, for if they came to a head the Chinese would support and incite the Arabs and upset the balance of power in the most politically sensitive area of the world. 'We know what needs to be done,' Tom said, 'but it is perhaps not possible.' And he put to them the proposal that they should make two trips, the first keeping within a 1,500-mile distance of Moscow in order to have a stabilising influence on the Russian leaders, and the second to Israel itself, where it was of vital importance that they should be between the 5th and the 13th of December. Between the trips, Tom said they must be in Ossining for the period 18–22 November, for this was the time allotted for the TV and radio intervention project and their energies would be needed for that. 'Can you arrange?' he asked. Daunted by neither the expense nor the awesome responsibility laid upon them, John and Andrija said they could.

'We've been looking at maps,' Andrija said at the beginning of the next day's communication, 'and we've found out those places that are within 1,500 miles of Moscow, and we have the feeling – at least I do – that this is to some extent a test exercise to see how well we can operate at such short notice and in foreign circumstances. One of the possibilities is that we could move from country to country around the perimeter of Russia ...'

Tom interrupted: 'We have told you many times that your thoughts are not your own, but there is one exception in this: it is not a test. Your moving is very important, because remember, every time you move, whether it be 500, 100, 50 or 5 of your miles, it then overlays. Do you understand? When you have been in an area, for twenty-eight to forty-eight hours afterwards the trace of you, of the three of you, remains.'

Andrija said, 'So if I may interpret what you say: if we could make a sweep, an arc, around the Soviet capital from the north all the way round to as far south and east as we can get conveniently, this will leave a trace around which will keep radiating. Is that the idea?'

Tom said he was right and John asked what difference it made with regard to intensity of influence to be actually in a place, for instance Moscow. Tom answered in effect that the intensity was in proportion to the proximity, which was the reason why they were here, within a few hundred miles of the US capital, and also why they had been asked to go to Israel, and if they could arrange to actually go to Moscow it would be so much the better. So the route decided on was to begin at Helsinki, proceed by way of Warsaw and Ankara to Tehran, then fly north to Moscow itself and return to the US with a stop-over in Copenhagen. 'Can you arrange to be in the Soviet by the tenth of November?' Tom said. They said they'd try, though the travel and visa arrangements were complicated and would take some days to complete.

Dr Henry Kissinger, of course, didn't have visa problems and he was able to fly to the Middle East without much delay. He was unaware as he jetted from Cairo to Riyadh and then to Jerusalem that back home near New York three people were daily meditating in a sealed metal box in order to channel energy that would protect him as he pursued his peace-keeping mission. This they did on Tom's instructions, for Kissinger, he said, was in danger of assassination and there was

191

nobody who could replace him at the present time. 'Your nation is no longer running on an intellectual plane, it is running on an emotional plane,' he said, and predicted that 'within six of your months there will be problems with your Dr Kissinger, simply because those in office that will be operating emotionally will not understand the intellectual and will plot to discredit and remove him'.

When they had arranged their itinerary, John and Andrija found that en route between Ankara and Tehran they had a wait of about an hour at Beirut Airport, and John asked if they could do anything to help the Israel situation at this time. Tom said, 'the fact that you are in the area creates a blanket', and instructed them to sit in meditation in the transit lounge during the hour they spent at Beirut. Again he stressed how critical the situation was, saying: 'The danger to Israel, if allowed to develop, will cause what you call a major confrontation, and it will be the beginning of the end.' By a major confrontation, they ascertained, he meant a nuclear war. At present (this was 5 November, the day Kissinger was conferring with President Sadat in Cairo), Tom said, the probability of war taking place was as high as ninety per cent, 'but, as in all of your worldly situations, this may be changed'.

'Do you think there is a real chance that if we are there at the proper time we can help to keep it down to minor local skirmishes?' Andrija asked.

'Yes,' Tom said. 'Your presence would do that because of the vortex of the three.'

Andrija asked whether, if the situation got worse, they should not spend time in Israel on their first trip, returning from Tehran that way instead of through Moscow. But Tom said: 'It is important that you go to Moscow. Within the time you will be in the area, and for four days afterwards, there will be major decisions made. The reason for you being in the area is to reverse some of the decisions that some of the Council of Soviet Russia would like to make. By your presence, you will bring light and sanity.'

So on 7 November the peace mission of the scientist, the psychic and the aristocrat set out from Kennedy Airport on the first leg of their journey, destination Helsinki. And a motley trio they must have looked, John wearing the blue track suit he often travelled in and carrying his only luggage, a shoulder bag, Andrija still managing to look professorial even in a blue denim jean suit, Phyllis encumbered with three suitcases and looking like any middle-aged American tourist doing Europe. The suitcases irritated John, who believed in travelling light, and so did Andrija's insistence on carrying with him a load of gadgetry for photography and recording. He reflected that under normal circumstances none of them would have chosen either of the others as a travelling companion. But this was no holiday.

As spokesman for the Nine, Tom assured them that 'as you proceed upon your journey to lessen the evils on your planet Earth, we will be with you each step of the way. This is a time when we shall not be separate, we shall be one, and when we are one our energies are not dispersed.' John had not been able to accept that meditation, particularly when performed by the trio alone, could achieve anything of the nature the Nine spoke of and even the idea that the three of them, when balanced, functioned as a kind of lens that focused energies from another source, as Tom had once explained, was hard enough. But there was more to it than that, apparently, for in the same communication Tom told them that 'when a decision is reached by the three of you, from the moment it is made that decision goes into effect and radiates out from you; so before you arrived here work that you had decided to do was put into action'.

Of Helsinki, Tom said: 'This area has its own vortex of energy which we are tapping, and which will then feed you more energy for you to radiate out.' In nearby Russia there were crucial discussions taking place about Middle East policy, and though some members of the council were 'coming to an area of sense in their human minds' they were not yet in the majority, 'so it is important for these next days that when you do your meditation you extend it for another period of time in order to bring all the leaders involved into the vibration'. In the next few days more was going to be demanded of them than ever before, Tom told them, and he concluded with the assurance: 'You are here together on a great mission. In your minds you could not possibly understand the extent of what you are in and why you are here. You are trusting and you do as we ask, and this we are grateful for, and though you may not see dramatics we wish to assure you that what you do is of the utmost importance to the universe, and we understand also that this may be difficult for you to comprehend.

They spent two nights in Helsinki, during which they held four thirty-minute meditation sessions and three communications. Tom had said that when they went out they should always remain together, which caused some problems because Andrija spent an entire afternoon going from shop to shop looking for a particular type of short-wave radio receiver. This irritated John because the addition to their load of gadgetry was still more heavy hand baggage and was likely to cause them longer delays as they passed through customs control in all the countries they visited.

The third Helsinki communication was held at 5.30 in the morning of 10 November, just before they left the hotel for the airport on the next leg of their journey, to Warsaw. Tom had asked them to communicate at this time at the end of the previous evening's session. He explained: 'The reason for requesting a meeting before proceeding with your journey is that there has been a meeting of your government and a date has been decided for proceeding with the plan. If the Israelis do not commence war on their own before approximately the twenty-ninth or thirtieth of your November, it will be commenced for them.' This was a staggering allegation, implying that Dr Kissinger's peace-keeping missions in the Middle East were a front for quite a contrary policy. But according to Tom he was not a party to these machinations: 'Your Dr Kissinger will be in a disturbed state because of the decisions of others.' When Andrija asked where the flashpoint would be if the plan for the 29th/30th November were put into effect, they learnt it would be Saudi Arabia and that 'the consequences of this aggressive act by the United States would be to mobilise those that are in fact already mobilised and are waiting for the opportunity'.

'So if the decision has been made to go ahead,' Andrija said, 'this means that we didn't succeed in Washington.'

'But remember, the energy can still change that,' Tom said. 'At this time, though, your physical presence and energy is needed to cover this area. The Russians have not yet agreed to the American plan.'

'Are they aware of it, then?'

'Not officially, but they have a thought, and for them to agree they must benefit. With you in the area, it may be prevented. Your purpose is to prevent.'

The scenario was becoming increasingly bizarre, more and more like the plot of an extravagant political thriller, a 'James Bond' fantasy. Recapitulating in a later conversation all the bits of information they had had over the past weeks, and drawing only the most obvious inferences from them, Andrija and John put together the following version of the alleged situation. The United States, foreseeing that the Arabs, armed with their 'oil weapon' and substantial capital reserves, could soon become a formidable and unpredictable third force in world politics, had decided to seek an opportunity to intervene militarily in the Middle East in order to gain control of the oil. The opportunity would arise if war broke out and they could move in ostensibly to prevent Israel being overrun, and if war didn't break out during the present period of high tension they could precipitate it by themselves mounting a simulated Israeli attack on Saudi Arabian targets. Their main problem was what Russia would do in these circumstances. Since World War II the two great powers had reached many tacit agreements as to where their respective spheres of influence should extend, agreements reached by a strategy in which the unofficial 'leak' of information in order to sound out the other side's reactions was standard practice. So they had now leaked their plan to the Russians and if the Russians agreed the two great powers would in effect share the Middle East between them. But if China in turn intervened the partition might not be so easily effected and there could be danger of world nuclear war.

It is very difficult to believe that such a cynical *realpolitik* could be entertained by a great nation in the present day and age, but such, unmistakably, was the gist of Tom's reports on the international situation during these weeks. In the light of it several items that were widely reported in the press at this time are interesting. A military member of the US Defense Department made a public speech in which he expressed strong anti-Israeli sentiments and had to be formally rebuked by the President. Ford himself made a statement implying that the US was prepared to recognise and negotiate with the PLO, issuing it just before Kissinger visited Jerusalem and thus in effect undermining the Secretary of State's peace-keeping efforts. Then the leader of the PLO, Yasser Arafat, was interviewed in Lebanon by an American television reporter, and the interview, in which he appealed to the American people to stop helping Israel, was widely shown in the States. Finally, and perhaps most significantly, it was publicly announced that President Ford was going to meet the Russian leaders at Vladivostock (near the Chinese frontier) on 24 November.

The radio receiver that Andrija had bought was not for their entertainment en route, but for experimental purposes. Tom had said that Ultima would try to come through directly if the receiver were kept tuned to a specified frequency, and also would try to co-operate in an experiment during one of their sessions, so at night Andrija slept with the receiver switched on and tuned, and during a communication they held in Warsaw he tried to set up an experiment.

This occasioned an amusing exchange. Having checked with Tom that it was all right to attempt the experiment at this time, Andrija said to John, 'Could you just carry on this interrogation while I get the machine ready?' John said he would, but, before he could ask a question, Tom put in: 'May we first of all say that your term "interrogation" we assume is in error.' Andrija laughed and apologised and Tom said: 'It is the influence of this country you have come into.'

While Andrija was adjusting his radio receiver, John asked some questions on Phyllis's behalf. She was puzzled and disturbed by information they had reported to her from earlier communications to the effect that of all of them she was the one who possessed no free will, but that after the landing she would be free to choose, if she so wished, to return home. Tom explained: 'When this Being made her commitment to return to this planet, her commitment was for the period to the end of the landing. This was the time limit that at that time she put on a physical existence.' Until the landing took place there would be limitations on her free will for she had voluntarily turned it over to the Nine at the time of her incarnation with a commitment which was total and irreversible, but after the event she would be free to return home, which meant not to her physical home but to her place of origin. Her commitment, however, would last as long as she opted to remain in the physical body, which the Council hoped that she would do because after the landing there would be years of follow-up work for all of them to do. The period between now and the landing, Tom said, was 'what your book has called Armageddon', and was going to make great demands on the three of them.

Andrija, who had completed his radio adjustments and was participating in the discussion again, remarked that, talking about demands, he had felt, during the last two days, uncommonly tired and drained of energy, and if he felt like this at the beginning of the work he wondered how it was going to be later on. Tom explained that his physical body had to adapt to working over a larger area than before, and that as more was demanded of them all they would find the resources within themselves to meet the demands. 'Sir John would understand,' he said, and used the analogy of driving a car for a long period non-stop, which presumably was a reference to John's former career as an international racing driver. The energies they had radiated over the last two days, he said, had 'created many thoughts of peace and suppression of aggression in those in the area in which we are working'. John, who still had difficulty with the idea of energy transfer, took the opportunity to express his doubts that the energies they channelled during their meditations could produce such great effects, particularly as, speaking for himself, he didn't feel at the time that he was giving anything out. 'We understand what you mean,' Tom said, 'but you spend no time and patience to feel. And we would ask you to remember: it is not action always that is necessary; being is necessary.'

This Warsaw communication session was suddenly terminated when the telephone rang in the hotel room in which they were holding it. Andrija answered it, but nobody spoke, although he was aware of somebody on the other end of the line for a few seconds before the connection was broken. 'They must be checking on us,' he said, and returned to continue the communication, but Tom was no longer there and he had to bring Phyllis out of trance.

They didn't have an opportunity to ask Tom for an explanation of this event until the following day, when they held their first session in their hotel in Ankara. The journey from Poland to Turkey gave rise to other experiences that they were also anxious to ask Tom about. A suitcase of Andrija's disappeared for an hour at the airport. Phyllis had seen it on the trolley coming from the plane but it didn't turn up in the collection area, and when Andrija reported it missing he had to wait an hour before it was brought, by a porter who spoke no English and who appeared with it from the opposite end of the building to the arrival area. Then John noticed a man at the airport who he suspected was observing them, and his suspicions increased when he saw the same man later in their hotel.

Could some authorities be taking an interest in their movements? It seemed a preposterous idea, but although their mission was essentially non-political and they were not taking sides in the Middle East situation, they were aware that if their activities were known it might not seem that way to the respective government authorities. They tended to have different views as to the degree of official interest in them, and consequently how they should behave, and these differences were a part of the interpersonal difficulties, problems and tensions that further heightened the drama of this trip.

Tom confirmed their suspicions in the first Ankara communication. He said that the break in communication in the Warsaw hotel was because a bugging device had been activated and 'if what had transpired had been recorded, you would have had great difficulty in explaining'. They were reproached for being careless in conversation: 'When you assume that all those around understand you not, you are assuming an error.' John asked when and where they had erred, and Tom answered, 'In places of consumption,' which reminded them that they had talked about the work in the dining-room in the hotel in Warsaw, and that twice there had been a man sitting alone at a table nearby. Their suspicion that the contents of Andrija's suitcase had been examined at the airport was correct, but nothing had been found. Part of the reason they were regarded with suspicion was that they hadn't been behaving sufficiently like tourists, and they should now spend an extra day in Ankara, taking pains to look and act like tourists. They should remain together at all times and be careful what they said in public places, but they would be able to talk freely in the hotel room. Meanwhile they could continue their good work of defusing the explosive political situation.

On the present state of play in the war game, Tom reported: 'Soviet Russia has not bowed to your nation, Doctor. They will go to a point, but not beyond that point, and at this time they are considering the possibility of doing it themselves and saying that your nation has done it. It is important that the power that the three of you generate negates the Soviet Russia's thinking. It is also of the utmost importance that you be in Israel not later than the twenty-fourth of your November.'

Andrija asked what they would be able to do in Israel since it seemed that all the important decisions were being made elsewhere, and Tom answered: 'It is through your energy that the leaders of Israel will be given the strength to make the proper decisions and proper negotiations without giving their souls.'

The plan to interrupt television and radio transmissions during the period 18–22 November was still on, they learnt, and would be carried out whatever the international situation was at the time. 'Speaking for the civilisation that is handling that project,' Tom said that 'it may not be with the fullest of force, but it will be the beginning.' Also, it might afford an opportunity to alert the people of the world to what their governments had in mind. 'We are already in effect overriding at this time with experiments,' he told them. As if to demonstrate the fact, Andrija's radio, which throughout the communication had remained tuned and silent on the specified frequency, began just as the session was coming to a close to emit curious noises, a cacophony of sounds made by musical instruments, with a cornet predominant. 'Is that Ultima's sound?' John asked. 'Yes, they are testing,' Tom said, and to listen to the tape today and hear that pat response makes one ask again the question: is he truth-teller or opportunist? The sounds are certainly unlike anything one would expect to hear on a radio, even in the Middle East: rather like a brass band frenziedly tuning up in the middle of a battlefield. But to paraphrase Shakespeare's Prospero, 'The air is full of noises.' And as Coué demonstrated, men are infinitely suggestible.

The extra day in Ankara afforded John and Andrija the leisure and opportunity to take a long look at certain problems that they felt were undermining their efficiency in the work. In the second Ankara session, they discussed these problems with Tom, and the discussion, which lasted an hour, is interesting both as evidence of Tom's insight and for the light it throws on the relationship and interpersonal problems of Phyllis, Andrija and John at this time. I will have to summarise it briefly in the present context, and such a summary will not convey so strongly as does listening to the tape of the discussion, with all its give and take and repetitions, the impressive way that Tom, by means of Socratic questioning and analysis, obliged John and Andrija fundamentally to change their view of the situation.

The situation, as they at first saw it, was that Phyllis was causing them problems by being moody and sometimes appearing reluctant to work, and as she had told Andrija some days ago that she was lonely he suggested that things might be better if she had her husband with her. 'This is not true,' Tom said, but Andrija argued that it must be, because Phyllis herself had said that she was lonely. 'You understand not,' Tom said categorically.

So John had a go, and explained that recently Phyllis had

come to need much more attention than formerly. She was like a child, and when it came to work she was always finding reasons to postpone it or to do it in a different way.

'You are reading into the situation things that are not there,' Tom said. 'Look within your own hearts, the two of you.' Andrija did, and admitted that he had the same problem to an extent and would feel better if he had an 'emotional companion on these trips', and he asked if it might not help alleviate some of their interpersonal strains and tensions if they travelled with such companions. Tom professed not to understand the question and Andrija had to spell it out in different terms before Tom said he would consult.

While he was consulting, John told Andrija that he didn't feel quite the same as he did about it, and Andrija said, 'I don't particularly need you know what, but there is this emotional thing in the air all the time,' and when Tom, having consulted, asked how they thought the presence of others would affect the work he repeated that he thought it would help by preventing 'ridiculous emotional problems' arising all the time.

'Whose are the emotional problems?' Tom said.

'Well, both John and I feel that it's the Being, Phyllis.'

'In what manner?'

'She is lonely. She says so.'

'You are creating the problem. You understand not.'

'I'm sorry, but you're wrong. She told me herself that that's her problem. She gets upset because of being lonely and takes it out in little ways on us.'

'And you have no knowledge of doing the same?'

Andrija was becoming exasperated. He said, 'I don't feel lonely. That's not my problem. And I think we're getting into an impasse here that isn't very elevated.'

'You are correct,' Tom said calmly, 'but you do not understand.'

'I don't think you're trying to understand us, and I don't know why.'

'We understand what is inside. Now would you speak, Sir John?'

After this exchange in which Andrija's exasperation came close to turning to anger, John tried to be conciliatory and reasonable. He said that part of Phyllis's problem was probably that he and Andrija didn't give her all the support they could, and that they could try to help in future by being closer and more supportive. But Tom wasn't satisfied with that. He wanted them to examine the question whether the central problem really was Phyllis's loneliness. With regard to the work, Andrija said, he felt that the problem was her lack of enthusiasm and unwillingness to accept all the responsibilities the work entailed. For instance, when they tried to play her the tapes of the communications her mind tended to wander, as if she didn't really want to face what the tapes said. John supported this interpretation, saying, 'Yes, there is this reluctance. She says she will always work, but many times she is rather morose before she does, and I don't understand that.'

'You understand not communication,' Tom said bluntly. 'The doctor should.' Had she, he asked, ever refused to work, or to go somewhere required by the work? They had to admit that she had never actually refused. 'And do you understand that it is important for many things not to be in the mind of the Being?' he said, implying that this was the reason for Phyllis's unwillingness to listen attentively to the tapes. This too they had to admit. So what was the problem?

'I think it is the situation of the relationship between the three of us that is the problem,' John said.

'Who has created it? One or the other or all three?' Andrija answered that undoubtedly all three of them had personal problems, but he thought that he and John were more successful in keeping them out of the work than Phyllis was.

'There have been times, Doctor, when you have involved yourself and have created problems, and we have not chastised you for that.' Andrija, and then John in turn, had to admit that this was true. Tom proceeded to demolish the theory that the root cause of the trouble was lack of emotional companionship, forcing them to contemplate what it would be like if their respective partners were with them on this trip, and to admit that in that situation 'there would be nothing but trouble'.

Then he said, 'May we bring into the open what is the core of the problem?'

'I wish you would,' said Andrija.

'The one who is most unbalanced is the one who is the balance. Sir John, have you looked within? Have you understood that it is your frustrations that have created the problem?' Suddenly transported, as it were, from the jury box to the dock, John was defenceless. He listened as Tom gave examples from his recent conduct of how he frequently got frustrated because the others, Andrija as well as Phyllis, did not do things as he thought they should be done or at the time he wanted them to be done, and of how these frustrations built up into resentment, which Phyllis felt and was affected by. There was nothing that John could deny or defend. He was chastened. He could only say, 'I'm sorry, but I think you know that my motivation is that I'm trying always to do the right thing to help the work.'

'You are not the only one who is trying,' Tom persisted. 'All three are trying and all three have frustrations, and no one is better than another. You say you must treat the Being as a child, but part of the reason you have a problem is because you treat her as a child. You must treat each other as equals, not even as man or woman, because this is not the nature of the three of you. Do you understand?

'Yes, I do,' John said, and he thanked Tom for his insight and his counsel.

'There are things that are going to be very difficult in the next two years,' Tom said in conclusion, 'and if you cannot deal with this how will you deal with those?' Andrija said that he was sure that with Tom's continuing help and guidance they would be able to deal with their interpersonal problems and maintain the harmonious balance of the triangle which they all understood was essential to the work.

In spite of their problems and very human failings, they were, according to Tom, succeeding in their apparently superhuman mission. En route from Ankara to Tehran, they unobtrusively held their meditation session in the transit lounge at Beirut Airport, and in the next communication they held Tom told them: 'What we have asked you to do you have done, and let us assure you that though you may not see or feel or think that there are any effects, there truly are. Because you see not a tangible result you understand not.' They had succeeded in preventing a Russian/American conspiracy, but they had still to 'negate the Soviet Russians of their intent'. Their influence was working to that effect, and from their present situation it was also spreading to the South and West and affecting the Arab leaders. Moreover, a little influence in Iran itself was not going to go amiss, for the country was going to play an increasingly important part as a balancing influence in the Middle East in the future. 'The Shah of Iran', Tom predicted, 'will become a strong and very important spokesman in deterring, though not at this time.'

They spent two nights in Tehran before setting out on the last leg of their journey, which would take them to Copenhagen via Moscow. They had not had time to obtain visas for Russia before leaving New York, but Tom had stressed that it was important that they should at least pass through the Russian capital, so they had scheduled the journey so that they had four hours in Moscow Airport in transit.

There were only four or five other passengers on the Iran Air Boeing 707 from Tehran to Moscow, so Andrija conceived the idea of taking the opportunity of the relative privacy to attempt to hold a communication. They waited until they had seen Mount Ararat on the left side of the plane and they were flying at 35,000 feet above southern Russia when they established contact with Tom. 'We wish to speak in another language,' was the first thing he said, and proceeded to utter a few phrases of musical chanting. He then explained: 'You are close to your homeland, and we wish that all adjustments were in order so we could speak to you in the original.' Recalling the earlier occasion when he had heard that chanting language, Andrija understood that by his 'homeland' Tom meant the Tarim Basin, and he asked if he could now tell them more about the civilisation of Aksu. 'Doctor, you were one of the founders,' Tom answered, 'and you are now coming full circle. You are now one of the savers. Remember, Sir John, that you carried on the thoughts and service of the founders, as this Being did at a later time.'

As conditions were not favourable for a prolonged communication, Tom changed the subject, giving them instructions as to what they should do in Moscow. He concluded with the shrewd comments on the Russian mind that I quoted in Chapter one (see p. 28). Then Phyllis came out of trance and described a place she had visited during her trance. 'There was something in the clay there that made it shine, and there were all kinds of bird symbols of some sort, all kinds of birds. The singing, it was fantastic. I can't describe it. It was like . . . talking in levels. And there were hundreds of people and they were singing, and it was like they were singing a hosanna. It was beautiful.' In earlier communications, John and Andrija had learnt that the original language of Aksu was a tonal language, which would sound like singing, and that the predominant symbology of the civilisation had featured birds, so Phyllis's description was consistent both with this earlier information and with the content of the communication that it followed.

Arriving in Moscow, they tried to get a special dispensation to tour the city in the company of an Intourist guide, but were refused. They had to spend the hours between flights in the transit lounge and do their meditation there. They found a quiet corner of the cafeteria, and as they were undisturbed John suggested when they had completed that they might attempt a second communication of the day under unusual circumstances. So as not to be too conspicuous they did not record this session, which was a short one, but later in the day they recorded the fact that it had contained one thing of significance. Tom had said that there was an assassination plot under way aimed at the PLO leader Yasser Arafat, and that they should meditate at three o'clock New York time in order to prevent it. The prescribed time fitted well into their day's schedule, for it fell shortly after they had settled into their hotel in Copenhagen in the evening. Shortly afterwards they held another communication and obtained a longer explanation of the Arafat situation. Tom informed them: 'A meeting was arranged for the leader Arafat to view installations of a military nature. There were to be journalists of different nations, and the plan was to have a conference and when the photographs were to be taken this would be the time. The conference is still in progress. There are two that have been pulled out because of previous knowledge, and that in effect is what you have done.'

This is the kind of information that should be checkable if one had access to the relevant records. From the newspapers all I have been able to ascertain is that Yasser Arafat was in Cuba on this day, 15 November. He had been in the news all the week because two days before he had made a speech to the United Nations Assembly in New York in which he had accused Israel of preparing for a fifth war in the Middle East. On 14 November he had flown to Cuba to spend two or three days, and it is certainly likely that his programme there would have included a press conference and a viewing of military installations, as Tom said.

Reviewing the past week, Tom went on to say: 'Your project has been successful. The Russians are no longer inclined to become involved. They have become more stable, and truly now because of your trip they are considering going forward with their own nation and the nations they control. There have been leadership problems, but they are stabilising, and they have also realised that they may be the goat. They like to be the bear, and they would not like to be the goat.'

The journey had also been a learning experience for the three of them. 'In reviewing the past eight of your days you will find that, besides the work which you have accomplished, there have been many things within you which you have mastered.' And they had learnt about the energy that they could channel and how doubts and negative thoughts could undermine a project. This was a thing they should never forget, and in the coming months they were going to have many demonstrations of the effects of their positive thinking. There was still a need for them to be in Israel the following week because 'by being in that area you will not only stabilise the leaders of Israel, but also put a dampener on the Arab leaders'.

But during the following week they should be, as originally planned, back at Ossining for the experiments in television intervention.

It was early on Sunday morning, 17 November, that John, Andrija and Phyllis arrived back at Ossining. They did not see the following day's issue of the London *Times*, though they would have been amused and perhaps gratified if they had, for it carried on its front page the headline: 'Threat of New Middle East War Recedes'.

On the face of it, the idea of communicating to the people of the world by using their radio and television networks would appear a most efficient way for an extra-terrestrial civilisation to get its message across. Beings capable of interstellar travel should not, we imagine, have any difficulty with the technology such intervention would require. This, however, may be an unwarranted assumption. Because we can form no conception of either technology we cannot assume that command over the one must imply an equal facility in the other. That would be illogical, but of course men are often illogical, particularly with regard to matters in which they have invested faith, love or money, and it is understandable that after all that had happened in the past weeks Andrija and John were eager to have some visible and irrefutable evidence of the reality of the intelligences and the forces that they were trafficking with. Tom had cautioned them about expecting too much: 'Ultima says you think he is what in your world you call a magician. He is a refined technician and he is a perfectionist, but he is not a magician, and he does not want to blow out the Being.' Nevertheless, they returned to Ossining expecting something like a miracle.

When they were in Ankara Tom had told them that the communications transmissions project could not be initiated 'with the fullest of force'. Andrija took up the point a couple of days later in Tehran, and asked: 'Is it not possible somehow to make a stronger showing during our communications initiation on 18th to 22nd November, in such a way that men's minds will be taken off war and will begin seriously to wonder about your presence and possible coming to Earth?'

Tom answered: 'We understand what you are speaking about, and we wish we could help. We wish there was the power to help. Remember that when we sent you Uri, this was a primitive power and a power that could do many things. But then there was the problem with Uri. Then we sent you Bobby, and we had the same difficulty. And so this Being and the two of you were willing to be used. But the work that had been done on this Being for many years was not in the field of what we are now attempting to do. This, you must understand, is a different power from that power we originally planned. We can put power through this Being of that nature, but it could create a problem for the physical body to the extent that we would no longer have a Being.'

The point behind this, and behind the earlier mention of the danger of a 'blow out', is that Phyllis was to function as the main channel for the energies required for the communications transmission. When transmission was being attempted, she was to sit in the Faraday cage, wired up to Andrija's electronic equipment, and all three of them were to meditate in order to focus the required energies. They did this three times daily for the four days 19–22 November inclusive, and all the time Andrija kept his radio tuned and connected to the tape recorder so that if anything came through they would have a record of it. Nothing did. On 21 November they had the television programmes on channels 9 and 3 videotaped between 2.30 and 3.30 in the afternoon, because they had been told that an attempt would be made to communicate on those channels at that time, but again nothing happened. It seemed that the entire project had been a failure, and at the end of the period Tom admitted that it had been in most areas, but nevertheless Ultima was satisfied because the experiment had been successful in twenty-seven per cent of the areas in which it had been attempted, and only regretted that these didn't include the areas monitored by the group at Ossining. 'He says that you as a scientist will understand,' Tom reported to Andrija, adding that after this moderately successful first attempt Ultima and his unit would continue working at the technical difficulties.

Even in the areas where intervention had been successful they had not succeeded in creating any effect that would start people asking questions. They had accomplished only short blackouts and faint superimpositions of images alien to the programme: irregularities that viewers would shrug off as technical faults. Ultima clearly had a great deal to learn before his technology awakened the world to his and his colleagues' existence. The project had first been mentioned in the course of the communications held in the Bahamas in June, and since then Andrija and John had built up great expectations around it, and though Tom had on several occasions told them about the problems involved and how Phyllis was really too sensitive a channel for the rather primitive energies that the project necessitated they were disappointed that the results of the 18–22 November series of experiments were not more positive and evidential.

One of the sessions held over these four days consisted of an hour-long and very impressive lecture that Tom addressed to his terrestrial colleagues. The Nine, he said, were disturbed by certain directions that their conduct and their thoughts were taking, and it was necessary to repeat and clarify a few points:

'We have told you before that zeal is futile. It is of great importance that this be understood, and especially by you, Sir John. And it is of importance – and we speak to the three of you now – that you do not think of yourselves as special. You have a special function, but this does not relieve you of the problems of the physical plane or give you a special dispensation to remove yourself from the affairs of the physical world. Your purpose is to help the physical world, and for that you must exist on the physical plane. What we have asked of you is that you balance it. There is no way you can help people if you understand them not, if you understand not the joys, the fears, the sadnesses, the despairs, the loves and the angers of people that exist in a physical world. In truth you are to master these things, but a person does not master them by escaping from them. A person masters them by existing among them. If you remove yourself from the physical world

209

you have no temptation, you have no anger, you have no joy, you have no love, and by removing, yes, you can master these things because there is no temptation and there is no touching of other beings . . .

'The most important of all, it is ego that must be dealt with, and all three have difficulty with that. Remember this: for the three of you to come as far as you have it was important to have an ego, and it is still important. We do not ask you to be ego-less, because if you were you would not have character. But it is important to be balanced and to exist in the world and to realise that you are not more important than any other. None of you is a perfect being, but each of you has qualities that, blended together, make a perfect being. And when you understand not each other, how can you understand the world that you are trying to raise the consciousness of? Remember, you cannot escape your destiny; you can only turn round and walk towards it; and the destiny of the three of you is to be involved with the peoples of the world to help them.'

The directness, the pertinence and the eloquence of this pep-talk impressed both John and Andrija. If Ultima had limitations as a technician, Tom made up for them by possessing in good measure those other attributes expected of super-human beings: wisdom and insight. Indeed it is largely on account of these latter qualities that the trio have kept faith over the years, and that I undertook this chronicle, considering it not unworthy of the attention of serious readers.

Two other passages from this long speech of Tom's are worth recording, the first for the light it throws on one of the most problematical themes of the communications, and the second for its wisdom and a nice touch of invention that it contains. The first has bearing on the problem posed by the previous lives material:

'We speak of the time in your lives when the three of you were beings together. In the first communication when we told you who you were, in your mind you asked a question because you were convinced that you could not have been who we told you you were. Because it was not of great importance then, we simply said that in truth it was so. Do you recall the conversation? It is important now that the three of you review that which is written of your past lives. If you do, it will give you greater understanding of what is important.'

The previous lives material is difficult and embarrassing because it seems to polarise the possibilities: either you accept it as literally true or you dismiss it as a monumental ego-trip, which would of course put the authenticity of the material of all the rest of the communications in doubt. This passage suggests another way of regarding the previous lives material: as symbolically true, as an instructional aid, a way of directing their attention to characteristics and possibilities pertaining to their present lives; which leaves open the possibility that the intelligence producing the information exists independently of the three of them. While we are on the subject of previous lives, one other piece of information divulged by Tom in this speech should be noted. They had not always incarnated as figures of extraordinary distinction, but had each lived many obscure lives. 'We understood not the physical world, and you did not either, and so you lived many times to try to understand, and although you are pure soul, each time you live on the physical planet you are open to be trapped by it.'

The second passage for the record was addressed to Andrija and referred to a conversation earlier in the day at which most of the household had been present:

'I will now speak to the doctor. In your speech to the group of your people, when you explained that all of your people had been gods or goddesses, this was in error. You cannot speak to people in that manner, for when you do they begin to believe that they are special, and the problem of the physical world has always been the people who think that they are special. It is only in humility that the people of the physical planet Earth can grow and understand.'

Andrija acknowledged the justice of this, but asked, 'Is there any other term that might be more appropriate and accurate so that these people might understand just a wee bit?'

Tom answered promptly, 'Would you be satisfied with the

term "messengers of the aeons"? – because in truth this is what they are.'

'Yes, that's beautiful,' Andrija said.

And so to Israel, where the greater part of the sequel of this story takes place. When Andrija, John and Phyllis arrived in Tel Aviv on 24 November 1974, they had specific instructions from the Management to be out of the country by 11 December because if they stayed longer they might be in danger. None of them had any idea at that time how prolonged and complex their relation to Israel would become.

To contemplate the various strands that relate the trio and their work to Israel is to be persuaded of the validity of the Jungian theory of synchronicity. Ostensibly they first went there because Israel was the potential flashpoint for a war situation which could engulf the world. But Andrija had worked there before, with Uri Geller, who of course is an Israeli. And the Israeli people, according to Tom, were genetically related to the space people, particularly those of the civilisation of Hoova. Also, Israel had been the place where the last attempt to upgrade human consciousness had been made, through the agency of the Nazarene, Jesus Christ. And the stress, in the teachings of Tom, on the importance of humility, love and service, is reminiscent of Christian beliefs, just as a great deal of the symbolism and some of the dramatic themes of the communications are reminiscent of esoteric Christianity and Judaism, of the Book of Revelation and the Kabbalah. Israel brings into focus, interrelates and catalyses many of the disparate themes of the communications; so much so that one is tempted to speculate that the trio's being drawn there when they were, at a time when their work needed to be given focus, direction and coherence, was not a fortuitous but a synchronistic event.

Andrija had had problems with the Israeli immigration and customs authorities before. When he last left Israel he had had all the notes, research documents and tape transcripts of his work with Uri confiscated for some time. Now when he presented his passport the immigration officer called another over and they went into a huddle for a couple of minutes before returning it to him. His arrival had been noticed. He wondered how it would have been if Uri had been with them. Some days before, Tom had said that it would be advantageous for Uri to join the party. Andrija had phoned him and at first he had said he would try and arrange it, but at the last minute he had backed down.

They had reserved a two-room suite at the Sheraton, a tall modern hotel overlooking the Mediterranean at the northern end of Tel Aviv, and they made this their base during the three weeks of their stay, using a hired car to get around the country and generally looking and behaving like tourists. According to Tom, in the first communication they held, there was no need for dissimulation, because the Israeli authorities were aware of their presence and some of the leaders knew their true mission and were grateful to them. But they could be in danger from other factions, and should be particularly cautious on 28, 29 and 30 November. They could begin their work, he said, by spending a day driving around Tel Aviv. This would spread a pacifying influence in this time of high tension. 'We are now in a time of war,' Tom said. 'A greater war has never happened, and when we say this we do not mean just on your planet Earth, but we mean in the surroundings and in the heavens and in the universe.' He was referring to Armageddon, the cosmic conflict of the Biblical 'End of Days' period, of which Earth's present troubles were but the microcosmic reflection. Motoring around the streets of Tel Aviv seemed to Andrija, Phyllis and John a modest way of contributing to the war effort, but for their second day the Management came up with a rather more dramatic situation.

In a state of waking consciousness, Phyllis got some figures which seemed like map co-ordinates. Andrija went out and bought a map, and when they checked the co-ordinates on it they found that they indicated Yavneh, which is the site of one of Israel's nuclear power stations, about twenty miles south of Tel Aviv. In a communication they asked Tom if there was any significance in Phyllis's getting these co-ordinates, and he said that there was, for a sabotage plot that could have very serious consequences had been formulated and it would be their task to help frustrate it by spending thirty minutes in meditation as near as possible to Yavneh. So they drove down the coast and sought a suitable spot where they might meditate without being too conspicuous. The power station area was enclosed by tall barbed wire, the roads around it were patrolled by security vehicles, and there was a low-flying helicopter overhead, and they had to settle for a place some four or five miles from Yavneh for their meditation. After about twenty minutes Phyllis said that Ultima had 'told' her that they could go now, and she described what she had 'seen': the dematerialisation of the core of a tube which she presumed was an explosive device of some sort. So when they held their evening communication in the hotel, Andrija's first question was, 'What did we accomplish at Yavneh?' and Tom answered, 'A complete de-fusing.'

During this period Phyllis again became very vulnerable to psychic attack when she was coming out of trance, perhaps because she no longer had the protection of the Faraday cage. She also became very visonary during the meditation sessions, getting imagery that seemed incomprehensible but which Tom could usually later elucidate. During one meditation she kept seeing four umbrellas. Tom explained that as they didn't have the cage it would be beneficial for them to use umbrellas during their communications because the metal frames would help concentrate energies and afford protection. 'It is sad that there is not among all the possessions of your world a copper umbrella,' he said, but suggested that the lack may be compensated by placing something of copper on the open umbrella. So the next day they bought umbrellas, and thereafter used them as Tom had suggested, attaching them to the backs of the upright chairs they sat in for communication in order to keep their hands free. If the Israeli authorities were, as Tom had said, keeping an eye on them, and if one of their agents had caught a glimpse of them sitting hour after hour in a darkened room in the Sheraton under open umbrellas while the woman pointed her two index fingers at the other two and talked in a strange voice, they would surely have been dismissed as a group of crazy American cultists. They themselves often joked and laughed as they made their preparations, imagining how they would appear to others, but the umbrellas and the copper bracelets really did seem to improve communications and minimise attacks.

In another meditation, Phyllis got a very strange sequence of images. It started with birds, large and colourfully bedecked birds. 'They're coming from North Bravna, that word's very clear,' she said. The birds swooped down to where people were signing a paper with a quill pen. 'I don't know if the paper is a surrender or a peace treaty,' Phyllis said. Then she saw scenes of savagery and wanton murder, the beheading of women and children, performed by men wielding curved swords and wearing ornamented robes. There was some connection between the men and the swooping birds. And perched on a wall were a number of eagles, just watching. They could quite easily stop the marauding birds, but they didn't move. The name North Bravna kept coming back. Where was North Bravna? she asked. Neither Andrija nor John knew, but Andrija suggested that the savage killers she saw were Saracens and that she was seeing a replay of historical events. 'Did the Saracens ever take the city of Jerusalem?' Phyllis asked, and Andrija was able to tell her that they had done so at the time of the Crusades. 'Well, that's what they're going to try to do this time,' Phyllis said.

Tom later confirmed that her interpretation was basically right. There had been a building up of terrorist infiltrators in the city of Jerusalem over the past three months. They were armed by supplies that originated from a munitions factory in a small Russian town named North Bravna. The eagle that watched and would not intervene was the United States. The outbreak of terrorist activity was imminent, and they should project their energies and their concentration over the next days to the city of Jerusalem. 'Should we physically go there?' John said, 'We can easily do so.' Tom had to consult before he could answer. 'There is danger,' he said. 'You will be protected, but we cannot make that decision for you.'

Of course they went. They spent the greater part of two

days wandering about the narrow alleys and visiting the holy sites of the old city of Jerusalem. This walled city within a city, this bustling relic of many pasts thriving in the present, fascinated Phyllis. She soon learnt how to haggle and joke with the Arab traders, which embarrassed John though he had to admit that she was playing the tourist pretty convincingly. Several times they lost her and had to retrace their steps up a thronged alley, looking into every shop as they went until they found her, bargaining with a trader over an embroidered galabeer or a piece of jewellery or an ornament. It was quite credible that some of these traders or some of the young Arabs lounging about or sitting drinking coffee should be the terrorist infiltrators that Tom had spoken about. There were plenty of heavily armed Israeli soldiers around, too, some casually patrolling the alleys and others posted on roofs and surveying the scene below. It wasn't difficult to imagine violence suddenly erupting and the panic that would ensue in the narrow streets if shooting started.

Accompanying them on this trip was Leon Berg, a friend of John's from England. Leon had been one of the helpers at the time of the May Lectures, but John hadn't seen much of him since that time. He had gone to Tel Aviv on an impulse. He knew that John was there, but assumed that he was on business and knew nothing about the work or his involvement with Andrija and Phyllis. He had contacted him at the Sheraton when he arrived in Tel Aviv, and he joined them on several of their trips over the next couple of weeks, though he still had little idea of what they were engaged on.

I have to bring Leon Berg into the story at this point because it was because of him that they went to Ein Kerem. Ein Kerem is a village just outside Jerusalem. Leon said he had some friends who lived there and would like to take the opportunity to pay them a visit. He had been told that they lived near the church, so when they reached Ein Kerem John drove up a lane which wound up towards the church, but only to find that it terminated in a cul-de-sac. Then an extraordinary thing happened. When John tried to reverse back to find a place to turn, the car simply wouldn't move. All four wheels were locked. He tried everything he knew to release them, but to no avail. The car was obstructing the lane, but the only way they could move it was by sliding it downhill. This they did with some help, and the car nearly veered into a wall as they negotiated a bend. Eventually they got to the bottom of the hill where the road was wider, and John tried again to release the locked brakes. It was a hydraulic system and in spite of his long motoring experience John couldn't imagine how all four wheels could remain locked in this way.

Leon went on foot to try to find his friends, hoping that they might be able to help at least by recommending a local mechanic. The car was stopped just outside the big church, which Phyllis said they should go into. She was quite insistent about it, so John and Andrija complied, as they always did when she got strong impulses to do something, knowing from experience that the thought wasn't always her own. The church was locked, but soon after they had tried the door it was opened from within by a priest. The church seemed ordinary enough, and after wandering around it for some minutes they were about to leave when the priest called them back and led them to a corner of the church that they had missed, where a short flight of steps led down into an illuminated grotto. Here, they learnt, was the spot where John the Baptist had lived. That was interesting. They spent some time reading the texts and looking at the pictures on the wall of the cave, then left the church and returned to the car. John could never explain why, but he knew with absolute certainty before he stepped into the car that the mysterious fault would be rectified. And he was right. After a couple of minutes Leon reappeared, still having failed to find his friends, and they drove back to Jerusalem without further trouble.

We have had occasion before to wonder whether the intelligence that is Tom is a clever opportunist, ingenious in thinking up explanations for events that fit them into his own scheme of things. With regard to this incident he admitted to being an opportunist, but in a rather different sense. He claimed that the Management had seized the opportunity of Andrija's being in Ein Kerem to make a point.

'It was Altea* using the energy of the Being. It was on our direction,' said Tom when Andrija asked for an explanation of the incident.

'And why did you have us stop right there?' Andrija said.

'You are the proclaimer,' Tom answered.

John the Baptist, of course, proclaimed the coming of Christ. Here, clearly, was a pointer to Andrija's role in the present-day situation. Tom spelt it out quite unambiguously: 'You are the proclaimer, and it is now the beginning.'

'What specifically is to be proclaimed at this time?' Andrija asked. He half expected to be reproached by Tom for asking something he already knew, but Tom didn't mention the landing, as he had anticipated, but said:

'It is important for you to have those of the nation of Israel understand from where they came, and for what purpose.'

Both Andrija and John understood the allusion. In earlier communications they had learnt that the Israelis were descendants of the extra-terrestrial civilisation of Hoova, whose leader was Jehovah. They were what Tom termed a 'species' nation. A 'species', he had explained, was a hybrid. 'All beings on this planet have lived on other planets, but there are those that are a mixture. Physical beings may be reborn on another planet. A species is a mixture of two or more planets at the time of its physical existence. It has a strong ego and it has free will.' The Israelites were not the only hybrid people on the planet, Tom said, but as they were the descendants of Hoova, the extra-terrestrial civilisation that had special responsibility and concern for the development of the planet Earth, they had a particularly important role to play in history.

This was the gist of the message that Andrija, as 'the proclaimer', was supposed to convey to the people of Israel. As it is one of the major themes of the communications from now on, and allegedly one of the most important things to get mankind to understand, I will digress to summarise the whole story and message as it emerged through a number of com-

* Tom explained that Ultima's true name was 'Altea' and that he would use that form in future. The true identity could not have been revealed before but they would later understand its significance.

munications held over this period. By way of introduction I should like to quote part of a communication which I recently participated in, when I was able to put a question and a point of view which I am sure many readers would want to put at this stage. This was in May 1976, when I paid a visit to Israel, and this particular conversation took place in a trance session with Phyllis in the Neptune hotel in Eilat. After spending nearly two weeks in Israel I had formed the impression that its people were efficient, aggressive, sensual, hidebound and quite unspiritual, and I couldn't reconcile this with what at that time I knew about their alleged role and history. So I put my problem and point of view to Tom:

'As the aim of your programme, as I understand it, is to heighten consciousness on this planet, and to unite the people of this planet, I find it very difficult to come to terms with the fact that the Israeli people are the chosen people for this work. It would seem that in this time the idea of a chosen people is a rather retrograde concept, and that if it has any meaning it is not racial but applies to people from all over the world and from different cultures.'

'Do you understand that in the nation of Israel there are represented all the nations of this planet Earth?' Tom asked. I said I realised that, and he continued: 'Do you understand that when we use the term "chosen" it is not necessary to relate to them that they are chosen, but what we are trying to say is that if they had followed their programme we would not be in the situation we are now in, for all of the nations on the planet Earth would be chosen. In this nation of Israel there are representatives of each of the nations on the planet, and if you reach this nation its energy will generate then to all of the other nations, and what should have been thousands of years ago will then come into being. It is not that they are chosen in specialness, for what they have chosen and been chosen for is similar to service. It must be understood that being chosen is not necessarily to be elite, for being chosen brings great difficulty.'

'Yes,' I said, 'I understand that, but my problem is that the Israelis as I see them today must be one of the most difficult people in the world to bring round to higher consciousness. I feel, though, that the higher consciousness is being generated by a large number of people scattered throughout the world, and that mankind's greatest hope lies with these people rather than with any special group.'

'We understand what you are saying,' Tom said, 'but if you imagine the universe as a whole and you see the planet Earth as a black spot in the universe which has bottlenecked the evolution of the universe and stopped the growth of the souls that should by this time have evolved further than they have, and if you then look upon the Earth as the universe and see the nation of Israel as the black spot of the planet Earth, you will then understand that it is important to reach the nation that has all nations within it in order to raise the level of all the nations.'

The logic may be difficult to follow, if you are not *au fait* with the view, which is central to Tom's philosophy, that events in the microcosm affect the macrocosm and vice versa, but the answer does quite ingeniously dispose of the suspicion that the Management are a kind of cosmic Zionist faction which must be the invention of some fanatic Zionist brain on Earth.

In the following paragraphs I will attempt to summarise the story of the history and role of the Jews using the framework of known Biblical history to supplement and elucidate the information volunteered by Tom over a period of time.

The land of Mesopotamia, which historians regard as the cradle of civilisation, was peopled by one of the groups that migrated from the nuclear civilisation of Aksu. About 2000 BC the space civilisation of Hoova launched another attempt to upgrade the planet Earth, and chose as the most promising group to work through the tribe living in Mesopotamia. It was Abraham of Ur who initiated the experiment, the aim of which was to produce an improved stock of human beings who would lead the planet into its next evolutionary stage. The improvement was to be accomplished by engineering into the genetic code the essence of Hoova in order to produce a new hybrid species on Earth. The children of Abraham were the first to be so implanted, and the plan was that they should eventually interbreed with all the nations and races of the world in order to produce a more highly evolved genetic strain, and also that they should raise human consciousness by teaching the skills and knowledge that were their heritage from Hoova. Chapter 17 of the Book of Genesis records Jehovah's covenant with Abraham: 'You shall be the father of a multitude of nations . . . and I will make thy seed as the dust of the earth, so that if a man can number the dust of the earth, then shall thy seed also be numbered.' But the plan went wrong, because the Jews forgot their role and their cosmic origins and became an inbred ethnic group, forced in upon themselves by the struggle for survival in harsh physical conditions and by the enmity and resentment of other people who did not understand them.

Hoova had to intervene again to attempt to bring its errant protégé people back to an understanding of their role and mission, in the thirteenth century BC, when Jehovah appeared as Moses. He led the Jewish people out of bondage and gave them the Law that was to become the basis of their religion. The purpose of the Law was to inculcate principle and self-discipline in the people. The forty years they spent wandering in the wilderness was a time of trial for the Jewish people, a test of their faith and their obedience, and though on occasion they denied God and rebelled against Moses' leadership, the generation that eventually inherited the Promised Land was a generation that had never known bondage and in whom a life of hardship had cultivated discipline and principle and its consummation had strengthened a faith in God.

There followed a time of internecine struggles and an attempt to build the earthly kingdom, and again the Jews made the error of forgetting their origins and their purpose. They isolated themselves from the world, they deified Moses and trivialised the Law by elaborating it into a code of religious observances. They enjoyed independence and sovereignty for a time, but they did not fulfil their intended function, and when this period ended with the Roman conquest Hoova took advantage of the conditions of social and spiritual upheaval and Jehovah incarnated again as Jesus of Nazareth, coming among his people as an example and a model of man's next phase of evolution. As Moses he had brought the principle of Law, and as Jesus he brought the principle of Love, in order to guide the Jewish people towards the fulfilment of their destiny.

'The book does not always tell the truth,' said Tom, referring to the Bible when Andrija said that as he understood it Jesus's betrayal and crucifixion were foreordained. The truth was that if the Jews had accepted Jesus as their leader and had followed him he would have shown them, and in turn the rest of the planet, the way to individual and global transformation. The crucifixion was not part of the plan, nor was the religion that centred its theology upon that event which only signified another failure on the part of the Jews to understand and fulfil their role in the process of planetary evolution. Thereafter they lost their homeland and were dispersed about the Earth, and though they contributed knowledge, invention and beauty to the other cultures they lived in, they never integrated completely with these other cultures but remained jealous of their traditions and their identity. The re-creation of the State of Israel in modern times presented the first opportunity since the diaspora for the Jews to be reached collectively and reminded of their true heritage and role. It is, however, now too late for the original plan of gradual planetary evolution through their agency to be carried out, and Hoova has adopted a new policy towards the Earth, a kind of shock-strategy because of the seriousness of the situation, in which a period of preparation will be followed by a landing on Earth. The process of preparation will not this time involve sending a special individual whom humanity might deify, but the appearance of a number of individuals endowed with the powers of Hoova, of whom Uri Geller was one, and at the same time the work of trying to develop planetary and cosmic consciousness in the people of Israel will continue, if only because of all the Earth's peoples they are the most intractable, and if they can be raised and made aware of their cosmic connections there is hope for the rest of the world.

To return to the communication that took place after the visit to the church at Ein Kerem:

'You didn't have to lead me to the grotto of St John the Baptist,' Andrija told Tom. 'I mean, as a proclaimer, I didn't need to know of that particular place. But now the subject has been raised, can you tell us more about the strange tale of how St John's life ended? Is it true that Herod's daughter requested his head to be cut off?'

'It was not Herod's daughter. It was his step-daughter.'

'And did she indeed order his head . . .'

'She was a child. She did it for her mother, for John spurned her.'

'I see. You mean that Herod's wife tried to lay St John?'

'We understand not that term,' Tom said. Andrija explained and he confirmed that this was in fact what had happened, and took the opportunity to give Andrija a bit of advice: 'You must be careful of your she-people who use the wiles of a she. You will not be beheaded, Doctor, but if you are not careful your personal life could interfere with your knowledge of truth, and that would be like a beheading.'

Andrija brought the conversation back to an earlier point. 'When one proclaims, one usually proclaims on the basis of knowledge, and that knowledge has a source . . .'

Tom didn't let him complete the sentence. He interrupted: 'John didn't have knowledge, and he proclaimed. Because he knew in his heart. You speak of knowledge as written or established. But true knowledge and wisdom is in the heart.'

There followed a long discussion of the means of proclaiming, and Tom said that Andrija should write another book, which would be based upon the communications and would serve as a source for material for television and film. They discussed what should go into the book and John raised the question of the past lifetime's material, pointing out that many mediums and other people in the past had totally discredited themselves by claiming to have been important people in other incarnations. 'We three are on the face of it very ordinary people,' he said, 'and people are going to wonder why we have this particular information.'

Tom had a suggestion. 'May it be possible in your publication to review your own lives in this lifetime in order to make sense of your past lives? Can you show the fine line of what you have brought forward?'

'Well yes, it would be possible if we knew more about our past lives,' Andrija said, 'and then we would have to decide if we could relate our present existence to the past ones. But the subject doesn't really concern us from a personal or ego point of view, and it isn't our main problem. The problem is, I'll tell you frankly, that we believe that you've given us what we call a "mission impossible". And when I say this I mean that for us, who are in this world as Gentiles, to try to convince the Jewish people, the Israelites, of their true origins and their true responsibilities, and of who is coming in the next few years, seems to me almost impossible.'

'Do you not understand that with the Nine and you three working together all things are possible?'

'Yes, you've told us that before, but we also know that there are certain things that you don't understand about the physical, about desire and about emotion, and it is we who have to deal directly with the emotions, with the blocks, with the negativity ...'

'Do you not think that we are learning when we deal with the emotions of the three of you?'

'Yes,' Andrija conceded, 'we know you're learning because you tell us quite clearly things about ourselves that we aren't aware of. But then you must also recognise the unusually stubborn, hard-headed and disbelieving nature of this Israeli people.'

'Are you not stubborn and hard-headed? If you were not you would not have come this far. And Sir John, he is very much of a stubborn nature and with a hard head. And this Being at times we cannot reach because of the closing. Do you understand that the three of you are of the nature of those of Israel? And if you can reach each other you can reach those of the nation of Israel.'

'Well, I accept that,' Andrija said, 'but you have to remember that we have had your presence and guidance and even so have made many mistakes.'

'And you will do for those what we have tried to do for you,'

Tom said with a note of finality.

They spent two days in Jerusalem on this first visit and at the end of the time were told by Tom that they had accomplished a great deal. 'Because of your presence and the energy that has been utilised from the three of you there is now greater hope and stability of emotion among the leaders of the nation,' he said, and went on to give an interesting brief analysis of the international political situation with regard to Israel: 'It was planned by the most powerful governments in your world that this nation would in fact be crucified. In the reasoning of the governments, it would have been justified. This has been averted at this time, but this does not mean there is complete peace. As you know, in all times of crisis those of the nation of Hoova have always taken the blame. It is because the rest of the people of the world need a reason for their emotion and it is projected on those of the nation of Hoova because of the lack of understanding. We are saddened that these people have come no further. It is true that those of the nation of Israel because of the physical conditions of the planet Earth have not followed the path of truth, but it is also true that those of the other nations have not done so either. In order to exonerate themselves they will cause a blemish upon another, and will throw the other into a pit of cobras. They will be ashamed at another time. But that has been the history of the planet Earth. We cannot have it so in the future, nor at this time. It is a time for each individual to stop, to respond, and to realise that it is within them that the blame lies, not within others.'

This was the kind of message that the three were now expected to proclaim, but as proclaiming was a new task laid upon them and one requiring some preparation, their activities during the rest of this stay in Israel were directed towards fulfilling their earlier instructions so travel about the country and thus help bring peace and stability to all its people.

There were a number of people in Israel who knew about Andrija's work in the parasciences and who somehow got to know that he was in Tel Aviv, and John kept answering calls from people who wanted to meet him or to ask him to give a talk. Andrija was feeling pretty exhausted with all the travelling and generally refused such requests, but one invitation that they accepted because it happened to fall in with their itinerary led to interesting developments. It came from a Mrs Judith Stahl who lived in Amirim, a village in the hills of Galilee which was well known throughout Israel as the home of a vegetarian community. Mrs Stahl herself was a dietician and, judging from her phone call, seemed to have some ideas worth getting acquainted with, and as Andrija, Phyllis and John were planning a trip to Safed in Galilee the day after she phoned, they said they would visit her on their return journey to Tel Aviv in the late afternoon.

They made an early start the next day because Andrija, who had done this trip before, wanted to take the others to and spend some time at the ancient site of Megiddo on the way to Galilee. There was something about Megiddo, he said, that drew him back and made him feel he could spend hours there. The site of settlements going back, according to the guide-book, to about 6000 BC, Megiddo, is a mound of fairly modest height and dimensions which commands a view over the largest and most fertile plains of Israel, the plains that are supposed to be the physical battlefield of Armageddon, on the other side of which rise the symmetrical Mount Tabor and beyond that the rugged hills of Galilee. Archaeologists have cut away sections through the mound of Megiddo, and in the deepest of these excavations is situated the old Canaanite altar, a circular platform of rough stones. This was the particular spot that Andrija said he felt drawn back to. There were hawks nesting in the rock face flanking the altar, and hawks had a particular significance for Andrija. They stopped to meditate for ten minutes in this spot before continuing their journey.

Galilee, John thought, could have been a Swiss or South German lake, but for the names familiar since the scripture lessons of childhood: Tiberias, Migdal, Capernaum. There was an east wind and the lake was green and choppy. The other side, where the Golan Heights rose, sand-coloured and streaked with gullies, looked uninhabited. After driving along the lakeside and visiting the sites they completed the journey to Safed, the hill town, ancient centre for the kabbalists, that from Galilee stood out conspicuously among all the other hills, crowned with a forest of tall trees. In Safed they spent some time walking through the narrow streets and up to the park, and they admired the view of the sun setting over the hills to the west. It was nearly dark when they arrived at Amirim and found the home of Mrs Stahl, who turned out to be a woman aged about forty-five, deeply tanned and bursting with energy. She was a woman of the commanding, insistent type, and her chief concern was to get Andrija to do research to validate her findings and theories about various diets. Andrija was interested in the theories but non-committal about working on them.

They had come to Amirim at a good time, said Mrs Stahl, because today was the festival of Hannuka and in the evening the children of the village were presenting a special Hannuka entertainment in the community hall, which they should certainly see. They went, and they enjoyed the entertainment despite the language barrier, for it was tuneful and zestful, and the drama was heightened by the conditions under which it took place, with soldiers standing around with uzi guns ready, for a neighbouring village had recently been attacked at night by infiltrators from Syria. One item in the entertainment made a particular impression on John, Phyllis and Andrija. A painted screen was brought on stage. It had a two-fold frame and therefore consisted of three panels. On the lower half of each panel were painted three figures, curiously slant-eyed and unearthly looking beings. On the top half were mushrooms of the *Amanita muscaria* type (the 'Sacred Mushroom' that Andrija had written about in his book of that title). The symbolism was so obviously apt to their situation that John, Phyllis and Andrija all registered it independently while the screen stood on stage and they were waiting for the sketch to begin. It was not only the way that the nine figures were arranged in three groups of three, but also the fact that they each had over their heads this mushroom, for in recent communications Tom had referred to the umbrellas they now regularly used as 'mushrooms'. Then, as if to reinforce the already staggering impression made upon the visitors, when

227

the sketch began nine children danced out from behind the screen carrying umbrellas. Once again, it seemed, synchronicity was at work, and the three could not help wondering whether their visit to this place was as accidental as it seemed.

It was not until the following day that they were able to confirm with Tom that the events of their trip were not mere chance coincidence. Andrija said, 'It was odd to find our symbol so clearly spelled out in this remote little village in the Galilee hills. The preparation for that must have been very long.'

'It was not overnight,' Tom said.

The screen had looked about thirty years old. To minds just getting emancipated from thinking in terms of cause and effect and of linear time the implications were mind-boggling. It was natural to assume that the village must have some special significance.

'Is there any lesson to be learned from the situation in Amirim,' Andrija said, 'and from the way those children are fed and brought up, which could be applied to the new generation of young people?'

'Those children are of a different nature,' Tom answered, 'and it could be said that the way they have been raised has in part given them this nature. But also they are all species, and all of them have within them the ability of Uri. Did you not see that?'

'Well, we saw that they were different,' Andrija said. 'We didn't know how it would manifest, though.'

'There is a difference. It is that Uri is aggressive and has fears, but there are no fears in these children.'

Amirim had another significance. 'It is a place of special importance to you, Sir John,' Tom explained, 'because of the many times that you have existed in the area. You were there for many of your physical lives before the time of the Nazarene. You knew of this.'

'Well, I did have a very special feeling for the place,' John said, 'but I didn't realise that was why.'

On a future visit to Israel, Tom said, they would go again to Amirim and spend more time there.

In the same communication they asked Tom about Megiddo and obtained an interesting response. The first settlement there was three thousand years earlier than generally supposed, in 9228 BC to be precise. Then a migrant group had come from afar 'at the time of the destruction of our great anger' (a phrase which will be explained later). 'It was a stronghold of those that were in truth, but those that opposed sought to destroy it.'

'How did Megiddo come to be associated with Armageddon?' Andrija asked.

'Have we not explained that those that opposed tried to destroy the colony that was of the essence of truth? It left in the area a vibration, and this was always an area of battle, both in the physical and in the spheres.'

'What puzzles me,' Andrija said, 'is that there's only one mention of Armageddon in the Bible, and that's almost a passing reference.'

'We did not control what men put in your Bible,' Tom said. 'Remember, there are parts of your Bible that are not *in* your Bible.'

In several communications over this period Tom reiterated that they must leave Israel by 11 December, and three days before this date Andrija mentioned in a communication session that they had not yet been able to cover the whole of Israel in their travels and asked if they should extend their stay in order to complete the project. Tom said that on no account should they leave later than midday on the twelfth, and that already they had accomplished enough to ensure stability in the Middle East situation for three months, but they ought to plan to return in February. This reminded Andrija of a report he had just read in a newspaper of a speech given by King Hussein of Jordan warning that war in the Middle East could develop to planetary proportions and stressing the importance of working towards peace in the area.

'Parts of the statement were almost word for word what you have said to us,' Andrija told Tom. 'Did you have any direct influence on him?'

'We had not. You had,' Tom said. 'Have we not explained

that you are here in order to stabilise the leaders, and that you have a radius of 1,500 of your miles?'

'Yes, we understand these things,' Andrija said, 'but I think you have to respect our modesty. It's hard for us to believe that we could have such influence.'

'We will explain again,' said Tom in that tone of indulgent patience that was becoming familiar. 'When a project is important and we request you to put aside your personal life and to proceed upon the project, each of you has three of us with you. Have you not seen what has been accomplished? Have you not noticed what has happened after you have been in an area? Have you not seen that there are those of the Arab nations that are now beginning to soften and to understand this nation? Have you not seen that within some of the Arab nations they are fearful that Arafat will begin to take over and control them? They are now turning their attention to internal problems.'

'Well,' said Andrija, 'we've been a little too busy these days to keep up with all of that detail, but thanks for putting us in the picture.'

On their last day in Israel, 10 December, they planned a trip that would take in as many as possible of the parts of the country they had not yet covered. They left Tel Aviv early and by mid-morning they were in Hebron, where they visited Abraham's tomb. They went to Bethlehem for lunch, then drove on to visit Jericho and the Dead Sea. In falling darkness they drove south along the road coasting the Dead Sea, then cut across the Negev to Beersheba, whence they planned to cross to the Mediterranean coastal road and drive directly back to Tel Aviv.

They were not long out of Beersheba when Phyllis got one of her flashes. She said that there was something wrong with the tyre on the right-hand front wheel. John pulled up and he, Andrija and Leon, who was accompanying them again, examined the tyre, but they could find no fault in it. John was a little irritated, because he suspected that Phyllis had said that just to slow down his driving. With a big distance to cover, he had tended throughout the day to drive faster than Phyllis found comfortable, and she had several times made her discomfort known, but John had only paid cursory attention because he knew he was driving safely. Not long after they had resumed their journey after examining the tyre John carelessly hit a kerbstone, and a few miles further on he felt on the steering the pull that signals a flat tyre. Fortunately it wasn't a burst but only a leak due to damage to the rim of the wheel when he had hit the kerb. It was the right-hand front wheel that was damaged, so obviously Phyllis had had a precognitive flash. They changed the wheel and continued their journey. They were about thirty-five kilometres from Tel Aviv when they ran into a quite spectacular storm, and suddenly, simultaneously with the occurrence of a particularly bright lightning flash, the car's engine cut dead. John found a suitable place to pull in off the road as the car coasted to a standstill. He tried several times to start the engine, but it did not fire once. Remembering the incident at Ein Kerem some days before, he said, 'What are we supposed to do this time, Phyllis? I don't see any church.'

'I guess we'd better just sit here and meditate,' Phyllis said. They did as she suggested for five minutes, then John tried to start the engine again but still nothing happened. Phyllis thought a longer meditation was required, but Andrija suggested that she should go into trance and try to find out what was happening. She did so, and came up with the information that there was a great battle taking place in the spheres and that in order to send helping energy to the forces of light they should immediately meditate for a longer period. Phyllis came out of trance and they meditated for a further twenty minutes. During this period of meditation John kept getting an image of two people, a man and a woman, the latter with her face badly mutilated as if she had been in an accident. After the twenty minutes John tried the starter again and this time the engine fired instantly and in another half hour they were back at the Sheraton.

It wasn't only Phyllis who was annoyed at the way John had driven on the trip. That night Tom chastised him severely saying that but for the protection of Hoova and Altea, 'you would no longer have been in existence on the physical planet

Earth, but you would have been returned with us'. A lot of energy had been deployed protecting them, which could have been put to other use if John had not put all their lives at risk. 'We cannot waste the energy of Hoova or of Altea or of you three to protect you from your own foolishness,' Tom reproached him. As for the stopping of the car, that too had been the work of Altea, for a contribution of energy from the three was required at that particular time.

'Was there some major event going on in the battle of Armageddon?' Andrija asked.

'The battle of Armageddon is between what you call the sons of light and the sons of dark, but remember that it also affects physical planets,' Tom said. 'Those that oppose had set in motion a situation to help those that they work through on the physical planet.' There had been a difficulty prevented at the Yavneh power station, though two lives had been lost in the process. They hadn't realised it at the time, but the place where the car had stopped was near Yavneh. The situation, Tom said, both in the spheres and on Earth, was now stabilised, and they would be able to leave as planned the following day.

'May we hold with you now ten minutes of prayer,' Tom said in conclusion. 'The twelve of us will pray together, and then we will close and leave.' And the prayer he proceeded to give them, which is also a summary of the main motifs of the communications, will make a fitting conclusion to the present chapter:

We pray that the children of the nation of Israel come to peace within themselves and come to recognise whence they came.

We pray that all the civilisations of the universe that are engaged in the balancing of the universe be given strength and peace within to carry on the work to which they are committed.

We pray that the physical beings of the planet Earth come into a state of awareness and understanding in order for their souls to evolve to raise the level of the planet Earth and to cleanse the heavens around the planet Earth so that the universe can progress.

We pray that those beings and civilisations that are opposing what we do come to the light of understanding so that they also come into perfect balance.

We pray that the day may soon come when all in the universe have the knowledge and the understanding that will make them whole.

We pray for understanding among ourselves, and for the strength that is needed so that each of us can guide the others to become perfect beings.

We pray for the souls of the children of Israel to be brought out of the dark and into the light.

# CHAPTER SEVEN

# *Revelations*

'We were wondering when you would ask,' Tom said when Andrija asked if there was any connection between the extra-terrestrial civilisations and the legend of Atlantis.

This was in November, before the first trip to the Middle East. There were two other sessions largely devoted to ancient history and Atlantis during the stay in Israel and which I have deferred writing about until now in order to bring all the material together in one place.

Atlantis, Tom explained in reply to Andrija's question, was a civilisation originated by a migrant group from Aksu. It had flourished for thousands of years and had come to a sudden cataclysmic end about 11000 BC. It had stretched from Greece to the Americas. The name Atlantis was in fact a corruption, and it should be known as the Altean civilisation, for its people 'were of the civilisation of Altea'.

'Could you give us a glimpse of the level of civilisation attained by the Alteans?' Andrija asked. 'What was their outstanding achievement?'

'In the field of what you call medicine they were far superior to what you are at this time. Also, your knowledge of electronics is primitive compared to their knowledge. And they knew how to use the mind to move objects and to move themselves. If it was not that below their waist they were always in trouble, it would have been a fine civilisation.'

'Was their medicine not able to help them with that part of their problem?' Andrija asked.

'They enjoyed it,' Tom said. 'We, as we have told you before, have no objections to enjoyment, except when it becomes the consuming. Instead of using the great medical knowledge that they had to improve their minds they used it to improve their sex organs.' Altean surgery, he explained, was capable of effecting transplants of all the vital organs of the body, even of brains, and 'those organs that were transplanted were far superior to those that had existed in the physical body'. The life expectancy of an Altean who had the best medical care could run into thousands of years.

The three had been on Earth at the time of the Altean civilisation, though they had not been together. The Doctor was in the area we now call Crete. Sir John was on a land off the coast of present-day South America, and the Being was near her present home, Florida, but in a place now submerged. They had all three functioned as teachers, and as they had not been physically born but had come to Earth on a mission, they had not had the same emotions as physical beings. They had underestimated the human desires and greed upon which the opposition could work. The Altean civilisation eventually became predominantly degenerate.

Andrija asked, 'Was the submergence of Atlantis an act of God or was it . . . ?'

'We were angry,' Tom said. 'It was perhaps our ignorance in not understanding the density of the planet Earth. We are more compassionate now.' At the time of 'the great anger', he further explained, there were some peripheral colonies that were not destroyed. But also there were, on the main land masses that were submerged, some individuals 'that were not of the nature of the majority', but they had been destroyed with the rest. They had understood the necessity for the act, and when these souls had incarnated again they had chosen to come in a different physical form. There were some of these reincarnated Altean souls on the planet Earth today. 'We are not sure that in the future their appearance in the manner in which they have appeared will benefit their soul growth,' Tom said, 'but it was their choice, and with their understanding of the physical nature of their past experience they decided that perhaps in this form they could be of service in a proper way.' And they were incarnated as dolphins.

Thus was first introduced a subject that was later to be elaborated upon and to lead to some interesting field work. Andrija did not pursue the subject of dolphin intelligence at this stage, however, but followed up the subject of the relation between the civilisation of Atlantis and that of other ancient civilisations.

'According to the Platonic legend,' he said, 'the desirable elements of Atlantean, or Altean, civilisation were brought to Egypt. Is this true?'

'Yes. After the destruction, you were each involved with the early civilisations of Egypt, Ur and China.'

Referring to the legend that the culture of Ur, or Sumer, was founded by the god Oa, and to a well-known picture of the god, Andrija asked why the founder of the civilisation of Ur had appeared in the form of a fish.

'It was not. It was a ram,' Tom said categorically.

'Then why did it come out of the sea, according to the legend?'

'That is not all of the legend. It was first as a bull, it was then as a ram, and finally, as recorded, it was as a fish. It was in truth a dolphin, and it was a merging of others with those of this planet.'

'Was it a true biological merging, or just for the occasion?' Andrija asked, and Tom explained that, as in Aksu, it had been a merging of the genes of beings from higher physical civilisations with those of the people of this planet, in order to strengthen and upgrade the species.

'How much knowledge from Atlantis was given to the early Egyptians?' Andrija asked.

'The knowledge of medicine, with the exception of what could be done with the sex organs, was given to them,' Tom said. 'But you must understand that the primitive people in the land that you call Egypt were a very fearful people. Because of their primitiveness they were also of such a nature that the genetic memory of the mind recalled the destruction, and therefore they built upon their structure a great worship.'

While they were talking about Egypt, John took the opportunity to put in a question. 'I'm very interested in the great pyramid and its meaning. Could you say something about that?' Which elicited a reproach that, considering the range of Andrija's questioning, seems rather unfair:

'Your curiosity and your anxiety at times make us itch! You cannot stay on one programme.'

'Well, I assumed that the great pyramid had something . . .,' John began, but he was interrupted.

'When the day arrives when there is understanding upon the planet Earth, and when those of other civilisations arrive to help the planet, that will be the day when the secret that you ask is given.'

Undaunted by the rebuff John had received, Andrija now changed the subject: 'We now know that there are different peoples and groups upon the planet. We know that the Israelites are the special project of Hoova, and so on. Can you tell us where the Nordic people fit in?'

'They came from the civilisation of Ashand.'

'And is there any particular significance in the fact that Uri and his work are most readily accepted in the Scandinavian countries?'

'They are in that knowledge the most evolved, because of the creativity of the civilisation of Ashand. And they have a core of understanding. It is unfortunate, though, that they have become so material.'

Tom declined to answer a similar question about the background of the Arab races 'until we are in the box', but when John asked about the blacks he came up with an interesting statement: 'They were the originals on this planet. They were not seeded. They were the souls that evolved here from what you would call the elementals.'

Briefly summarising the history of Earth civilisations, Tom said: 'That time [32400 BC, the time of the foundation of Aksu] was the beginning of the rising of civilisations and populations. You understand that there was a collapse of the civilisation of Aksu. Then there was of course the collapse of what you call Atlantis. And then there was the collapse of Egypt. And if you continue, there has been the collapse of many other civilisations. And have you now discovered why?'

'Well, from all you have told us,' Andrija answered, 'we understand that it has always collapsed when the desire life has overcome the higher evolutionary development of the soul.'

'That is in part true,' Tom said, and went on to explain that the other part of the truth was that the people of Israel had failed to understand and to fulfil their historical mission.

Let us now compare this Earth history material with some of the findings and conjectures of scholars.

The evolutionary theory of the origins of *homo sapiens* and of Earth's civilisations has in recent years suffered some setbacks. Though palaeontologists have found evidence of the existence of anthropoid species going back over a million years, it is generally acknowledged today that these could never have evolved into human beings, and that true man appeared on Earth about 35,000 years ago. As one writer on the subject has put it: '*Homo sapiens* appears, suddenly, out of the blue, complete, intelligent, with clothing, weapons, fire. With a curious mythology that owes nothing to an animal ancestor, and with an ability that, at the beginning, is at least equal to that of today.'

There is no consensus among historians and anthropologists as to where what Joseph Campbell has called 'the nuclear folk' first appeared. Mid-Europe, the Middle East and central Asia have all been suggested as locations. The latter would, of course, coincide with Tom's information, for the Tarim Basin is in the Sinkiang province of Western China, and in fact some interesting material has recently come to light which not only seems to bear this out but also supports the theory of extra-terrestrial intervention.

In 1965 a Chinese archaeologist published the results of a twenty-five-year study of some strange stone disks found in caves in the Bayan-Kara-Ula mountains on the borders of Tibet and Western China. The disks belonged to the Ham and Dropa tribesmen who still live in these caves, and who have puzzled anthropologists for they seem unrelated to any other ethnic group, being of frail build and little over four feet in height.

Eventually the key to deciphering the hieroglyphics on the stone disks was discovered, and one of them read: 'The dropas came down from the clouds in their gliders. Our men, women and children hid in the caves ten times before sunrise. When at last they understood the sign language of the Dropas, they realised that the newcomers had peaceful intentions.'

The Chinese archaeologist speculated that these disks and the present occupants of the caves were connected with ancient Chinese legends which speak of small, yellow-skinned men who came down from the clouds. The Chinese Academy of Pre-History banned publication of his discoveries and theories for many years, but when he finally did publish them a Russian writer, Vyachedlev Zeitsev, reported the work in an article titled 'Visitors from Outer Space' in the magazine *Sputnik* in 1967. I am indebted to a book, *Uninvited Visitors*, by the American writer Ivan T. Sanderson, for this information, which of course is particularly interesting in the light of what Tom has repeatedly said about the origins of civilisation on Earth.

Now as regards Atlantis: all the theories about the nature, location and dating of this prediluvian civilisation are highly speculative, but Tom's dating corresponds with the general view that a cataclysmic event, the origin of world-wide flood legends, took place between 10000 and 12000 BC. In Plato's *Critias* there is a passage about the reason for the destruction of the Atlantean civilisation which Tom's account corresponds with, and which also suggests that the people of Atlantis were a hybrid species: 'When the portion of divinity within them was becoming weak and faint through being oft times blended with a large measure of mortality, and the human temper was becoming dominant . . . Zeus, the God of gods, desired to inflict punishment upon them.' The punishment, according to both Plato's and Tom's versions of the story, was inflicted overnight, and resulted in the submergence of the civilisation of Atlantis. It is interesting to note in passing that the trio later learned that Zeus, Altea and Atlas were synonymous.

With regard to Sumer and Egypt, many historians have puzzled over the sudden appearance of high civilisations in these regions about the middle of the fourth millennium BC, and some have speculated that such a substantial body of knowledge must have been taught to the Sumerians rather than developed by them. The view is supported by a passage by the Chaldean historian Berosus, a contemporary of Alexander the Great, who reported a tradition already ancient in his day that: 'There appeared, coming out of the sea where it touches Babylonia, an intelligent creature that men called Oannes, who had the face and limbs of a man and who used human speech, but was covered with what appeared to be the skin of a great fish. . . . The entire day this strange being, without taking any human nourishment, would pass in discussions, teaching men written language, the sciences, and the principles of arts and crafts, including city and temple construction, land survey and measurement, agriculture, and those arts which beautify life and constitute culture. But each night, beginning at sundown, this marvellous being would return to the sea and spend the night far beyond the shore. Finally he wrote a book on the origin of things and the principles of government, which he left with men before his departure. The records add that during later reigns of the prediluvian kings other appearances of similar beings were witnessed.'

This was the origin of the legend, referred to by Andrija, that the founder of Ur appeared in the form of a fish. Tom's statement that 'it was first as a bull, it was then as a ram', is difficult to verify, though the symbology is consistent with what we know of the period. When Sir Leonard Woolley excavated the royal tombs of Ur he found artifacts which associated the bull with the moon and the ram with the sun.

All this is fairly recondite knowledge, and the agreement of Tom's account with these traditions again raises the question whether the communications are derivative or corroborative Of the trio, Andrija is the person most likely to be familiar with the sources, and as he asks most of the questions it is possible to regard the communications, on the 'normal paranormal' hypothesis, as a dialogue he is conducting with his own unconscious, using Phyllis's telepathic receptivity as a feedback channel. Alternatively, it might be surmised that Phyllis in trance can exercise an extraordinary clairvoyant ability to pick up information from remote sources.

While we are on the subject of recondite knowledge, I should like to bring up one more point. In the course of a discussion in which John was trying to get a clear distinction between the Supreme God, minor gods and superior beings, Tom said, 'We in truth are Aeons.' And in an earlier communication he had suggested that all their people connected with their work might be collectively known as 'messengers of the Aeons'. Now, the term 'aeon', meaning an eternity, is quite commonly used, but is use in the sense of 'a being beyond space and time' is only to be found in certain rare texts of the Gnostic philosophers. Moreover, there are other aspects of the philosophy of the communications, which I shall discuss in the final chapter, that have much in common with the esoteric philosophy of the Gnostics.

After spending the festive season separately with friends and family, Phyllis, John and Andrija reassembled at Ossining at the beginning of January 1975. The two months they spent there before returning to Israel were not externally eventful though they were not lacking in drama at the interpersonal level. Communications were held every three days, and familiar subjects were elaborated and some new ones introduced. The series began on 3 January, with a talk by Tom on the subject of doubt and belief, which they all found very pertinent after having had three weeks to think over the events of the past months.

'You have doubted yourself, Doctor,' he began. 'You have doubted your ability, and you have doubted that within you and within the three of you, you have the power to accomplish all that we ask. We wish you from this moment to remove your doubts. When we inform you that you three have the power and the love and the strength to prevent chaos, tragedy and loss of life on your planet we mean this with all that we are, and we ask you to remove your doubts.'

'Thank you for that strong reassurance,' Andrija said. 'John and I do live with doubt and questions, based on the fact that we cannot see the results of our work, for example when we were in Israel last month.'

'We understand that, and there will come a time when that problem will be removed. But may we ask you to hold in your heart the faith that you have in knowing that this universe is not operated by chance or simply by what many people on the planet call nature. You are aware of and do not doubt this, so may we ask you to remove the doubt that you have within you the energies to do what we ask. Do you understand of what we speak?'

'Yes, we understand,' Andrija said, 'and I think it's a very relevant lesson for both of us, and . . ,'

'Can you see God?'

'I cannot, no.'

'Sir John, do you believe that there is a God?'

'Yes, I do.'

'Then if you can believe that, why can you not believe that you have the ability and the energy and the power? For remember this ability and energy and power comes from the love and the desire within you, and when I say desire I mean the desire to help, which is different from the desire which seeks to control.'

Andrija asked how the existence of doubts in them had affected the work, and in explanation Tom used the analogy of a cable consisting of millions of copper wires. If some of the wires were broken, he said, it would not break the cable, but the cable would not be perfect and communications going through it would be affected. 'You have doubts,' he concluded, 'because in your explanations to yourselves and to each other you cannot comprehend the nature of who you are. Yes, Sir John?'

The inquiry must have been prompted by an act of mind-reading, for John did have a point to make. He said, 'One of my main difficulties is our acute awareness of our inadequacies on a physical level.'

'Sir John, you are not so inadequate as you would like to

242

believe. To believe that you are inadequate may be used at times as an excuse,' Tom said shrewdly.

Andrija suggested that it would help their understanding if Tom could give them a specific example of an occasion when their doubts had adversely affected the outcome of some project. But, Tom explained, that hadn't happened; projects had been accomplished in spite of their doubts. Had he not said that the cable with the defective wires would not break but it would be weakened? He referred to the incident of their last day in Israel, when their car had been immobilised near Yavneh for an hour. 'You prevented an explosion which, if it had taken place, the three of you would not be in your physical, you would have been returned with us. We cannot prove that to you, but must we have an explosion to prove to you what we say? You have come here with complete faith. That is your mission, as it has been in many of your existences. But sometimes we peer at you and we say, "The three of them have forgotten who they are, and they are trapped in the physical and the thinking of the physical, because in the physical it is necessary to see an object or to hold an object in order to believe." But you, Doctor, above all, should understand, for what you have accomplished in your years could not be seen before. Parts of the secret knowledge that you have held within you for many years have now been proven to this physical world.'

'Yes, that's very true,' Andrija said.

Sixty-three per cent of the people in the United States, Tom said, were now aware of the existence of other beings, and were beginning to ask, 'Who are they?'

'Yes, and not only that,' Andrija said, 'but they also ask, "Are they good or evil?"'

'When they ask that,' Tom said, 'you must say, "They are good, and they wish to help." And if there are those who say, "But we have seen those of evil," then we would ask you to ask them to look within themselves and to understand that within each physical being there are all the elements of good and all the elements of what they call evil. But we do not like that word "evil".'

'No, neither do I,' Andrija said.

'I'd like to return to the subject of doubt and belief,' John said. 'I understand completely what you say about the effects of doubting, but on the other hand I think that blind faith can be equally dangerous, and that for us to draw the fine line between the two is difficult.'

'We do not ask blind faith of you ever,' Tom said. 'You must never just accept, and you must at all times ask questions. But if you will review your communications you will find that many things that we have related to you have already come to pass.'

'Yes,' Andrija said, 'John and I have been reviewing some of the tapes over the past week, and we are quite astounded at how much we have grown over the last few months under your tutelage.'

'Remember that we have grown with you, because when you grow, we grow.'

'That's a difficult one,' Andrija said. 'I mean the idea that growth potential still exists at your level, the level of the Nine, is quite amazing to us.'

'It is because you are in the physical and we are in the zone called cold,' Tom explained, 'and through you we are growing in understanding of the physical. If some one relates an experience to you, you might believe it but you will not have had the emotion, and what has happened with us is that because there are three of us attached to each of you and we are within your emotions, we are beginning to learn and to understand.'

'That's interesting,' Andrija said. 'We didn't realise that you were getting a refresher course in Earth experience.'

'It is not just Earth, Doctor, it is the physical. The Earth is only one of many physical planets, but it is the densest, which is unfortunate for you but means that it is the best place for us to learn.'

Concluding the session, Tom said: 'We have begun a new time in your land and your universe, and it is a time for you to drop and to remove the string that attaches you to the past time in the physical, and to remove also your doubts. We ask this of you, and we know that it is much, and we know that it is difficult for you to prove what you say to those around you.

But it is not necessary, for the proof will come in time. In this world in which you exist, they use a term, "Happy of your New Year". We wish to say to you, "Happy of your New Universe".'

As if in response to the call of the new time, during January and February 1975 contacts were re-established with old associates and there was a continual flow of visitors to Ossining, including Bobby, Lyall Watson, Dr Neil Hitchen and Jim Hurtak. On 19 January I paid the visit described in the first chapter of this book, which the reader may refer back to for an impression of what daily life in the community was like at this time. It is very much an outsider's impression, though, and since writing it I have listened to the tapes and talked to the people involved and got a clearer picture of the interpersonal conflicts and underlying tensions of the time. In this narrative I have had to focus on Phyllis, Andrija and John, and have only been able to mention very briefly relationships they each had outside the trio. Nor have I been able to make more than a passing mention of the fact that when he was at home in Ossining, Andrija sometimes held communications through other psychics.

In order to preserve the anonymity of certain of these, when we speak of 'Colette' in the rest of this narrative, the reader should understand that the name is used for more than one person.

The first communication that Colette participated in is interesting both for its content and for the fact that it was the only communication of this period that was terminated abruptly, allegedly because of the activities of the opposition.

Tom chose this occasion to address the group on the subject of spurious physical and spiritual experience and the different orders of non-physical existence.

'We know that what you have done you have done in faith,' he began. 'We have asked you to understand that the nature of the project will take from all three of you great energy. You will also recall that those that oppose have not finished opposing. Now we wish you to understand clearly that what we ask we are asking from a universal point, and not from an earthly or a spirit point. There are many things in which you on the planet Earth are involved that in truth do not have the nature of the universe but only of the planet Earth or of the spirit planes that surround the planet Earth. And you have the belief that this is a way of attaining what you call the spiritual. There are many processes in which you are involved which are a waste of time and which also create a problem because you believe that this is the path on which you must go. We wish you to know that when a physical body is ill, the person often has what is called a spiritual experience. Do you understand why this is so?'

'Is it because the so-called separation of the spirit from the body occurs?' Andrija said.

'It is in a sense, but what happens is that when the physical body is ill not all the vital organs operate upon the proper vitality rate in order for the physical body to function properly. This in turn gives the feeling to the physical being that they are having a spiritual experience. It is simply because they are between two worlds. They are closer then to the spirit world than they are to the physical world.'

'Is that what we call the astral?' Andrija asked.

'There are different planes of existence in the spirit world,' Tom explained. 'But it is not a universal world. Each planetary civilisation has in its midst or around it a spirit plane or numerous spirit planes. And there are within the physical planet Earth many forms of communication with different levels within the spirit planes. There is a difference between what the Being calls Intellions and we have asked you to call Aeons, and those of the spirit planes. We wish you to understand clearly with whom you are dealing.'

'Do you wish me to end communications with the astral plane?' Colette asked.

'It serves no purpose except to drive you into its pits,' Tom answered. Then, returning to the subject of spurious spiritual experience, he went on: 'And it also came into the minds of physical beings that they could perhaps bring to themselves the experience of spiritual awareness by the intake in their bodies of substances that would bring them to this awareness.

The reason that the intake of what you would call drugs gave them the sense that they had become spiritually aware was simply because they affected the vital organs and brought them in fact closer to death, so therefore they would be between the spiritual and the physical. But if you operate an automobile on inferior oil, how long will it work without being clogged?'

A number of other topics were raised and discussed in this communication before Tom interrupted a question of Andrija's to say, 'We are having difficulty.' Suddenly Phyllis came out of trance. 'How can they do that?' she said when she had got her bearings. 'How can they bring me out so quickly?' John said he supposed they could do anything when they had to, but the question was, why had they had to? There was only one way to find out, so after a pause Phyllis went back into trance and Andrija asked Tom for an explanation of what had happened. He explained that the opposition had suddenly launched an attack of intensified vigour and all energy resources had been required to combat it, leaving none for continuation of the communication. The battle was still in progress, he said, so it would be better if they stopped again and met later in the day for further discussion.

When they met again just before midnight, Colette was not a participant, and Tom was able to explain more fully the cause of the earlier difficulty: 'The trouble arose because of the lady. There was within the lady a problem of ego. She does not mean to be of that nature, but there is a weakness in her, and as you have learned, all weaknesses can be used. This does not mean that she is not to work and to serve, but is only for you to understand that physical beings have these weaknesses, which you must have the wisdom to discern. Do you understand?'

'Yes, I understand about the lady,' Andrija said, 'but I don't understand how it relates to the opposition.'

'When there exists a problem within a physical being and they are within your box, that energy may be used. We are only telling you this out of love for you and the lady. There is within her, as there was within all three of you at one time,

247

a great deal that needs to be purified. And you do not have the time, so she must do her own perfecting. It is important for you both to beware of those that are involved in what you call the psychic field. It is a new field for Sir John, but our Doctor knows it well. But there is one thing within him which he is aware of but does not attend to. Of all the beings and species that exist on the planet Earth, those that are involved in what you call psychic work have great difficulty with the ego. It is important for you – and we know not how to say this to you, but beware of your weaknesses and be careful of your traps and do not permit yourself to be used to perpetuate the ego of those that are psychic. Your weakness, Doctor, has been sirens. It is an element in your nature that needs to be controlled. We ask you in the future on meeting a siren to stand back and be objective. Do not bring those with whom you have a personal relationship into the work. It cannot be. They will use you.'

Andrija did not at the time react to this advice and view of his situation, but apparently acquiesced to it, but in a later discussion with John and Phyllis he said that there were times when he disagreed with the Nine. When they spoke from their universal point of view they were no doubt infallible, but with regard to the physical he believed that they could sometimes be wrong, for on their own admission they did not fully understand physical life and its problems. John and Phyllis both felt that he was rationalising an unwillingness to acknowledge what they both considered a very relevant warning, and there followed a discussion in which they each expressed quite frankly their views of and problems with the other two. The idea behind the discussion was to clear out, as John said, 'anything that has an energy in it that can disrupt the work', and over a period of a couple of hours there was certainly a great deal of energy discharged, though the problems were not, as John hoped, once and for all disposed of.

Since the psychology of the three and of the relationships between them may be relevant to the question of the nature and origin of the communications, I have judged that to report this personal material can be construed neither an unwarranted infringement of privacy nor as a gingering up of the narrative with spicy revelations. He who seeks a psychological explanation of the phenomenon of the communications may find something here to his purpose, and for other readers the spectacle of the three laundering their dirty linen may serve to counteract the uncomfortable implications of elitism that have emerged in earlier chapters.

The discussion developed out of a report Phyllis gave the other two of an experience she had had that morning during her session on the electronic equipment, which is why it was recorded. She had fallen into trance and been taken out of the body to appear before the Nine, where she had been given a lecture and instructed to report it to the other two. The Nine had told her that they must have the triangle in perfect balance for their work, and that at present they were not balanced, for they each had an ego problem that they were not aware of and that could ruin all their work and plans. They had stressed, Phyllis said, that the three were physical beings and were not different from or better than others on the planet, and that if they didn't understand that they wouldn't be able to function. They had analysed the faults of each of them and told Phyllis that she must convey this part of the message quite clearly. She didn't know how she could, though, because some of the things they had said were so personal.

John said she must just come out with it, for he and Andrija wouldn't hold her responsible for what the Nine had said, and he personally had no doubt that at this time she was functioning as spokesman for the Nine. Andrija agreed. Phyllis said she knew she had to do it but it wasn't going to be easy, so perhaps she could start with what they had said about herself. They had told her that she was too emotional in relating what they said and what she felt to the others, and that the reason for her excessive emotionality was a lack of confidence and a tendency to doubt. As regards John, they had said that he was sometimes like a spoiled child, that he was given to unreasonable resentments, was prone to self-pity, and that in everything he did he tried too hard. Both John and Andrija, they had said, sometimes misinterpreted what was said in the communications, and made them mean what they wanted them to mean. But it was what they had said about Andrija that she found most difficult to relate. They had said that he had not really mastered his emotions, though he thought he had, and that this made him susceptible to the manipulations of sirens. In conclusion they had stressed again that the energy of the three was vital and that if their mission failed the consequences for the Earth would be dire and they would be entirely responsible.

Andrija was apparently moved by Phyllis's account and at first showed no resentment about what had been said about himself nor any doubt that the strictures and advice that Phyllis reported emanated from the Nine. He said: 'Let's recognise that there is an outside world that presses upon us, and let's make a pledge to each other never to let any outside thing get inside the group and disrupt the work. I'm prepared to make that pledge right now.'

'Right,' Phyllis said. 'They said that unless we're in harmony we can't do anything.'

'So we must recognise where the disharmony comes from,' Andrija said, 'and help each other understand and deal with it.'

So they agreed, as they had done before, to be more 'up front' with each other in future, not to hide their feelings or thoughts, to talk frankly about any problems that could cause disharmony, to be willing, each of them, to accept criticism from the other two, and to put before all other considerations the maintenance of the harmonious balance of the triangle. John said that he acknowledged that the Management were right about him, and that the problem he needed help with was the problem of his intensity.

'Sure,' Andrija said, 'your adrenaline system is just hyperactive. You've trained yourself all your life to be competitive, aggressive, a sportsman, all that stuff, and you can't get rid of it that easily. You could take a tranquilliser and you wouldn't be so hyperactive. And Phyllis should go to a gynaecologist and get her menopausal problem under control.'

'Andrija, I went through a hysterectomy three years ago,'

Phyllis protested.

'I know,' Andrija said, 'and you're still in menopause, kid. You think it ends with a hysterectomy? This is a definite problem that we should be realistic about. There's no shame, there's no nothing, it's just a problem. And I'm speaking as a physician. We have to take into account the biochemistry of the body. We should look at that very carefully, and it shouldn't give rise to any more emotion than looking into the functioning of a machine would.'

They discussed at some length problems of decision-making both in the context of their work and in the context of their community life, and agreed that anything the Nine asked of them should be discussed and agreed upon unanimously before any action was taken, but that they might each act on their own initiative regarding minor decisions. It was at this point that Andrija said he retained the right to disagree with the Nine about physical matters that they admitted they knew little about. Then Phyllis brought up a problem of hers for discussion. She said she sometimes got a strong feeling that she should say something that had a bearing on their work or their safety, but she got so afraid that they would misunderstand that she avoided saying anything at all. 'For instance,' she said, 'I have to talk to Andrija about something right now, and I want him to understand that I do it because I'm fearful about what could happen if I don't.'

'We have to understand each other's personality,' Andrija said, 'and one thing you must know about me is that it's no good trying to impress me with the consequences of anything. If, like that time in Israel, you get the impression that there's going to be a blow-out in the right front wheel, just say so in a matter-of-fact way, and don't scream out as you did in a panic and say that it's going to kill me. That's what I resent, because that's laying a trip on me that I don't believe in. I don't believe in fear or death.'

'Okay, okay, I dig that, Andrija,' Phyllis said.

'You have to remember you're dealing with two very unusual people in John and me. We both, I guess, love to play games with death. That's why we've done some of the stupid things we have done in life.'

'Andrija!'

'It's our nature. You're not that type, we know that. So there's a huge imbalance in our perspectives . . .'

'Andrija! Hey!'

'. . . on life, on death, on safety.'

'Wow! You didn't even hear what I said.'

'Let me try to mediate a bit,' John said, and he tried to explain to Phyllis that what Andrija was saying was that he had no problem with the content of the messages Phyllis brought across, but what created the problem was the emotional way she expressed things. 'As I understand it,' he said, 'you get a message from the Management from time to time which you need to pass on to us. What we're saying is that if you put it in a calm way then we feel absolutely cool about it and there's no problem.'

'But none of this has anything to do with what I wanted to talk to Andrija about,' Phyllis said. 'You're both browbeating me.'

'Oh, come on, Phyllis,' said Andrija. 'Browbeating! You use such heavy words.'

'Just let me finish, okay?'

'Okay, but choose your words more carefully, please.'

'I know you've no fear, Andrija, but that's not what I was talking about.'

'We were talking about predictions,' Andrija explained 'and the way predictions are loaded with fears of consequences.'

'Were we? I thought I was talking about a problem I have and asking for your help with it.'

'So let's come back to what you wanted to say to Andrija,' John said.

Phyllis was silent for some time, then she said, 'We'll finish the conversation another time.'

'Phyllis, you mustn't get emotional about anything we say, That's the first thing you must learn.'

'Oh God! Please! I know that, Andrija . . . I . . . I . . .'

'You're being emotional right now, and you must stop and

say, "Phyllis, I'm being emotional." '

Phyllis shouted, 'I know it!'

'Okay, then stop it, baby!' Andrija shouted back, but with a laugh.

'What makes me so goddam mad is that you don't listen half the time,' Phyllis said.

'I'm listening to every word, but you don't use words very carefully. You don't realise how loaded some of your words are. I'm a very sensitive person to words.'

'And I'm a very sensitive person to feelings,' Phyllis flashed back.

John tried to mediate again, and eventually succeeded in coaxing Phyllis to say what she wanted to say to Andrija. It turned out to be that Colette had taken her aside and told her that she had come to Ossining to take care of Andrija's needs, that she had a personal relationship with him, and that she wasn't going to stand any interference from Phyllis. 'I didn't know what to say at the time,' Phyllis went on. 'Andrija, you know there's never been anything between you and me, so I don't understand someone talking to me like that.'

'Well, I don't even want to discuss it because it's in the area of competition between women, and total irrationality,' Andrija said.

John didn't agree with him. He said he knew Colette had spoken to all the other women in the house in the same terms, and that because what she had said had been hurtful to Phyllis it couldn't be lightly dismissed. Phyllis said she wasn't so much concerned about the personal hurt as about Colette interfering in the work, because another thing she had told Phyllis was that she knew about the work and was a part of it. And John reminded Andrija that they had had a warning about a siren.

'Look, I'm not involved,' Andrija protested. 'The warning was that this siren was going to take me over, right? Well, I tell you, forget it. It's a joke. It's just a case of jealousy between women.'

'Jesus Christ! I'm not jealous of her,' Phyllis shouted.

'Then you wouldn't have brought it up,' Andrija said.

Gently but emphatically John said, 'Andrija, it's not such a joke if there has been a warning about a siren. The Management do have a thing about you not getting involved with a siren.'

'Well, how about yourself?' Andrija retaliated, and the subsequent discussion must have become even more personal and recriminatory because the recording ends abruptly at this point.

This material is relevant to the study of the communications, I would suggest, because it is highly revealing both as regards the psychology of the three and of their relationships and as regards their attitudes to Tom and the Nine. Though Andrija doesn't like some of the things the Management have said, and though he regards Phyllis as too disposed to indulge her personal emotions, he doesn't suggest that the material she has channelled has been influenced by those emotions. At this point in time he preferred to think that the Nine were wrong about some physical matters that, on their own admission, they did not fully understand.

The communication held the day after this discussion constitutes further weighty evidence of the independent reality of Tom, for the intelligence, objectively and breadth of view expressed in it are greater than we could expect any member of the trio to manifest, particularly in the light of what we have learnt of them through eavesdropping on their discussion.

'We were saddened and we were grieved when we saw the great discord among the three of you,' Tom said. 'The sadness we feel is because there is so much difficulty among all in the manner in which you communicate. We have observed that what you speak is often not what you think. It is tragic that your manner of communication is used in this way. The day when all can see clearly what is in truth in the mind of another will be of the greatest importance, because then no one will speak in a manner that is not of truth.

'Misunderstanding is a different thing. We realise that at times you misunderstand what we say, just as you sometimes misunderstand each other. But one thing that must not be misunderstood is that when we speak to you we speak through this Being, and perhaps if you would understand the manner and the difficulties of our communications it would be the foundation of future understanding.'

Andrija said that the manner in which the Nine communicated was indeed a mystery and that he would welcome more information about it. Tom proceeded to give a very informative and lucid talk on the subject of channelling, which was not only interesting but also opportune, for it had the effect of establishing Phyllis's uniqueness as a channel at a time when Andrija might have been prevailed upon to doubt it.

'In many thousands of years of communications from other dimensions to species and beings upon the physical planet Earth there has always been great difficulty,' Tom began. 'There have been but few that permit complete control. Without complete control, and without the relinquishing of the personality of the individual, there cannot be clear communication. The one whom we communicate through is in truth a physical transmitter, and it has to be a being that is willing, that will become passive in order for us to be active. We have said to you before that this Being is the greatest of the communicators, and we wish you to understand that this is because this Being transcends the individual.

'In order to communicate with you, we must take over the subconscious of the Being and at the same time control the physical body. We must, with great effort, maintain a balance in the body. We must cause the body to have its heart operating, its lungs breathing and all its major organs functioning. The reason for the drain of energy many times from the two of you is that we are maintaining the body in a suspended state. When we maintain the Being, it is as if we take a million threads, and we weave these threads together to communicate with you. If there is a situation in which the Being is not physically in condition, if for example there is difficulty of digestion or of elimination or difficulty in emotion, or if there is a negative vibration within the Being or either of you, or an anger or a disturbance in you, we cannot then use the energy from you because it would only cause a breakdown in the threads which we weave with the Being in order to communicate. So therefore we communicate at times with great effort, which in turn causes more of a depletion in the Being. It is also very difficult, when conditions are not proper, to present the images so that they may be related, for you must understand that we do not have a vocal language and we have to communicate with the mind of the Being and it is the Being's subconscious that translates our communications into words.

'We have told you before and we will tell you again to be of extreme caution with those you use as communicators. It is important for you to understand that this Being is upon the physical planet Earth the only one to give completely to the Nine. Communications which you receive through other beings or species are of a different sort. They are relayed. You must also understand that the conscious mind of others may desire to use you. We have asked you, Doctor, to be cautious of communications through other channels. We are again giving to you, not a warning for we do not warn you we alert you, so we are giving you an alert, for although the civilisation that speaks through them may be trying with great difficulty to relay a truth to you, for them it presents an opportunity to use you.'

'Is there any reason why this kind of deception goes on?' Andrija asked. 'Are they the opposition, or are they misinformed, or what?'

'It is a consequence of their physical nature,' Tom said. 'We wish you to know that the most destructive element – and we have talked to you of this before – is the ego that controls. It is true that all three of you have what you would call a giant ego, but one thing is clear with the three of you and that is your commitment is true. Your ego does not create difficulty when we communicate. It has sometimes caused difficulty within the cage when you have brought with you your anger and your problems of dealing with each other. But this is different from the ego of ambition and manipulation. We say this to you – and we speak now to the Doctor – because in truth we are in Armageddon, and this is one area the opposition may use, even though the communicator may not be aware. Do you understand?'

'Yes,' Andrija said, 'that's very serious.'

'We just ask you to be responsive to souls,' Tom continued. 'If you are responsive to souls, we will take care of the rest. You are ambassadors for us. We have asked you before to remember who you are, and that it would behove you to act as the Nazarene. Do as he would do. You have, the three of you, the most difficult of assignments. You have a special mission but you are not special. You are no different from any other physical being. The reason for this is that it is important for you to understand their difficulties. It is important for you not to withdraw from the common folk, for it is they who will hear the message and of whom the demands will be made. When we say that you are no different, we mean in your feelings, your emotions and your sufferings. The common man must exist upon this physical planet, with all its hurt, all its sorrows and all its joys, and this is the existence of you three also. You chose this existence so that you could relate to the common man, and in this area the Being is of the three of you the most able, and is your teacher, our Doctor and Sir John, as in other areas you are her teacher.'

Andrija wasn't too happy with this last statement, and he pointed out that he had been born in the slums, had served in the army and had worked for years among simple people doing medical work.

'But you are superior in mind,' Tom said. 'They look upon you as someone special. They tell you only the things you wish to know. They do not tell you their deepest feelings. You are two different beings. You can, from a clinical position, understand the common man, but you are – and you know this – superior.'

Andrija proceeded to bring the discussion back to the subject of channelling with a question that brought an interesting answer from Tom. 'It might help us to understand what you were saying about the nature and problems of communication if you could give us an idea as to who in the past, among known historical figures, you would call perfect communicators as you say this Being is.'

'There was the one called Jesus of Nazareth. You know of him.'

'Yes.'

'There was the one that you call Socrates. There was the one that gave to you in code: Nostradamus. There was the one that was one and the same as Jesus: Buddha. But remember this: there was perfect communication, and it was in translation that it became obscure.'

'Of which figure are you speaking now?'

'In all of the translations. Then there was one, Elijah. And there was the one called Joseph.'

'Which Joseph would that be?' Andrija asked. 'There are several in the Bible.'

'It would be the one that was in Egypt. And there was one whose name was da Vinci. We speak to you only of those that have been recorded historically. There have been others.'

'To come to more recent times,' Andrija said, 'would a figure like Helen Blavatsky qualify?'

'I must consult,' Tom said, and after a pause returned with the information, 'Blavatsky was true.'

'Well, thank you,' Andrija said. 'That information answers a lot of questions. Before we go on, I have just one more along those lines. Who was it that received the communication that we call the Revelation of St John the Divine?'

Tom had to consult again, and this time he returned with a question: 'Would you be able to understand that it was John the Baptist?'

'I would never have imagined that,' Andrija said. 'That really is a surprise.'

'It was before the baptism. It was that that brought the understanding of who Jesus was.'

'And was Jesus a witness to this Revelation?'

'Yes. He was a young boy.'

'And did he actually say this Revelation to St John, or did it come direct?'

'It came as we speak to you,' Tom said.

258

It was later explained that after John the Baptist's death, the Revelation was transmitted by him to St John the Divine who received it as a vision while in exile on the island of Patmos.

Though the powers of the opposition were supposed to have diminished since October, it was during these weeks of January and February that the balance and togetherness of the trio came under the severest pressure. It was, perhaps, the more severe for being pressure from within. In October they had rallied to withstand a common enemy, but there was no rallying against the more insidious enemy of this time, which was a disruptive force that drew its strength from their own egos, their resentments, their insecurities and their pride. Two years later, looking back on the big scene between Phyllis and Andrija in which he had acted as mediator, John said: 'I thought that Phyllis's emotions had as much right to be heard as Andrija's opinions, but at the same time my mediating wasn't perhaps as selfless and as balanced as it might seem. For one thing, I felt some guilt because in the past I'd done what Andrija was doing now, and not paid attention to Phyllis's emotions, and to an extent I was compensating for that. But also I didn't want to fall into disfavour with Andrija because I regarded him as an ally. So there was an element of self-interest in my playing the middle of the road.'

John's own crisis occurred at the beginning of February. They had agreed to split up for a short while so that John could spend some time with Diana in the Bahamas and Phyllis could go and see her daughters in Florida, and the last session they had before John's departure had a dramatic conclusion. John, no less than Andrija, had balked at Tom's statement that in certain respects Phyllis was their teacher, and also in the last weeks he had been repeatedly irritated by certain aspects of Phyllis's conduct. 'I was very much into the idea of community living,' he later explained, 'and sometimes the way Phyllis insisted on doing her own thing and set herself apart really got up my nose.'

As if exasperated by observing their interpersonal conflicts, Tom said: 'We cannot impress on the three of you the importance of what we say. When there is difficulty among you it is more serious than the difficulty that would arise among others. Your energies are of a different nature, and if they cannot be in balance they will be the destruction of the three of you. You must understand that if one of you is on a collision course it affects all three. There is great anxiety among us. We do not wish to speak of bringing you back to us, but we want you to be clear that now there are but three choices. First, we can remove the Being and return her home, and that will leave the two of you. Second, we can remove the Being from the two of you and still have her in physical existence so that her energy would still be available for us or for the civilisation of Altea to use. Or we can keep the Being with the two of you, which is in truth the situation which you originally chose. As we have told you, when the three of you are together and in harmony this creates a perfect unit which because of the power that comes through you, can prevent catastrophes. It is your choice. We cannot interfere. We give you the three.'

Andrija recalled that in an earlier communication Tom had said that sometimes Phyllis served as a thorn to goad himself and John, and he asked, 'Is this a part of your plan?'

'No,' Tom replied. 'When we said she was a thorn it was from observation. It is difficult for the two of you to accept that the Being sees to the core of the truth of a situation. It is not always a situation that she understands, and she is not always aware that she sees the truth, and it is as difficult for her as it is for you to understand how she knows. When we said she was as a thorn, it was because we realised that the Being knows the truth upon immediate communication with other people. And it is not always the truth that they would recognise in their own minds. It is the truth of what is the truth.'

This claim for Phyllis's infallibility was very difficult for John to swallow in view of the dissensions they had had over the last few weeks. He mentioned that she had sometimes accused him of generating a negative energy, and he accepted that possibly he sometimes did, but, he protested, 'I cannot help but be aware that the Being herself is sometimes the source of a negative energy that affects not only me but others around here. This she doesn't seem to see at all, and this is possibly where our problem lies.'

'We have just explained and we will explain again,' Tom said. 'The Being sees through the situation. Immediately upon observation, without thinking, she knows. You have said that there is a creation of negative energy. What we have explained to you is that the negative energy of which you are aware comes from what the Being sees, though she knows not from where it comes.'

'So what you're saying is that she's perfect,' said John, a little irascibly, 'and that the negative energy all comes from other people and not from her.'

'We did not say that. You are not perfect, the Doctor is not perfect, and the Being is not perfect. We have asked you to work in harmony, and if you allow others to implant in you a great disharmony, then you have done a great injustice to yourself and to the three.'

'Well, may I just say this,' John said. 'I feel that you've quite rightly admonished me several times for my feelings of frustration and my shortness of temper with the Being. But very often she produces those very same characteristics that you've admonished me for, and this is something I find very difficult to accept and deal with. And it's not as if it's me alone that has noticed this. I think there's a general feeling around here that she does not fit in, and she does tend to cause difficulties . . .'

John was externally being cool and reasonable, but a surge of violent anger welled up in him, and he later attributed to this the alarming and unprecedented thing that happened next. Tom interrupted him and said in a level voice but with a chilling note of finality: 'We will remove the Being.' Instantly, Phyllis slumped out of trance, and for an awful moment John thought that she was dead.

That peremptory statement echoed through John's mind

repeatedly during the days he was in the Bahamas. He phoned Andrija twice a day to see if there was any news of Phyllis from Florida, still fearing drastic consequences. To 'remove the Being and return her home', Tom had said, was the first option available to them. The second was to 'remove the Being from the two of you'. So either she was to die or to stop working with them. Either eventuality would be catastrophic and was unthinkable, and John agonised over the thought that he had brought this situation about. He sat on the beach alone and went through harrowing hours of reappraisal of himself and of the extent to which his ego had caused the conflict with Phyllis. At first he was unclear how he had been so wrong but he accepted that the Nine knew best and that he would understand in time. He resolved that if the work with Phyllis continued he would finally and unconditionally surrender his personal will to that of the higher purpose of the work.

When John returned to Ossining after a few days the news of Phyllis was encouraging. She was going to be back on 25 February. But also John recalled that some time before, Tom had said that they should be in Israel again by the end of February, and he was apprehensive lest their interpersonal discord should have created a setback for the Management's plans.

It was a great relief for John to find, in the first communication they held after Phyllis's return, that nothing had substantially changed, except within him. He and Andrija reaffirmed their dedication and readiness to work wherever the Management required, and Tom said that as they were all in a low state and not fit for channelling the necessary energies they should not go to Israel yet. The situation would hold a little longer, and meanwhile there were many things to be communicated.

It was in this period just before they went to Israel for the second time that the subject of the Book of Revelation came up and was elaborated by Tom over a number of communications. I propose now to bring all this material together, but first would like to make a few points by way of preface.

The material on the Book of Revelation is in many ways the most intriguing in all the communications, for the familiarity Tom shows with the text and the ingenuity he exercises in interpreting it raise and focus the basic problems posed by the communications as a whole. Do they emanate from the mind of one or other of the participants? or from a combination of them in psychic concert? or are they explainable in terms of Phyllis's cryptomnesia? or of Andrija's telepathic projection? Are they a collusive hoax? or are they the product of an intelligence or a combination of intelligences of unknown origin endowed with extraordinary powers of invention and improvisation? Any member of the group might have been or become familiar with the text of Revelation, so a 'normal' explanation (hoax) or a 'normal paranormal' one (telepathy, cryptomnesia) might be tenable. But close study of the material raises problems for these explanations, for Tom sometimes explains the symbolism of Revelation in terms consistent with information contained in communications channelled months before the Book was first mentioned. Which would seem to reduce the choice of explanations to two: brilliant improvisation or truth.

The subject first came up when Tom volunteered the information that the opposition forces had been in control of the planet for the last 1,300 years.

'Was this foreseen in the book of the Bible that we call Revelation?' Andrija asked. Tom complimented him on his insight and said 'There are messengers who reveal the nature of what is in the cosmos. Those that are of the opposition had until this time period. It did not matter if those upon the planet Earth evolved or did not evolve. But the fact that those that oppose have kept the planet in bondage makes Armageddon more difficult.'

'So we're to understand that we chose to come back to be prepared for the moment when Armageddon started.'

'Yes.'

'There are many obscure passages in Revelation,' Andrija said. 'Could you clarify one that bothers me? After the sixth trumpet sounds there is the appearance of the two witnesses

263

on Earth. And it says that the two witnesses would go around in sackcloth for 1,260 days and then they would be slaughtered by the mob and their bodies would lie in the street for three and a half days unattended, then they would get up and walk away. Is that the scenario?'

'It is not in the sense of a physical experience,' Tom said. 'You understand that the passages of the final book are in symbolical language?'

'Yes, of course. But what is the true interpretation of that symbolism?'

'It is that the witnesses will not be understood. There will be great anger against them because they reveal what they are to reveal, and those who are knowledgeable and recognise that they have the truth will live in great fear of them. And they will say that those that are coming to this planet, who you know are coming to save the planet, are coming to control it. Remember also that the time of what you call the Bible is a different time from your time. When it speaks of the rising, it is simply saying that the recognition then will be given and they will come to the witnesses for help and understanding. It is true that they will first strip them of their dignity, and that is the reason for the terminology.'

'Will this occur before the landing?' Andrija asked.

'It will be after,' was the answer.

Andrija took a copy of the Bible into the next session they held, and resumed his questioning: 'As history is unfolding now, where would you say that we are in the Book of Revelation? What chapter and verse are we actively living out right now on the Earth and cosmic scene?'

'I will consult,' Tom said, and after a brief pause he gave the information: 'In your chapter number six, and it is in your five.'

'Chapters five and six, okay just let me look that up,' Andrija said, and when he had found the place he said, 'That has to do with the opening of the seals.'

'It is the third,' Tom said.

Andrija read out the passage about the opening of the third seal (which is verse five of chapter six, so Tom's reference was exact to the chapter and verse and Andrija had at first misunderstood it), which in the translation he had went as follows: 'When he broke the third seal I heard the third creature say, "Come!" And there as I looked was a black horse, and its rider held in his hand a pair of scales, and I heard what sounded like a voice from the midst of the living creatures, which said, "A whole day's wage for a quart of flour, a whole day's wage for three quarts of barley meal, but spare the olive and the vine."'

'There is an error in part of the translation, but not enough to cause a difficulty,' Tom said. 'As you understand, the planet upon which you are existing must now be brought into balance. The scale is a symbol of balance. If the Earth is brought into balance, then the rest need not happen. So it is in truth when it says to spare the olive and the vine. It is important that you understand that the month of your December 1971 was the beginning of the first seal.'

'That would be the time when I was with Uri in Israel,' Andrija said. 'Was the awakening of Uri the opening of the first seal?'

'In a sense,' Tom said, and Andrija read out the symbolism of the first seal:

'I saw a white horse, and its rider held a bow; he was given a crown and he rode forth conquering and to conquer.'

In explanation of this, Tom said, 'You must understand what in fact happened in December 1971. It was the beginning of the arrangements for the coming of Jehovah. You understand about the Hoovids?'

'Yes,' Andrija said, 'that's beautiful. I'm really grateful to you for giving us these explanations.'

'You must also understand,' Tom continued, 'that in the Book of Revelation each of the seals depends upon the completion or non-completion of the one before. If you can bring into harmony and into understanding the peoples of the planet Earth, it will not be necessary for the fourth seal.'

'I see,' Andrija said. 'Then presumably the seven trumpets would not have to be blown. I mean, the trumpets of the seven angels all spell disaster for Earth and for man.'

265

'That's correct.'

'And there's obviously a timetable for the opening of the seals, and there's one verse that seems to indicate the start of the final phase. It's the first verse of chapter eight: "Now when the Lamb had opened the seventh seal, there was silence in heaven about the space of half an hour. And I saw the seven angels which stood before God; and to them were given seven trumpets." The way I understand this now,' Andrija continued, 'is that if we complete the work we're doing before or at the time of the seventh seal, then the first trumpet will not have to sound.'

'Yes, this is what we explained.'

'So it's impossible to overemphasise how important it is that the three of us strive for perfection.'

'Yes. But may we say this to you. We do not wish you to berate yourself looking for perfection. There is not perfection upon the physical planet. But the three of you together are a perfect being. You must understand that by being, by the three of you just being, we are, and that by the three of you being together and being in harmony all things may be done. We do not ask you to do any particular thing if you are in harmony, because one perfect being can bring it all into balance and the three of you can make one perfect being.'

The number seven is central in the symbolism of the Book of Revelation. In one of the first communications with Tom, in the Bahamas in June 1974, the group had learnt that they were 'the primary hub' of a world-wide plan and organisation consisting of groups of seven working in different areas. In a number of other communications over the months they had also learnt that they would eventually have six co-workers. The apparent anomaly was now elucidated in a communication of three weeks after the one quoted above:

'There are seven, and we wish you to understand this. We have explained to you before that the three of you are one, and that there will be six others. This is a core, and it is no more than seven. Six and the three make seven and at the same time make nine. If you review your Book of Revelation we ask you to review particularly chapter number two, because in truth the seven are the seven angels.'

'Excuse me, but there are the seven churches and the seven angels,' Andrija said.

'That is true. The angels are the seven that will relate to the churches. The churches are different areas of beings and people. And it is as if you were in the centre and you had under you six pillars, and these pillars were giving you strength and supporting you. Do you understand that for the three of you to be complete here, upon the planet Earth, you need six supports?'

'No, we didn't realise that,' Andrija said.

'We ask you to review and to study your Book of Revelation. There are many truths and there are many symbols, but there are more truths than there are symbols. We ask you to review and to have in your heart the openness to understand the verses nineteen to twenty-two of chapter two.'

'We'll do that right after this session,' Andrija said. 'While we're talking about numbers, what does the Book refer to when it speaks about God sitting on a throne surrounded by four beasts and twenty-four elders? Is this a literal situation or is it symbolic?'

'It is a symbolism. The four beasts are the four corners of your world, your north, your south, your east and your west. The twenty-four elders are of the civilisations.'

'Do we deal with any of these civilisations? I'm thinking of Altea, Hoova, Aragon, Ashand.'

'These are among the civilisations, and they are part of the Lower Council.'

'I see,' Andrija said. 'Now for my own interest I'd like to ask about a passage in chapter ten, the eleventh verse. Speaking about the angels, it says, "Then they said to me, 'Once again you must utter prophecies over peoples and nations and languages and many kings.'" Now it seems clear to me that this means that a John the Baptist comes back and has to utter prophecies . . .'

'Are you not a proclaimer?' Tom put in.

'Yes, well, my question is, when is this process to begin? Because according to this text it comes after the seven trum-

267

pets, which we now understand may not have to be sounded.'

Tom explained: 'You must understand that it also involves what you call the Battle of Armageddon. The trumpets would be in the spheres. If you complete what you have to complete, that area will not affect the physical planet Earth. Then you would be a witness in explaining the nature of what had happened, and how close the people came.'

The second chapter of Revelation contains messages to four of the seven churches, and in the Authorised Version the specific verses referred to by Tom read as follows: 'I know your works, your love and faith and service, and that your latter works exceed the first. But I have this against you, that you tolerate the woman Jezebel, who calls herself a prophetess and is teaching and beguiling my servants to practise immorality and to eat food sacrificed to idols. I gave her time to repent, but she refuses to repent of her immorality.' In view of the interpersonal conflicts that were going on at Ossining at this time, and the discussions in the communications on the subject of authentic channelling, there is certainly no ambiguity about the relevance of this passage. Furthermore, it constitutes convincing evidence against the Andrija-as-telepath explanation of the communications, for Andrija would surely not produce, either consciously or unconsciously, a reference so pertinent to a situation that he vehemently denied existed.

When Andrija introduced the subject of the quotation in the course of the next session, Tom immediately said, 'Are you at this time of an open mind and without anger?'

'Yes,' Andrija said.

'We wish to speak to you, but before we do we ask you to remember who you are, and to be guarded and forgiving. We have tried many times to nudge you gently, but now we have decided not to nudge you but to speak directly. There is one among you – and we speak not of among the three, but in your home – that has been a catalyst that started the whirlpool that removed one from the aura of us.'

Andrija and John knew immediately that Tom was referring to Colette. While they had been away in Israel something had happened between her and another of the psychics living at Ossining who had now left.

'Listen carefully to what we say,' he continued. 'There is nothing cleverer in the universe than one that is looking for control of others. But remember, we do not work with those that are not disciplined. Such beings and species are used by civilisations, some of which are in service to us but most of which are not evolved. Do you in your heart believe that a sophisticated civilisation would use a being or species that is not stable? The tragedy of your planet Earth is that throughout the years this situation has existed and has created great problems in that our work and your forerunner work and the work of others has been discredited because of lack of stability. And remember that there are civilisations also that have ambition. You are aware that the world that exists immediately around your planet is the spirit world, and that there are those in the spirit world that claim to be different than they are? Well, it is the same with the civilisations.'

'May I say something?' Andrija interrupted. 'May I just say you must be more direct with me? We know who you're speaking about and we want the truth, so just come out with it directly. Don't treat me like a child.'

'We asked you not to be disturbed with us when we spoke to you of this,' Tom reminded him.

'I'm not disturbed. I want the truth. Specifically, is the woman lying?'

'We are explaining to you, our Doctor.'

'Well, be direct, please. Don't give us these long-winded stories,' Andrija said vehemently.

Tom waited for his vehemence to subside and after about half a minute said, 'May we speak now?' Andrija said 'Yes' and he continued: 'You have many interpretations of your Book. The essence is there, but there were times when there was an error made here and an error made there as it was handed down and as it was translated from language to language. Parts were lost and parts were misguided. Now what we said to you was that when there is a spirit world there are situations in which things are related and there are those who say they are something that they are not, but they are receiving it perhaps at times from another source.'

'This is not an answer to my question,' Andrija interrupted. 'Is the woman lying?'

'She does not understand. This is why we have a great . . .'

'Is she lying or not? Say yes or no. You're beating about the bush.'

'We are not beating. Can a species or a being lie when they do not know what is in themselves? This is what we have tried to explain to you.'

'You suggested she's on a power trip. Therefore she's lying,' said Andrija, seemingly losing his logic as well as his temper.

'We have explained to you very patiently that it is a manipulation by other civilisations, and also that she in truth does not know,' Tom said. This was in fact a perfectly clear and direct answer to Andrija's question, but he was not prepared to acknowledge it as such. He adopted another line of attack.

'May I say something very bluntly to you, please? May I speak very directly and honestly?'

'Yes.'

'A year ago the Being that sits before me did not know that you were speaking through her. She thought it was a spirit. She exorcised Bobby. She made all these mistakes. How do I know she is not making a mistake now in what she is transmitting to me? Can you prove that to me?'

'What would you like to have as proof?' Tom asked, but Andrija burst out:

'When I say something, would you simply say it is a lie or it is not a lie? You give me all these phoney stories that leave us all confused. Don't you see how confused we are? If the woman's false, say she's false and we'll throw her out. But this way we're not getting at the truth and you're not being fair to me.'

'Will you understand that we are attempting?' Tom said. Andrija gave up and asked John to continue the conversation. John said he thought it would be best to drop the subject and discuss it between themselves afterwards. Tom said that perhaps Andrija now understood why they hadn't spoken to him directly before.

'I can take any amount of straight talking,' Andrija said. 'What I can't stand is all this bullshit.'

John said, 'Andrija, it may not be bullshit if we explore it.'

'I'm trying to explore it, but I just don't get answers,' Andrija said. 'If they spoke clearly there wouldn't be any ambiguity.'

'Well, to me there isn't any ambiguity, Andrija,' John said. 'So let you and I discuss it.'

'We will leave now,' Tom said suddenly. 'And we leave you with love and we leave you with peace, and we will return at your convenience.'

'Love and peace,' John said, and Andrija echoed the last word rather wearily.

This was not a mere ephemeral fit of temper on Andrija's part, but a genuine crisis of confidence. He shut himself away in his room for two days and would allow no one to see him. In the evening of the second day, John held a communication alone, and at the beginning of it Tom said:

'It is a sad time when one of us in isolation must go through our own purgatory. But each of us has been in that state of consciousness. It is the one aspect of your physical existence that we understand, because it is not in truth part of your physical existence but of your soul existence. Each of us must evolve within ourselves, and we must resolve within ourselves our crises and difficulties.'

'I was wondering what to do about the Doctor's feeling that this Being is distorted the channelling,' John said. 'I'm very anxious that we should re-establish his confidence in her.'

'Distortion is not possible, for the Being is not in control,' Tom said. 'In time all will be proven and the truth will be made known within the soul of each.'

'So there's nothing particular we can do?'

'You can only love as we love.'

'Yes, of course, we do that.'

'May we say that the greatest sorrow in the Doctor is because he feels that he has been tricked, and it is his pride that is hurt. He has in fact not been tricked, either by the channel or by us. There is no black and there is no white. As we explained at the time of the communication, he must hold in his heart forgiveness and understanding, and he must remove from himself the resentments he holds against people who do not live up to his principles. And when we say this we do not speak of either the channel or this Being, but we speak of the being Uri and of others. It is only in forgiving that they are returned.'

Tom went on to explain that Andrija's going through his personal purgatory was a thing that was essential to the continuation of the work, and he did so in terms consistent with the general philosophy expounded in earlier communications.

'Many of our communications ago we explained to you that to be all positive is as senseless as to be all negative. And we also explained that the opposing forces and the negative vibrations are more powerful because they operate on emotions which temporarily create more strength than positive emotions, because a positive emotion is a feeling and a true manifestation of love, and love is peace and calmness, it is joy within the heart, and it is steady. In each soul, in order for that soul to be balanced, it must have both of these elements, of the positive and the negative. The emotion of anger, the emotion of hate, the emotion of bitterness, the emotion of fear are powerful, damaging and devastating, but in order for a soul to evolve to a perfect balance it must in its evolution go through all of these emotions. This time of the Doctor's personal purgatory was necessary in order for him to bring the other side of himself into balance and in order for our work to continue.'

At this time, and over the past few days, there had been a number of odd events in the house. All the clocks had started going haywire, jumping ninety minutes ahead of or falling ninety minutes behind the correct time. There had been many paranormal movements of objects, and things like coins and keys apparently dropping from the ceiling. Sometimes they were things that nobody in the house had ever seen before, for instance two coins appeared on the floor of John's bedroom, side by side, and on examination one turned out to be an Israeli coin and the other an Arab one. Whether these events helped Andrija over his crisis of confidence I do not know, but the day after John's solo communication he was back in the cage, and he began the session by reaffirming his commitment.

'Welcome, Tom,' he said. 'We have come to rededicate ourselves to the Nine and to the cause of peace on Earth, and we confess that we have lost our way temporarily with regard to immediate tasks, direction and purpose, and we want to start a fresh dialogue which will bring us back to the path of the Nine on Earth. So perhaps you could begin by assessing for us the present international situation and telling us what you would have us do to be of aid.'

'Your planet Earth is in a time of confusion,' Tom said, 'and the nation of Israel is in a serious situation, for aggressions are planned at the time of the holidays that you call Passover and Easter. But we can give you this promise: that with your prayers, with your dedication and with your permission that the civilisations working for what you would call the light may use your physical energies to stop aggressive acts, the nation of Israel will be sustained.'

'What civilisations are these that we would give our energies to?' Andrija asked.

'We are speaking of the civilisations that are involved in the saving. Those of Hoova, or Aragon and of Altea are the three of major importance.'

Andrija and John had no hesitation in giving their permission and they said they were sure they could also speak for Phyllis. They should then arrange, Tom said, to be in Israel by the 13th of March (it was now the 7th), and he proceeded to give a scenario of the events that could lead up to a major concerted offensive against Israel at the end of the month. There would be, he said, a stepping up of guerrilla activities first from Syria and Lebanon, which would appear to be the work of small independent groups but would in reality be an organised national project, and as the end of the month approached Saudi Arabia and (reluctantly) Jordan would become involved. If the plans as at present laid out were carried through, there would eventually be a full-scale missile war.

Andrija asked if there wasn't a danger of the Israelis learning about the Arab plans and launching a pre-emptive attack.

'With you in the area, you will also temper the nation of Israel,' Tom said. 'If you will do what we say, your energies will be used in two ways and two areas, and the timing is important in order for the leaders of Israel to be of open mind and not to become also aggressive. It is important that you spend a minimum of three of your first days at Megiddo. It is a source of energy.'

Andrija asked how many of them should go to Israel, and Tom said that only the three were needed, but 'if you wish others to go, if they will not deplete your energy or entertain their physical needs, it will be permissible for your peace and comfort, but it would be important to have them clearly understand before you go'. The community remaining at Ossining, he went on to explain, would have an important function, for Ossining, like Megiddo, was a power centre and the two were linked. The trio in Israel were to meditate for thirty minutes every afternoon from three o'clock, and the Ossining group were to do the same at the corresponding New York time and in addition hold fifteen-minute meditations together at three o'clock and nine o'clock New York time. To facilitate the concentration and focusing of the energy, they should put a crystal on a map of Israel in the middle of their circle. 'What sort of crystal should be used?' Andrija asked. Tom said he would have to consult for the answer, and after a pause said that Joseph of Aragon (the leader of Aragon, the civilisation concerned with healing, who had recently incarnated on Earth as the Brazilian healer Jose Arigó) had said that Andrija had a blue crystal of great healing power. 'Okay, we'll use that one,' said Andrija, showing no surprise at Joseph of Aragon's clairvoyance.

When the Israel crisis was over, Tom said, they must turn their attention to the work of using all possible media for the purpose of making the world aware of what was happening and what was going to happen. 'You must explain that there have been communications. It is in your hands how you explain the communications. We leave to you that decision. But you must explain that there will be of the nature of a landing.'

'If people can relate the landing to something known,' Andrija said, 'like the Book of Revelation, it will make our work a little easier. Will such information be forthcoming?'

'Are you requesting a complete interpretation of the Book of Revelation?' Tom asked.

'No, I'm asking if Revelation, as it refers essentially to the Second Coming of Christ, is a guide to what is happening with respect to the landing.'

'You are now in the fourth seal and the sixth church, so what you say is true, yes.'

'The biggest puzzle I have with Revelation,' Andrija said, 'is that half hour of silence in heaven before the first trumpet sounds. Could you explain that?'

'The vehicles which will come,' Tom replied, 'will come in silence, and also there will be silence upon the Earth as those upon the planet come to recognise what is happening.'

'I take it, then, that the half hour would be the nine days that you once gave us as the duration of the landing?'

'That is true. You understand that our time is not as yours. There will be great days of silence, for with the work that will follow the landing there will be some that will have fear in their hearts, but most will begin to take account of themselves.'

Over these weeks Tom had identified the six co-workers who, with the trio counting as one, would constitute the initial nuclear working party of seven, though he stressed that as the work progressed some members of the peripheral six might relinquish the work and others take their place. For the final communication session before the trio left for Israel, Andrija and John, at Tom's request, managed to get Lyall Watson, Dr Neil Hitchen and Jim Hurtak to come to Ossining. So with Phyllis, Andrija, John and Colette, there were seven of them crammed into the Faraday cage for the communication. Tom began with a short speech of encouragement and exhortation for the benefit of the visitors:

'For what you have chosen to do, and for what you have

been chosen to do, in our heart there is great love for you. You take upon yourselves a great task, but it is done with love and it is this love that will sustain you and bring to completion that which you have chosen. Remember this: it is only through the helping with the physical difficulties of the physical beings upon your planet Earth that the true message may be received. When it is not possible for their governments, their religious leaders, their medical profession and their society to give them the help they need, it will be possible for you, through your faith and what you have put into motion, to be of help to them. They will begin to ask questions and to demand answers from their leaders, and when their leaders do not give them the answers they will begin to see that there is more in this universe than they had been led to believe. And this is part of the preparation for the landing, for how can we arrive, how can we make our presence known, if those upon your physical planet Earth do not believe in our existence? You have upon you one of the greatest services that can be performed, and we know that you will do it with humility, with sincerity, with compassion and with balance.'

Andrija said he would like to give the visitors an opportunity to ask questions, and Lyall Watson was the first to speak:

'As this group reaches working strength, we can begin to appreciate why each of us has been chosen, each in a different area. Yet I'm concerned that we're a white Anglo-Saxon group and that there are talents and powers in other cultures that we don't seem to be availing ourselves of. Do you have comparable groups in other cultures, or do we need to incorporate other cultures in our work?'

Tom answered, 'Each of you in the core of the original group of seven, which in truth is nine, will be in the centre of another group of seven, and such groups will multiply and spread across the planet Earth and will involve other cultures. You have in each of you special knowledge, special abilities, and you are all unusual people upon this planet, and there are six others that will be drawn to each of you.'

Although it had been many months since Lyall had directly

participated in the work of the group, Tom said, 'in this time there have been other communications and there have been arrangements'. Lyall understood what was referred to. He said, 'ever since last March, when I received an "opening" in the Philippines, a lot of things have happened to me. I'm not disturbed by these things, because I feel that I'm responsible for most of them, that the access to power I achieved at that time has resulted in a lot of random occurrences around me. Am I right in thinking that these are accidental side products of what I'm supposed to be doing?' (Any reader interested in knowing more about what Lyall was talking about here should read his fascinating book, *Gifts of Unknown Things*.)

'You have analysed correctly that the energy within you and the power that has been transferred to you was sometimes out of control,' Tom said. 'It is important, Dr Watson, for you to understand that there are those that do not seek the greatest benefit for the planet Earth. And you must understand that when there is a fear within you or a negative force, those who would not benefit the planet Earth take from you that energy and create a situation. They cannot function and they cannot produce a phenomenon without the physical energy of those that exist on the physical planet Earth. But by the same token, those that work with you in understanding and who wish to benefit the planet Earth may use the energy of your goodness, your positiveness and your enthusiasm to produce also, and to bring to you those things that are necessary for you to proceed.'

'These phenomena don't seem to end with me,' Lyall said. 'They involve my family now.' He had recently met his brother Andrew after a separation of some ten years, and had found that he was working in South Africa with another person named Walton serving as channel and holding communications with alleged extra-terrestrial contacts. 'I believe he's been in contact for about a year,' Lyall said.

'It is more than that,' Tom said. 'It is since the third week of your August 1971. He is in communication with the civilisation of Aragon.'

277

I have recently met Andrew Watson and he confirmed to me that it was in the second half of August 1971, that his communications began, and also that the actual name 'Aragon' occurs in them.

Jim Hurtak, John's eccentric erstwhile guru from California, a man with his own extra-terrestrial contacts who had regaled his students at the California Institute of the Arts with reports of his conversations with contacts with names like Enoch, Maitreya and Metatron, learnt from Tom that he was from Altea.

'This I have known,' he said.

'Yes,' Tom said. 'And have you known that those from Altea are those of what you call Atlantis?'

'This has been told me,' Jim said.

'Because of the knowledge that is within your soul, and because of who you are, you have great ability,' Tom told him. 'But remember that you are dealing with a physical planet that is caught in heaviness. It is important that you find a way in the language of the people with whom you communicate to speak in terms that they may clearly understand, for they understand not in the abstract as you do. You must bring your knowledge into focus for them. You have come a long way, and with your help and with the three, the message that must be communicated to the nation of Israel will prevent massacre and catastrophe.'

'I should like to ask the meaning of the Golden Wreath that is to be laid in Israel,' Jim said, referring to something that had come through one of his own communicators and that nobody present understood, except apparently Tom, who answered:

'It will be when the nation recognises from where it comes and the reason for its existence. It means that only when the people of Israel become awakened and aware can this planet be saved.'

Jim Hurtak and his wife were to remain at Ossining while the three were away, and Tom said that Jim should be the spiritual leader of the group, should ensure that the meditation and prayer sessions were conducted properly and that nobody participated in them while they were in a negative frame of mind. He gave elaborate instructions for the operation of a proxy system to ensure that each member of the support group of six should be present at every session either in person or by proxy, and said that each of them should find on the hillside behind the house a small stone, put it in a box and carry it on their person for a short time to imbue it with their energy so that if no personal proxy were available it could be used in a last resort.

'Are we to understand that the stones will be the equivalent of the Urim and Thummim to be directed to the vehicle of Kishon?' Jim asked, again using terms that nobody understood.

'Yes,' Tom said. 'But remember that there is also one in this area where you are now, and it will be directed to that and from that it will be directed to Kishon and it will also go through the subterranean areas and perform a complete circle. Do you understand?'

'Yes. Thank you,' Jim said.

When it was Colette's turn to put a question, she said, 'I'm very disturbed by a channelling I did in January concerning certain visions about Israel which still haunt me. Can you tell me if I am to eliminate them or if they are still pertinent?'

Tom answered this with a display of Socratic virtuosity.

'It is important you understand that there is knowledge released in the universe that many civilisations have access to. Let us give you an example. If you were in this nation, and you went perhaps to an oriental nation and spent some time there, and then left and went let us say to Brazil, and if in the three nations you visited you learned only a portion of the language you would only receive a portion of the information released. Do you follow this?'

'Yes, I do,' said Colette.

'And do you understand that the civilisations that exist within the universe are all physical civilisations?'

'Yes.'

'And that those that are physical have emotions?'

'Yes.'

'And that perhaps at times the emotion is misguided?'

'Yes.'

'To return to your question: we ask you to eliminate these visions from your mind, and we give you the reason why. Your power – and you have got power, as all in this room have – is a special power and if it is misused, which it may be in error and not deliberately, or if a fear is created within you, this power may then be used by others to create a situation. There are those that exist in the universe that would like each of you to have a fear within you so that your power then may be misused. Remember, your power is the type of power that if it is not in balance may be used by either the positive or the negative.'

'And what we have said to this lady we say to each of you,' Tom concluded.

Neil Hitchen next asked a number of questions and received answers that were significant for him personally, and when the visitors had all had their say Andrija had a final question to ask. 'In the last week,' he said, 'we've had many things happening in the house here that cannot be explained scientifically, like clocks going backwards and forward, coins and things appearing and disappearing, events too innumerable to mention. Now are we to assume that this is your work, or that of one of your civilisations?'

'You asked for a proof, did you not?' Tom said.

'Yes,' Andrija said with a laugh. 'Well, thank you. We've had a lot of proofs.'

'If we had given you but one,' Tom said, 'you would have said it was an accident.'

# CHAPTER EIGHT

# *Walking on Eggs*

Of all Tom's predictions, the one that there would be a brink of war situation in the Middle East over the Passover/Easter holidays at the end of March is the second most impressive. (I will be writing about his most impressive prediction later in this chapter.) At the time it was made, the world's Press and politicians were expressing optimistic views of the Middle East situation, for Dr Kissinger was just embarking on another peace-seeking mission and hopes ran high that he would be able to persuade the Israelis to cede some of their strategic 1973 gains in Sinai in exchange for an Egyptian non-aggression agreement. Nobody foresaw at the beginning of March that Kissinger's mission would be a total failure and that before the end of the month the Arabs and the Israelis would be making missile-rattling pronouncements. On 24 March Kissinger returned to Washington a disappointed man, and a *Times* headline asked 'Has Dr Kissinger made his last stand as the American Superman?' Correspondents from Egypt quoted the Foreign Minister as saying that 'the breakdown had brought the Middle East to a "dim point" due to "Israel arrogance" and a new military conflict could not be excluded', and from Israel came the report that the Prime Minister 'accused Egypt of making exorbitant demands and causing the collapse of Dr Kissinger's peace mission with the aim of facilitating its war deployment'. There were reports of Egyptian troop movements on the East Bank of Suez and of a massive troop build-up on the West bank. With three days to go before the critical time predicted by Tom in the communication of 7 March, the situation seemed quite as dire

281

as he had said it would be.

It is worth noting in passing that two earlier predictions could be taken as referring to the events of these days. On 9 November 1974, Tom had said that within six months Kissinger would have problems and there would be attempts to discredit and remove him. And before they had left Israel in December, Tom had told them that the situation was now stabilised and would hold for three months.

The intervening three months hadn't exactly been peaceful. In January, skirmishing on the Israel–Lebanon border had escalated into what the *Times* called a 'mini-war', when the Lebanese army had apparently lent support to the Al Fatah guerrillas operating from Lebanese territory. Then there had been an audacious and suicidal terrorist attack from the sea on a Tel Aviv hotel, and the Israelis had learnt from the one prisoner they took that Syria was involved in this operation. Border raids and terrorist activities were everyday news, and by March there was a widespread feeling that the Kissinger initiative was the last hope for peace.

Andrija, John and Phyllis arrived in Israel on 12 March. They picked up their hired car at the airport and drove at a leisurely speed over the rocky but green hills of Judea and through the Arab towns of Ramallah, Nablus, Tubas and Jenin to their destination, Nazareth, where they checked into the best hotel they could find, a place that managed to be at once modern and seedy.

Tom had said that they should be at Megiddo on the 13th, so after an early breakfast they drove the twelve miles across the plain to the historic site. They spent the morning strolling over the mound, exploring it and collecting shards of ancient pottery which lay in profusion on the ground. They also collected specimens of a curious black stone which, Andrija said, was to be found only at Megiddo. They wandered around separately for some time, then found themselves together at the so-called Canaanite altar, the circular platform of rough stones situated in the middle of the deepest excavation and from which there is a panoramic view across the plain to the hills of Galilee. Here they were sufficiently undisturbed by tourists to hold a brief communication, which they did seated upon the altar.

Tom complimented them on so precisely locating the nucleus of the energy centre of Megiddo, and said that the middle of the altar was 'the core of a giant wheel that vibrates in twelve directions'.

Andrija asked, 'Was the Nazarene aware of this energy centre?'

'Yes,' Tom said. 'It was what fed him. It was from where the light came to keep him alight.'

Andrija asked about the black rocks and was given an explanation of their origin: 'We go back to a time of ten to twelve thousand of your BC. It was the time of the collapse of the continents upon which the Alteans existed. There were great explosions, and there also came from the sky the wrath of those that were in utter disgust at the perversion of the Alteans. Part of this came and landed upon the area of Megiddo and made a giant crater which then created a giant natural spring. There was a bombardment from the sky and the natives of the area were fearful, but because it had created water it represented those that had given them life.'

Tom stressed the importance of their holding their three o'clock meditation session, synchronised with that of the 'troops' back at Ossining, at this spot for the next three days. And tomorrow, the 14th, he said, was going to be a particularly demanding day, for the Israelis were planning a pre-emptive attack, a simultaneous foray into Lebanon and Syria, and it was important that the plan should not be put into action. 'If you may be upon the centre of Megiddo by twelve o'clock and be quiet between then and your three o'clock meditation, it will suffice,' he said. And after their three days of charging up, as it were, at the power centre of Megiddo, they should tour the northern frontier areas to spread the energy into Lebanon and Syria.

When they had completed this brief communication, the trio left Megiddo and went to the nearby town of Afula to get a meal. In the afternoon they returned to the power centre for the three o'clock meditation, then they drove to Mount Tabor.

Back at their hotel in Nazareth that evening, they held a communication in which they elicited some of Tom's fullest and most coherent statements on the subjects of cosmology, philosophy and teleology. It began with Andrija asking the question:

'Are the Nine the ultimate source of knowledge, wisdom and power in the universe?'

'The Nine together are what you would call the infinite intelligence,' was Tom's answer.

'Yes, well, we speak of "the fountainhead" or "the unmoved mover",' Andrija said, 'and in our theologies the idea is common that God initiates the thought but the action is always carried out by others, by subsidiaries.'

'That is correct. It is by the civilisations.'

'I see. And didn't you indicate at one time that there are twenty-four civilisations?'

'No, there are many. But there are twenty-four heads of civilisations. It might be compared to your Congress.'

John put in a question: 'And are all these working on the positive side?'

Tom had to remind him of one of the basic tenets of the philosophy of the Nine. 'Sir John, the positive and the negative must be blended to make it whole. As we have explained to you, to be positive without sense is not good. They are the balanced civilisations. When you speak of positive, Sir John, refer to it as a balanced positive.'

'Okay, I think we understand that part,' Andrija said. 'To take Jehovah as an example, I assume that he is one of the twenty-four and under him is his civilisation, Hoova.'

'Yes, and there would be, like a pyramid, many civilisations under that.'

'Okay. Now let's take human existence. Where do human beings come from, why do they come here, and where do they go?'

'All beings and species come from us,' Tom answered. 'Your questions: Who am I? Where did I come from? and Where am I going? are asked by all, and the answer is that all species and all beings are particles of us.'

284

'And they go through many existences before they reach Earth, is that not so?'

'It may be. But remember, the planet Earth is not so evolved.'

'So is there a regular sequence through which they must go before they come to this planet and through which they go after leaving it?'

'No. It depends on the needs of the soul. There are levels of intelligence and there are levels of consciousness, and some souls need more than others. Visualise a giant electric spark and smaller sparks coming off it. Each of those sparks would be part of the giant spark, which is us, and each would either die out or continue to grow. Some would create a fire and some would grow slowly. It would depend on the ambition of the spark.'

'Now when that spark cycles through Earth and achieves its full growth,' Andrija said, 'does it go through other civilisations or does it return directly to you?'

'It must continue for millions of years,' Tom answered, 'but it cannot continue if it stays upon the planet Earth. If you recall, in a previous conversation we have explained to you that the planet Earth is the only planet in the Universe that has upon it the variety of animal and the variety of plant. It is of all the planets in the universe what you would call the most beautiful because of its great variety. This attracts the souls, and they have desires to remain upon it. In other civilisations the souls have feelings and all the qualities that you have, but existence is more physical upon the planet Earth.'

'If I may ask a very broad question,' John said, 'what is the soul's purpose in existing in all those different civilisations?'

'If a soul becomes what you would call perfect, then it is . . .' Tom began, but he stopped abruptly and said, 'If we explain this to you, Sir John, you may think that we are cannibals.'

John and Andrija laughed and Andrija said, 'Well, I think you know us well enough to know that we won't jump to erroneous conclusions. Let's put the question this way: if we had to tell a human being what the purpose of life is . . .'

'You may tell them what has been told to them many times but has not been clearly understood: that the purpose of their existence is to return whence they came.'

'In other words, to be swallowed up by you,' said John with a laugh, now appreciating the 'cannibals' reference.

'And while they are on this Earth with all its problems,' Andrija said, 'what is it they can best do in order to return to the source?'

'If they treat all as they would desire to be treated, if they walk in dignity and neither attempt to remove from another nor permit to be removed from themselves their dignity, and if they have love for their fellow men and for all that they come in touch with, this in turn sends love to us.'

'So in essence,' Andrija said, 'we may say that God feeds on this kind of nectar, this love?'

'Yes.'

'And is this love totally immaterial? Is it something that has no material or physical existence?'

'It is an energy. It is not something you may hold in your hand. It is a spark that emanates and grows and becomes a shining sun and then returns to us.'

'In the future,' John said, 'we are likely to be asked, "What is God?" Of course we have some idea ourselves, but we would like to be able to give consistent and understandable answers to those who ask.'

'Sir John, what is God to you?' Tom asked.

'Well, there are various ways I could answer that. I could say that God is the Nine, or is a unified intelligence . . .'

Tom interrupted to take up John's last phrase and expand it to: 'A unified infinite intelligence supported by pure love and which grows with pure love.'

That was a conversation stopper. John and Andrija were both silent for a time while they took in this elegant and elliptical definition, then Andrija resumed the questioning:

'Now, how do the other creatures on the planet Earth fit into this cosmic scheme of things?'

'They have more love and more understanding of us than many humans,' Tom said.

'And do they also come back as sparks directly without having to go through a human form?'

'They are never of a human form. They are upon the planet Earth in order to make the souls there ask, What created this? How did this come to be? They are here to jog the mind. Do you understand?'

'Yes, I think so,' Andrija said. 'For example, at Megiddo today we were watching two hawks. They were mating on the wing and they were incredible and beautiful, and we wondered about them. They live in such freedom and, apparently, love, and . . .'

'It is the purest love,' Tom said.

'Yes. So would their soul spark if it achieved perfection go directly back to you?'

'Our doctor, you must understand that of all the creatures that exist upon the planet Earth only man and the porpoise has an intelligent soul that is a spark of us.'

'I see. So when we work with porpoises, as we expect to be doing in the future, we are to consider that they have souls equivalent to human souls?'

'Their souls have grown stronger and with more light than many human souls. They only desire to help the human race.'

John asked, 'Have some souls now in human beings ever been incarnated as dolphins? Is that possible?'

'Yes. But only in that relationship, and never in an animal. If you had the desire to come as a porpoise, you could do so.'

'That raises an interesting question,' Andrija said. 'You have told us that after the destruction of Atlantis, or Altea, many souls chose to return as dolphins. But did dolphins and porpoises have intelligent souls before that time?'

'Yes,' Tom said.

'So I take it that in dolphins, as in humans, there are souls at different stages of development.'

'Yes.'

'And are there any of what we might call advanced porpoises in this area of Israel and Egypt at this time?'

'I must consult,' Tom said, and after a pause continued:

287

'Altea has said that arrangements are being made for them to be in all areas so that men might recognise them for what they are. You understand that they, like you, are in service, but it is difficult for them to perform true service without the link with human beings.'

'Yes, well, when this crisis is over we must see what we can do to establish and strengthen those links,' Andrija said.

This was the most sustained discursive communication of this period, for throughout the next few days Tom was chiefly concerned with the political situation. The trio followed his instructions to be at Megiddo from noon the next day in order to pre-empt the pre-emptive strike into Lebanon and Syria that the Israelis were alleged to be planning. In the evening Andrija asked Tom whether their efforts had produced the desired effect and Tom said that they had:

'A decision was made at two-thirty. There was a vote, and it was finalised within the hour. But remember, there are among the Israelis, as among their enemies, those that are fanatics.'

'And is there any danger that these fanatics will be able to reverse the decision made today?' Andrija asked.

'We will alert you if there is danger of that,' Tom said. 'It is still important for you to go to the north now to prevent those that are fanatics on the other side.'

'Yes, we've made plans to go the day after tomorrow, after we've completed our three days here at Megiddo.'

'Our major concern,' Tom said, 'is if there should be what you would call a mushrooming of acts of aggression by and against the nation of Israel to the point where it would be very difficult for your energies and strength to hold it.'

So with the belief that their journey would prevent this eventuality, Andrija, John and Phyllis set out from Nazareth in a loaded station wagon on the morning of 16 March. They drove west to join the Mediterranean coast road, then after passing through the picturesque and sleepy towns of Acre and Nahariyya climbed by a winding road into the hills of the frontier area. Behind a high, double fence of barbed wire lay Lebanon, apparently utterly deserted except in the valleys, where occasionally Arab farmers were to be seen. The Israeli side of the frontier was fortified with military installations every few miles, and twice they were turned back by soldiers and directed to a parallel road further from the border. By two-thirty they found themselves on Mount Hermon at a kind of makeshift militarised skiing resort, with temporary portable buildings and tanks everywhere. For their three o'clock meditation the top of Mount Hermon, which commanded sweeping views over Lebanon and Syria, would be, they agreed, the ideal spot, so they took a chair-lift up the ski-slope and found a secluded place to sit. A mercilessly sharp wind from the east whipped round them and at the end of the meditation they were all shivering and glad to get back to the chair-lift and down to a more hospitable altitude. Further down still they came to a village named Banias, a place that echoed with the continuous rush of mountain streams, and here in a grove of ancient and gnarled olive trees they attempted to hold a communication. It was a short one because Tom said that conditions were not favourable, but he had time to congratulate them on a successful 'sweep of the north' and said that they should communicate at greater length that evening. So they drove in two hours to Tiberias on the lake of Galilee where they booked into the Galei Kinnereth, a luxury lakeside hotel. At the beginning of the communication they held that night, after dining and taking a walk around the town, Tom reviewed the effects of their day's work:

'Throughout the area where you have been this day you have accomplished a great deal more . . . we cannot say than we anticipated or planned, and we do not wish to anger those with whom you battle, so we must at this time speak with care. But you accomplished much. We wish you to visualise that as you pass through an area there spreads and dissipates behind you a bright glowing light that would be similar to a stream, but in truth it does not dissipate but reaches over a wide area. Do you understand?'

'Yes,' Andrija said, 'we can visualise it as what we could call a vapour trail.'

'Yes. And this day you have with your vapour trail caused a settlement of anger in many and you have spread a blanket that will keep the passions and the ambitions of those that oppose the nation of Israel under control. And you have done more than this. Within the area through which you have passed there were spirits that still existed from the history of that area, and because of their ignorance and refusal of understanding they have created difficulties for those of the nation of Israel and also of the nations of Lebanon and Syria through their strong desire to continue their battles. What you have done is negated the energy of those spirits that are used by those that oppose. You have done a great service because you have opened their minds to see greater things. These were some of the spirits that we have spoken to you about before and that have created a bottleneck in the spirit planes of the planet Earth, and through your work this day they have been released.'

Tom said that they should regard the following day as a day of rest, then they should go to the south and work on Jordan, Saudi Arabia and Egypt from the vantage points of Eilat and Sharm-el-Sheik. The prospects of success in their work were good, but there were going to be some very taxing days ahead so they should take full advantage of the present opportunity to recuperate their energies.

So the next day they took it easy, enjoyed the excellent amenities of the hotel including the lakeside swimming pool, wrote letters, strolled around the town, paid a visit to the ruins at Capernaum, the place where Jesus had begun his ministry, and at three o'clock in the afternoon found a spot beside the lake where a bank and a belt of trees hid them from the road and settled down, seated on rocks and with their feet in the water, for their half-hour meditation. Some twenty minutes had elapsed when a man's voice shouted from the trees behind them, 'Hey, what you do?' When he got no response, the man shouted his question again, then a third time, and Phyllis turned round to see an Arab in European dress standing on the bank above them. He asked, 'You are praying?' Phyllis said they were and the Arab asked what for. 'For peace,'

Phyllis said, and he said 'That's good,' and walked away. Just a few moments later a lone Israeli soldier appeared, removed his boots and socks and sat near them with his feet in the water.

When they held a communication later that day, Andrija referred to this incident and Tom said that the Arab who had spoken to them was a Syrian. Andrija wondered whether the incident signified that there was a possibility that the Arabs and the Israelis would sit down at a table together and work for peace. Tom said that it was indeed possible, but indicated that they would have a lot of work to do before it came to that. Moreover, there was a new cause for concern. There were plans being made to assassinate Dr Kissinger during his present tour of Middle East capitals, and the event could trigger a full-scale war.

'That's terrible,' Andrija said. 'And you speak as if it's a foregone conclusion.'

'In your world nothing is a foregone conclusion,' Tom said. 'We tell you these things so that we may use you.' And he instructed them to include Dr Kissinger in their meditations and prayers so that they could send energy to protect him. 'You three together are an energy field,' he told them, 'and you are as powerful as the energy of Megiddo, or of your home, or of a pyramid. When you are together we can take from you and weave a cable.' And this 'cable', he said, could be used to protect Dr Kissinger.

The talk about energy brought up the subject of the 'troops' at Ossining and the extent to which they were contributing support through their meditation sessions. Tom said that they were doing quite well but there were certain disturbances among them and they needed to understand the importance of discipline in their work.

'If they could have a sign from Altea or Hoova, I think it would encourage them,' John said.

'Tell them to watch their clocks,' Tom said.

John was in the habit of phoning Ossining every other day, and the next time he did so he conveyed Tom's message. When he phoned again two days after that, Jim Hurtak confirmed that the clocks had started behaving erratically again.

The contributions of the 'troops', Tom said, would probably not be needed after the end of the month and they could make plans to disband them if they wished to, but Andrija, John and Phyllis might be required to extend their stay in Israel. It would depend on the trend of events, but they should be prepared to stay longer than originally planned, and if they wished to make provisional arrangements for their respective partners to join them they could do so.

After spending three nights in Tiberias and being assured that their presence and meditations had helped to moderate the more extreme factions in 'the nation that is across', Andrija, John and Phyllis set out early on 20 March to drive to the south.

Eilat, a resort surrounded by desert and with big modern impersonal hotels, all glass and plastic, seemed to John a sort of poor man's Las Vegas. They held a communication that evening in a hotel room that smelled of fresh paint. It was a fairly brief session, a general situation report from Tom and advice for each of them on various small points. They retired early and by agreement were at breakfast by seven o'clock the following morning and shortly afterwards ready for the long run down the gulf to Sharm-el-Sheik. They were in Sharm, or Ofira as the Israelis have renamed it, by noon, and they found a town that was little more than a garrison and a construction site. The heat was intense and they were dusty from the journey through the desert, so as soon as they had settled in Andrija and John went for a swim. They had been told that the coral here was some of the best in the world, so they hired masks and snorkels and spent half an hour observing and marvelling at the underwater world of breathtaking colour and variety that contrasted so sharply with the unrelieved sandy monotone of the surrounding desert. Tom's point about Earth being the planet of greatest beauty and variety was certainly illustrated here.

But they were not here to marvel. They had work to do at three o'clock, and the map indicated that the best place for their meditation, the place nearest both to Egypt and to Saudi

Arabia, was the peninsula of Ras Muhamed, some fifty kilometres away. There was a road only part of the way to Ras Muhamed. The rest was a track across the desert marked by little piles of stones every fifty yards or so, but they found their way there in good time and managed to get to the very farthest point of the peninsula to do their meditation. It was a beautiful spot, utterly silent and deserted, where the sea washed the shore gently and a heat haze shimmered over the land.

They held a communication before dinner that evening in their room. Andrija had to begin by apologising for the noise, because there was a generator thundering just outside and somebody in a neighbouring room was playing a radio, but Tom said, 'We are secure,' and asked what questions they had.

'Well, as you know, we did our meditation facing Egypt and Saudi Arabia today,' Andrija said, 'and we'd like to know how effective that was.'

'It was of the greatest effect in creating sense in the leaders of those nations,' Tom said. The problem now was going to be to stabilise the leaders in Jerusalem after Kissinger's visit, and to this end they should go through Jerusalem on their way back to the north and hold a meditation as near as possible to the Knesset on 23 March. The Kissinger negotiations were not going well and his life was still in danger and the next days were going to be crucial for him, so they should continue sending him energy and protection.

Andrija had a question on another subject. Just before they had settled down for this communication they had learnt that during the afternoon there had been great excitement because about twenty porpoises had appeared in the bay. This, apparently, was an unprecedented event, so Andrija asked Tom if it had anything to do with their presence.

'Did you not ask?' Tom said. 'May we say to you, our doctor and Sir John, and you will relate this to our Being: we have in the past explained to you many times about your power. We have warned you, and we have cautioned you to be careful what you ask, have we not?'

'Yes,' said Andrija.

'We have asked you to be of extreme caution with your angers, your displeasures and your despairs because of your power. And it is the same with your happiness, your joy and your enthusiasms. Those creatures heard what you asked and came because of your asking.'

'Should we try and make contact with the porpoises tomorrow?' Andrija asked, and Tom said that provided they were able to fulfil their instructions for the 23rd it was up to them how they organised their time.

John was keeping a diary all through this period, and I am now going to quote verbatim his entry for 22 March, for it provides a better background than a second-hand report for the communication they held later that day.

'Got up early, and as I was keen to get to the Dead Sea that afternoon for the meditation I insisted on an early start, though Andrija wanted to hang about on the beach till noon and Phyllis wanted to talk to the porpoises. Anyway we got going at 9 a.m. and Phyllis was rather down so I became frustrated with her. On the road to Eilat we discussed many things about biblical history and Andrija had two minor arguments with Phyllis, one about "nine cancelling out" and the other about "truth" and "perfection". My thinking goes on much the same lines as Andrija's and I often find Phyllis's non-sequential and non-specific discussion irritating, and I did on this occasion. During the first argument her earring dematerialised and later reappeared, which with hindsight I see was a warning, and during the second we came upon a couple of Israelis beside a broken-down jeep. We stopped only briefly and didn't offer much help, which was a thing we were to hear more about later. We had a slow lunch in Eilat and left there at 1.10 to attempt to reach the Dead Sea for our 3 p.m. meditation. I drove faster than usual but quite safely I thought, and Phyllis slept most of the way and we reached the Dead Sea at ten minutes to three. We stood in the water for the meditation and then went to check in at the very touristy Galei Zohar hotel at Ein Bokek. Again Andrija and I went down to the beach to experience floating in the crazy water, which was fun. Then back to the hotel for a communication, and the bombshell hit us.'

During the meditation, John had had an unusual experience. He had heard very clearly a voice saying several times, 'I am Dennis Dunsmore. I am a reporter.' He told the others about the experience afterwards, but neither Andrija nor Phyllis had heard it.

The 'bombshell' John referred to at the end of his diary entry was the severest reprimand that Tom had ever handed out to them. At the beginning of the communication he said he had a great deal to say to them but would first answer any questions. John asked who Dennis Dunsmore was, and Tom answered, 'a spirit in the area of death'. Then Andrija said they had no important questions and would rather hear what Tom wanted to say to them, and he and John were both amazed and chastened by the long speech that Tom now proceeded to deliver to them.

'We have given you bouquets when you have deserved them, but we are now going to give you thorns. Today you took upon your physical selves a situation of great danger. You gave to those that oppose the opportunity to eliminate all three of you completely. We are angry, and we will not tolerate this in future. We speak to each of you. Those that oppose what you do wait for opportunities to eliminate you. Today it has taken the energies of Altea and Hoova and of Joseph of Aragon to protect the three of you. Those energies were needed to protect areas for which you have prayed. There is a word in your language that we must use for the first time in speaking to you, and that word is "stupid". If we understand that word, it means non-thinking and ignorant.

'Sir John, we will speak first to you, and then we will speak to our doctor and our Being. In the future, none of the three of you has the right or our permission to create dangers for the other two. When you take upon yourself the situation of the universe, you take upon yourself also the responsibilities of the universe. You have tested us today in a vehicle that is not of the greatest stability and that could have eliminated all three of you. We gave you signs but you did not pay attention. And we speak to the three of you. Each of you is as re-

295

sponsible as the others. We have been with you this day because of the necessity to be with you, and you have spoken of many things and we have listened. You have spoken of truth and you have spoken of perfection, and if you really have the desire to be perfect we will teach you how perfection is attained on your physical planet Earth. There is but one law to attain perfection. There are no complexities. It is a very simple law. And it is to treat each and every soul and every animal and every plant as you would desire them to treat you. That is the golden law, the law of the universe.

'There was upon your journey today a time of necessity for you to stop. We had made arrangements for that. Because of your testing of us, we tested you. And we were angry. You do not treat your fellow man as you would desire to be treated, not any of you. You cannot reach the people on your planet if you do not have consideration for them. It is time you learnt that if there is an inconvenience you should accept that inconvenience in order to give you strength and understanding. When you begin to feel that you are of a righteous nature, then you are no longer righteous. When you begin to feel you are more important than others, then you are no longer important. And when you begin to feel that you may do as you desire to save the world, then you will destroy the world.

'And today there was another disaster. There was the loss of a dolphin. We admonish the two of you because you did not explain to our Being as we asked you to about the strength of the three of you. You will now tell our Being that in the future arrangements will not be made unless there is certainty that they will be kept. We will tolerate no more losses, and we will not permit any one of the three of you to manipulate the other two. You spoke with spirits today, Sir John, because that is where you nearly went. And one of the dolphins made its transition today, in its difficulty in waiting for the Being. This caused great disturbance with Altea, for you should remember where the dolphin comes from. It is true that our Being asked the dolphin to come, and you must tell her that in future if she will not be there she should send as strongly for them not to come. And you, our Doctor, may we ask you if in your heart you can in truth – and you spoke of truth today – say that you did not permit endangerment of your lives?'

'I'm sorry, but I wasn't aware of any danger today at all,' Andrija said. 'Can you say what it was?'

'The car was dangerous. We have asked you before to pay attention to the wheels. Sir John, remember that when irritations grow out of proportion, then you have been reached by those that oppose. Today they were able to reach you. You do not know how close you came.'

John said he wasn't aware of failing to pay attention to any warnings, and Tom reminded him that 'we removed an earring from the Being and not one of you asked why'. Andrija asked whether in future warnings couldn't be clearer and quite unambiguous, for instance like the car horn suddenly sounding. Tom had to consult about that one, and after a pause he reported: 'The Council has said that you are asking us to do for you things that you should have the sense to do yourself, and that if we make that arrangement for you it will be the same as making a law, and it is not good to depend upon a law.'

Which was consistent with their frequently expressed attitude towards human free will, but a little ironical coming at the end of a harangue in which Tom had laid down the law as never before.

John and Andrija discussed the gist of this communication with Phyllis when she came out of trance, and that night a rather subdued and thoughtful trio of world savers went to their beds in the Galei Zohar hotel at Ein Bokek.

There was nothing obviously wrong with the wheels or tyres of the car when they examined them the next morning, but John drove slowly and with great caution nevertheless. The three of them talked frankly about the previous night's communication and the understandings and feelings that they had got from it, and by the time they reached Jerusalem they agreed that it had been a good thing because it had had the effect of bringing them closer together. In Jerusalem they sought a place for their meditation near the parliament buildings, but they could find nowhere very close where they would not be conspicuous, and they had to settle for the grounds of the University, about half a mile from the Knesset. Tom had said that they should get back to Galilee that day, so after the meditation they paid a brief visit to the old city to enable Phyllis to do some shopping then set off to drive to Tiberias via Ramallah, Nablus and Beit Shean. They bought a copy of an English language newspaper printed in Jerusalem which carried the headline 'PLO Plans Attack from Syria', and wondered whether this had anything to do with Tom's insisting that they return to Galilee. They arrived back at the Galei Kinnereth in time for dinner, and when a suitable time had elapsed after dinner they held a brief communication.

This day, the 23rd, was the day on which Dr Kissinger had to concede the failure of his negotiations, and the following morning he flew back to Washington. He had been unable to persuade the Israelis to surrender territory in exchange for Egyptian promises, and he was returning, Tom said, 'in great sadness', though with the failure of the talks the danger of his assassination had passed. Over the next few days the world's press was to be fairly unanimously critical of Israel's 'intransigence', and many commentators spoke of the likelihood of a re-opening of hostilities.

The following is how Tom analysed the situation in the communication held on the night of the 23rd: 'The nation of Egypt sought to make the nation of Israel bend its knee, and when it could not it began to lay a plot to involve the other nations. But Egypt did not in truth have in mind to bring the other nations to war. It was more the way of using a threat. In wanting the nation of Israel to bow its knee, Egypt showed its ignorance, and when Israel would not concede the requests of Egypt the thought was planted that if it would be brought to the attention of the other nations that their God demanded this war, then they could force the knees of the nation of Israel to bend. But through their ignorance they have set up an explosive situation. It has now been picked up by the nation across from where you are. It is the only idea that could pull all the nations that oppose together. It was only done to bring the nation of Israel to its knees, and it was to be but a bluff, but it has gathered strength and it must be negated. There is a plot to launch an attack when the holidays of the Christians are over and those of the nation of Israel are still in celebration. Israel, we give you our promise, will not be destroyed, but what is in the minds of those that oppose could cause the greatest devastation and, Doctor, it is tragic but your country will not intervene.'

For the next two weeks, the period that Tom had said when they were in Ossining would be the most critical, Andrija, John and Phyllis remained in Tiberias, ostensibly tourists, and followed Tom's instructions to stand in the lake of Galilee and 'face the nation of Syria and pray from the heart' for certain periods each day. 'You are in a very special place,' Tom told them. 'This area where you now are is special because of the Nazarene. We have explained to you about the energy field that is Megiddo and the spokes that go out and the pockets of energy at the extensions. Well, this place is one of the extensions. In this area the Nazarene performed many miracles. Remember who he was and who you are and remember that he promised there would be those that would perform more and stronger miracles.'

The incognito of the 'successors' of the Nazarene was impeccable during this period. When they were not meditating, praying or communicating with Tom, they looked and behaved exactly like tourists. John went water-skiing on Lake Galilee with the hotel lifeguard, a thirty-one-year-old Israeli who as an immigrant some years ago had boldly adopted the double eponym Israel Carmel. Israel was intense, aggressive, athletic and intelligent. He became a friend of the trio, accompanied them on sightseeing expeditions in the area and introduced them to friends of his in Tiberias. The friendship was strengthened when one afternoon he joined them in their three o'clock meditation as if it were the most natural thing in the world, though of course they did not tell him the purpose of it.

'In your meditations today,' Tom told them on 25 March, 'you have not succeeded in averting the war threat, but you have achieved delay until three days after your twenty-eight.

And may we say to you that if you can prevent difficulties for the nation of Israel through the month of your July, then the nation of Israel will stand firm for ever.' Which was the second indication they had that they weren't going to be based back in Ossining as soon as they had thought.

On the following day, the 26th, there was apparently danger once again of Israel embarking on a suicidal pre-emptive attack strategy. 'It is important for you,' Tom told the trio, 'in your next meditations to pray and to love and to give to those that are in authority in the nation of Israel the strength to be wise in their decisions. They feel that they are in a situation where they will have no choice but to be the aggressor. It must not happen. And we will tell you the truth of another situation. If it should come to pass that the people of this nation should ever come near the point of their total destruction, they will not only remain until they are no longer, but they will also take the rest of the planet Earth with them. They will release nine missiles. It is important that this not be permitted. The children of the nation of Israel have in their hearts the knowledge of who they are, but with this knowledge they are determined that before they will have to kiss the feet of others they will eliminate all their people. They know that if the country of our Doctor is not on their side there is no hope for their existence, and they are prepared to take the planet with them. They have nine missiles situated in three different areas, all pointed in directions to cause the greatest devastation.'

This was consistent with reports that appeared in the press shortly thereafter that Israel had achieved nuclear capability.

Tension was maintained at a high pitch throughout the next five or six days, both by the information Tom conveyed and by the news emanating from the newspapers and from radio and television. The latter did not corroborate the former, for Tom's information had to do with events and decisions that would not be available to the media anyway, but suspense ran at a parallel pitch in the two sources of information. Among the Israelis there was a growing sense that war was imminent and inevitable, and indeed many of them seemed to be spoiling for it.

Communications with Tom over these days tended to be brief and to the point, for the opposition was apparently trying to use the opportunity to put its oar in and there was a need for energy conservation in order to maximise the output for preventing an escalation of hostile posturings and plottings into open war. In addition to continually reassuring the trio that their energy, augmented by that of the 'troops' at Ossining, was proving effective, and exhorting them to stand firm in their faith and not relax their efforts, Tom vouchsafed some political information. Since Kissinger's return to Washington the US had decided to abandon Israel to her fate. In Syria the government was in cahoots with the PLO and a plot had been concocted to unite the Arab nations against Israel by engineering a political assassination which would look as if it had been done by Israelis. He wasn't named specifically, but there were hints that the intended victim of this plot was King Hussein of Jordan. All over Israel, including Tiberias, there were Arab infiltrators, and they were being organised to strike simultaneously in order to throw the Israelis into disarray just before the main military offensive started. 'For the next six or seven days,' Tom said on 28 March, 'we are walking on eggs.' There was a situation of supreme crisis coming which would demand of them a great concerted effort, and even if it were passed successfully it would not mean the end of their work here, for the situation would remain serious until July.

On 30 March Tom said that the moment of crisis would probably come at nine o'clock the following evening, and that from two o'clock in the afternoon they should be in prayer for an hour and should communicate at nine o'clock. This would be the last effort the Ossining 'troops' would be required to participate in, for after it they would not be in a condition to continue, so they would be free to disband.

So at 8.45 on 31 March, D-day as they called it, Andrija, John and Phyllis assembled in a hotel room in Tiberias which overlooked one of the most contentious territories in the world, the Golan Heights. It was an apparently peaceful night, with a near-full moon riding over distant Safed and casting a bridge of light across the still lake, but the assembled trio shared a sense of foreboding and of the great solemnity of the occasion. Phyllis went into trance quickly, and when her body stiffened and her forearms rose and Tom announced in a weak and halting voice, 'We are here,' Andrija said:

'Welcome Tom. We very much wanted to be with you in this fateful hour in human affairs, and we would like to do whatever we can to help. Can you advise us what the state of affairs is?'

During the session Tom was rather less coherent than usual and there were long pauses before he answered questions and between his statements, but the reason for this, they soon learned, was that he was simultaneously eavesdropping on a meeting of Arab leaders who were debating whether to give the order for missiles to be launched against Israel.

It was some time before he answered Andrija's opening question, then he said: 'At this time . . . [pause] . . . if there would be but six decisions – and there are four that are affirmative and two that are not . . . [pause] . . . We are sorry, you will bear with us when we must hesitate.'

'Yes, of course,' Andrija said, 'we understand.'

'It has come to the notice of those that are across the water from where you are that there is difficulty in – what is the word? it is not machinery . . . but they are having difficulty. It is for us and for you a good situation, but there are those who say that what is left in balance should be pushed . . . [pause].'

'I take it there's a decision meeting going on,' Andrija said.

'Yes, at this moment. We will say this to you . . . [pause] . . . There is much consternation, and there is much thumping.'

'Is Israel aware of this moment of peril?' Andrija asked.

'They have of this knowledge,' Tom said. 'We must pray.'

'Shall we pray to give them stability and strength?'

'Yes. The nation of Israel will not push the button without notification . . . [pause] . . . We are in a precarious time. We will hold each other.'

Andrija and John each took one of Phyllis's ice-cold hands and joined their own to complete the circuit. Andrija whispered into the microphone for the record: 'The time is exactly 9 p.m. local time.'

'We will send strength to those of the nation of Israel,' Tom said. 'If we may hold but four minutes we will in truth – how do you say? – we will have won a round.'

The three sat in silence with joined hands for what seemed a long time, and then Tom delivered a speech, slower and more hesitantly than usual:

'In these moments when we are together we ask you to call upon all your reserves, all your strength, all your love and your compassion. Convert your frustrations into harmony, bring out your understanding of all that is around you, and of each other, and spread it abroad and give it to the children of the nation of Israel. Plant in the minds of those that oppose the nation of Israel a seed, so that they may step out of their hate. It is important at this time that those that oppose be in confusion, and it is sad that in the confusion they cause more confusion, but it is the only thing that will keep them in separate doors. We would say this to you, for the work and the strength of the three of you, that if this night passes in peace, then those that oppose this nation of Israel will ask within ten to seventeen days for a meeting with Dr Kissinger, and this will bring great hope, but until that time we are on eggs . . . [pause] . . . We pray for peace, and that all of our strength be permitted to be used to the maximum to blanket this land and these people with love and with understanding, and to bring them out of the bondage of their minds.'

This was followed by a long wait, and then Tom announced success: 'Egypt is dismantled . . . [pause] . . . Lebanon is ineffective . . . [pause] . . . and four in Syria are non-functional. With the others there is difficulty . . . [pause] . . .'

Another suspenseful silence was followed by the announcement that brought a surge of relief to both Andrija and John: 'We have passed.'

'Are you holding in Syria now?' Andrija asked.

'There are three missiles functioning.'

'Have you not neutralised those yet?'

'With only three they will not attempt. We have passed.

303

Do you understand that if we had not succeeded you would be with us?'

Andrija laughed. 'Yes, we were very aware of that. Though I think it would be a pleasure to be with you, to tell the truth.'

'You cannot return. You have not completed.'

'No, we realise that, and of course we're anxious to complete our task on Earth,' Andrija said.

'We must tell you that in three of your days there will be those fringes that in their anger will create difficulty. Your energies may be used at that time to thin out the fringes.

'Okay, well, we'll be available for that mopping-up operation,' Andrija said.

I don't know about my readers, but I need to take a breather at this stage. This ready-made last chapter of the present narrative, which seems to be plotted and structured like a stage play or a movie scenario, is leaving even me breathless and incredulous as it unfolds. I mean, if it isn't literally true, whose fantasy is it? If it's invention, then the intelligence that invented it had an extraordinary endowment of dramatic skills, knew how to build up a *dénouement* progressively through a series of episodes, how to create suspense, how to plot and lay foundations for future developments. And there's another staggering thing I've just discovered. The ending of this book was foreseen by Tom in December 1974, some fifteen months before I began to write it and four months before the events recounted above.

At that time the intention was that Andrija should write the book, and in a communication on 5 December 1974 (part of which I have reported above, pp. 223–4), he discussed with Tom some of the problems he was having. He said, 'Right now, I'm really looking at a huge pile of rubble and trying to create an edifice out of it. I really don't know where to start, in what order to pick up the stones, what form and shape to give it.'

I know how he felt. But Tom had a simple answer to that: 'May we say to you, Doctor, that you have within you the nature of a ring of truth, and that is all that is necessary.'

So he should tell the story straightforwardly and just as it had happened. But what aboūt the ending? Andrija asked: 'I'd like to have your advice as to where the first publication and the report of the first series of your communications should conclude in order to set the stage for the next series of events. What would be a kind of climactic ending that in effect would whet the appetite for more knowledge?'

Tom's answer didn't seem particularly exceptional at the time, but in the light of what we now know about events, and considering how this book has taken shape and approached its maximum possible length at this stage of the story, it is quite an amazing answer:

'In the month of February of your coming year, towards the end of that month, it will be necessary for the three of you to return to this nation of Israel. You will return, and we know – you know not, but we know – that you with your presence will avert another attempt of war, and you may then if you desire end your book on that particular note.'

Though Tom was two weeks out, as their intended departure for Israel in February was delayed by the inter-personal difficulties they were going through at that time, what an uncanny prediction this is. And what a felicitous sense of literary structure it shows.

And so to the final scene of the drama, which appropriately contains suspense, villainy, miracle, the resolution of this particular climacteric and intimations of future developments.

On 1 April Tom gave them a summary of the consequences of the previous night's events: 'At this time there is great confusion in the nations that oppose the nation of Israel. There is contact between the nation across from where you are and the nation of Soviet Russia. There is great disturbance because the Syrians are blaming the Russians for the bad missiles. It will create a difficulty in two ways.'

'Yes,' Andrija said, 'I imagine the Syrians will blame Russia for sabotaging their plans with poor equipment, and the Russians will blame the Syrians for not knowing how to operate it properly.'

'Yes. At great cost. There will be more shipments. But when it has happened two or three times they may begin to understand what really happened.'

'So may we assume that we're safe now?' Andrija asked.

'Until the third of this month you are in.'

'Yes, you mentioned the third and the mopping-up of the fringes last night.'

John said, 'Can you give us some idea of the kind of thing our energies will be required for on the third?'

'Sir John, there is a plan to take you, our Doctor and our Being on a visit by the youth of where you are. It would be of benefit because it is closer to where you need to be. We would have you understand that it is only the nation of Syria that we will be concerned with at that time.'

It was true that the young man they had befriended, Israel Carmel, had proposed that he and a friend of his named Giddon should take them to see an interesting natural phenomenon known as the hexagon pools, in the former Syrian territory of Golan, and the date suggested for this trip was the third. Israel had thought that the trip was his idea, but now it seemed that it was an idea that the Management had planted as a part of their advance planning.

They received no further details of the plan in this communication, and when they attempted to communicate the following day a most unexpected thing happened. Phyllis was unable to get into deep trance. She got down to a certain level where she came up against some sort of blockage and was subjected to a psychic attack. She described the experience to John and Andrija and they discussed it with her.

'I was going in, and this fire was burning all around me. Villages were being burnt, and I thought I was in a situation like Africa. I saw these burning villages, and I saw skin being peeled off people, and all that kind of stuff. But I can handle that because it's like I'm an outside observer. Then all of a sudden all these kind of things are coming at me, and they're pulling at my tongue and at my eyes and they're biting me and sticking things into me. And they're the ugliest things I've ever seen. I've been in prehistoric times, but they're worse than prehistoric. Then they turn to human and their eyes are red and they laugh at you. And I can't get past that level. I can't get to the Nine.'

'Well, the Management have warned us,' John said, 'that the opposition would try to stop our communications and would try to do so by creating a fear.'

'Fear is one thing, John,' Phyllis said. 'I can rationalise in my mind: this can't hurt me, it's an illusion. Okay. When I go down there and see all these things I can say to myself, "It's an illusion, it's a nightmare, they can't do anything to you." But when they start ripping at you and it hurts, that's another thing.'

'Yes, that's when they're getting at your etheric, and it's dangerous,' Andrija said.

'And where are the Nine?' cried Phyllis, with a note of exasperation.

'Wait a minute,' John said. 'As I see it, the opposition believe that if they can prevent our communicating they can make us ineffective. So shouldn't we just go ahead and do tomorrow what we know or think is the right thing to do, and not worry too much about holding this communication, particularly in view of the risks involved.'

Andrija agreed in principle, but he said he thought they should try once more. This was the first time that the opposition had succeeded in blocking communication, and he was worried that there might be a reason for it. Perhaps the opposition wanted to prevent them getting information that would be important for tomorrow.

So they tried again, and this time Phyllis managed to get out of her 'etheric envelope', secure from the depredations of the creatures of the opposition, and in due course Tom made his presence known. His visit was brief, though, and his message urgent: 'There is within the spheres a battle that is creating difficulty. We can stay but for a moment. It is important for you to know that on your morrow there will be an attempt by those across the water from where you are to send destruction by poison. It is important that it be stopped. You will go where you planned to go. We must leave now.'

They got more details at nine o'clock the following morning, when communication was established without any problem. 'Between the hours of four and six,' Tom said, 'those that are across intend to create illnesses for the people of Israel by poisoning. It is important that you continue your plan to go within the reach of the nation of Syria and meditate. It is the anger of those that had a failure, and it is not done by the heads of the nation but by those that are fanatical. We cannot permit this destruction, but we need your physical energy to cause a neutralisation. As we have explained to you before, with enough series of failures, those that oppose will begin to see the light.'

Explaining the difficulty they had had in communicating the previous evening, Tom gave an interesting comment on the subject of Armageddon: 'In your physical world, when there is a war there are portions of that war that remain in the mind, portions that are memorials to freedoms and also memorials to slavery. What was happening last evening was one of those memorials. It was partly a physical battle, but it was more of a mental power struggle for the gaining of the minds. You understand that in this battle you call Armageddon the important thing is to gain control of the souls and the minds?'

Which prompts a brief digression. Several of the present-day 'awareness' psychologies and techniques maintain that man is kept in confusion and his development is retarded by what they call 'uncleared engrams', i.e. residual memories or emotions from earlier stages of life or from former lives. Tom seems to be saying much the same thing in this passage, and I think the idea helps us make sense of the concept of the Battle of Armageddon, particularly if we recall also that thought, and therefore memory, is an energetic field phenomenon.

Getting back to the subject of the day's work, Tom said that they should make Phyllis fully aware of the situation, and that if they alerted her that there was danger at any time they should all 'flee like deer'. He said, 'It is unfortunate that we must send you where we are sending you for you to be as close as possible for this particular situation. But we cannot afford to have any error. It must be completely neutralised. It cannot be merely in portion neutralised. It must be turned to pure water. Do you understand?'

'Yes,' Andrija said. 'Could you give us some idea what the nature of the toxin is?'

'I do not understand chemistry,' Tom said, but he consulted briefly with Altea and then continued: 'They have explained that it is of a viral nature that will work in slowly until it would be too late to recognise what had happened.'

'Yes, I understand,' said Andrija. 'A virus with a slow incubation period. Do you know how long that incubation period would be?'

'They say between three and seven of your days.'

'And presumably the plan is to release this material into the waters somewhere so that it pollutes the lake of Galilee?'

'Yes.'

'So it's a thing that can be done by one person surreptitiously?'

'By two.'

To get to the hexagon pools you take a rough track off a main road in the Golan hills and follow it for about three miles as it winds up and round a hillside. Then you have to scramble for fifteen minutes down a steep path into a narrow gorge, and all the time as you descend the sound of rushing water gets louder. At the bottom of the gorge there is this geological enigma. It is a rocky place, and all the rocks are hexagonal. You stand on a natural platform which is a mosaic of hexagons, each about eighteen inches across, and see identical-shaped rocks below and all around you. There is a large pool into which the water cascades over these hexagonal rocks, and the sheer cliff face that rises from it is ribbed with a profusion of hexagon-shaped outcrops, like stalactites and stalagmites. The whole is one of nature's most impressive sculptures.

This was the place that their Israeli friends brought John, Phyllis and Andrija to in the afternoon of 3 April. Israel and Giddon knew nothing about the dramatic background of the trip. However, they knew about their eccentric friends' habit of sitting in meditation with their feet in water for fifteen minutes every afternoon, and when they had all done admiring and commenting on the scene and John said it was time for their meditation the Israelis took off their shoes and socks as well. This created a dilemma, which John and Andrija discussed in private for a minute. They had formed the idea that their presence was needed in this particular spot at this time because it was the water of this stream, which ran into Galilee, that was going to be poisoned, and that by sitting in meditation with their feet in the stream they would be able to neutralise it. But what, they wondered, would happen if some of the stuff remained active and they got it on their feet? It was perhaps a minimal risk, but was it one they could let others take unwittingly? John was doubtful, but Andrija was of the opinion that they could trust the Management to look after everything and certainly shouldn't allow any doubts to jeopardise their work at this time, so the two Israelis joined them in their meditation unaware of any possible danger.

The water was pretty cold and after fifteen minutes their feet were numb and they had to massage the life back into them. 'Did you get anything, Phyllis?' John asked, for often her clairvoyance in meditation tied in significantly with what they later discovered had happened. Phyllis said that she had got something but she would have to tell them later.

When they were alone, just the three of them, back at the Galei Kinnereth, they compared notes and agreed that at the time of the meditation, and after, they had all felt quite depleted of energy. That was probably a sign that their energies had been effectively channelled. Phyllis's vision also suggested that they had. She had clearly seen two people dressed as bedouin in a field near a stream. One was dressed as a woman but she knew by the vibration that it was a man disguised. They were going towards two canisters which had just been dropped from a helicopter. They got to where the canisters lay and were going to pick them up when suddenly the canisters dematerialised. The Arabs were in consternation, they gesticulated and shouted at each other and rushed about the place searching for the vanished canisters. Phyllis said she felt quite sorry for them, for she could pick up the fear they had of going back to their leaders and having to say they had lost the canisters. They would probably pretend they had done the job, she surmised, and hope that some other explanation why it wasn't successful would be found.

The information Tom gave them when they held a communication at nine o'clock that evening seemed to confirm that Phyllis's vision was in essentials correct. 'You have upon this day completed,' he said. 'Though not in the minds of those that oppose, for it will take a few days for them to realise that there is no consequence. What you have done this day was a necessity, because in their blindness and ignorance those that oppose would not only have caused destruction and disease in this nation of Israel, but in other nations too. It would have caused contamination of their own water, and of that of the nation of Jordan. You are dealing with those that are not of great mental capacity, but only have anger and hate and emotion without reason.'

'Yes,' Andrija said, 'and what actually happened this afternoon? Did you successfully neutralise the toxin?'

'It did not even enter the water.'

'Did you in fact dematerialise the containers and the poison?'

'Yes. That is the reason there is weakness in the three of you, and particularly in the Being. It is now important that you rejuvenate your physical bodies. It is important for the blending that you rebuild your etherics.'

They may, he went on, now take a short break to attend to their personal affairs, but they should be back in Israel together within two weeks, for there was a great deal to be done in the months ahead.

Andrija asked if they might just summarise the various work projects. There was Altea's communications transmission project, which he understood was a long-term project that would begin with radio and television reception of anomalous signals and pictures. Then there was the work of communicating the message of the Nine to the world at large and particularly to the nation of Israel. Thirdly, there was the work of contacting and helping children with paranormal powers. There was healing work: an area in which Phyllis had been increasingly engaged and was to produce some impressive results in the months ahead. Then there was the dolphin communication project.

'Yes,' Tom said, 'but war must be the first of your priorities. It is important for you to keep in your mind and heart the seriousness of the situation in the nation of Israel. As we have explained to you, you must spend most of your time here until the end of your month of July, for if July can pass without a war in this nation of Israel, it will be the ending of all war.'

This was the most impressive of all Tom's predictions, for at the time it was made Arab-Israeli relations were just about as bad as they had ever been, and a peaceful settlement of their differences seemed a very remote possibility. However, by mid-July Egypt and Israel were each willing to make some concessions, and in August Dr Kissinger was able to announce that as a result of the negotiations of the past few weeks the Sinai Agreement was virtually concluded and all that remained was the dotting of the i's. In the eighteen months that have elapsed between then and the time of this writing, not only has there been no fresh outbreak or serious threat of war, but there has also been a discernible improvement of relations between Israel and the Arab world.

During these eighteen months, too, the communications and the work of Andrija, John and Phyllis have continued. But that will have to be another story, for it is as long, as complex and as eventful as the one this book has told.

# CHAPTER NINE

# *Anatomy of a Mystery*

To conclude, I propose to discuss a few key questions and make a few observations of the material presented in this book.

Let us begin with what is probably the most crucial question of all:

*Who or what is Tom?*

As I see it, there are five possibilities to be taken into consideration:

1. Tom is a pure invention, a creation of Andrija, Phyllis or John or of the three of them in collusion.

2. Tom is an unconscious invention, a composite created out of information contained in the minds of the sitters by the well-known mediumistic process of 'withdrawal' of such information.

3. Tom is a secondary personality of Phyllis's, endowed with psi abilities, that takes over when she is in a dissociated state of consciousness.

4. Tom is a spirit, a discarnate entity with extraordinary powers of invention and cognition.

5. Tom is what he says he is, an intelligent being from another part of the cosmos.

The possibility of fraud and invention can, I think, be quite definitely ruled out on the basis of what we now know of the personalities of John, Andrija and Phyllis, the manner of their coming together, and their sustained commitment and dedication. Some hyper-sceptical readers may not agree, and some, it occurs to me, may even suspect that *I* have made the whole thing up, but I think that the majority will agree with me that possibility number 1 can be eliminated. So we are left with two parapsychological hypotheses (possibilities 2 and 3) and two hypotheses that we may call transcendental (possibilities 4 and 5), all four of which come down to the basic question whether Tom exists independently of the three and their shared situation. Let us see what relevant evidence we can marshal from the communications that might throw some light on this question. In view of the complexity of the material and of the problem it poses, the most convenient approach will be to break down and analyse the evidence under a number of sub-headings.

### Alleged identity and abilities

Tom states repeatedly in the communications that he represents, as spokesman, and is one of the Nine governing principles and powers of the universe. 'But,' he insists, 'we are not God. All of you and all of us make God.' He is always insistent that man's tendency to worship and deify what he does not understand only inhibits his own and the planet's development. 'We are not your gods,' he says, 'we do not rule you or control you. We are all one and we work in harmony with you.' Men have conceived God as being omnipotent and omniscient, and according to Tom this erroneous belief has made the work of the Nine very difficult. Far from being omniscient, they are puzzled by the ways of the world and of men. 'It is important for us to learn, through you, of the nature of the physical,' says Tom, and again, 'We cannot do for this planet what this planet must do for itself.' But if the abilities of the Nine and their associated civilisations are limited, they are certainly impressive by human standards. They include mind-reading, prophecy, materialisation and dematerialisation, the ability to interfere with the mechanisms of motor cars and clocks, to mention but a few. Such alleged abilities, particularly the psychophysical ones that suggest an advanced technology, would argue in favour of possibility number 5 if they could be both consistently demonstrated and proved to be effects with no conceivable natural causes. But the Nine, according to Tom, are disinclined to produce signs and wonders to order, for they have tried such tactics in the past and have only been deified for their trouble, which annoys them because it is man's co-operation and not his worship that they need in order to accomplish their purpose.

This is a coherent attitude. Tom exhibits a robust intelligence and a consistency of purpose and attitude that is suggestive if not evidential of his independent existence. As William James remarked, most mediumistic trance utterances have 'a generic similarity in different individuals' and consist of 'a curiously vague optimistic philosophy-and-water' and could have been written by the same author. The Ossining group's communications do not fall into this category. Whoever or whatever Tom is, he is impressively original. But of course so are the people he is involved with. The question is, is he original in a different way? One way of approaching this question is to consider how he interrelates with the others.

## Patterns of relationships

Both as a teacher and as a colleague in an undertaking, Tom consistently exhibits superior wisdom, knowledge and psychological insight. He understands the problems the three have with their own personalities and in their relations with others and particularly the problems they have encountered through their involvement with and dedication to the work. He has repeatedly warned them, collectively and individually, of the dangers of excessive zeal.

When reporting the communications, I have had to be very selective for in the period covered by this book there were more than one hundred hours of taped material. From that I have selected some passages to bring in at this point as examples of psychological and moral statements that suggest Tom's independence of mind.

Early in the work, Phyllis had marital and family problems as a result of her commitment, and in one communication that she channelled Tom made a strong statement à propos this: 'The Being is confused. There is within her the essence of truth, but remember there is also the strong desire to be involved with you. It is true that she is dedicated to what she believes is her dedication, but you do not remove yourself from what you are responsible for without doing it in a manner that does not cause a friction of great hurt to someone else, because you also are responsible for the soul of that person . . . She cannot run from what she must settle first before she can be free.'

John, too, has on several occasions been admonished for his excessive zeal, which tends to take the form of an intense and unremitting application to the work. 'We ask you to relax,' Tom told him. 'It does not help your work for you to be intense. It is important that you have some form of what you call relaxation or diversion, such as to turn on your television, to listen to music, or to read, or to walk, or to visit with gentle friends on a different subject. It is important in your physical world to maintain a balance, and you cannot maintain a balance if there is not a diversion. You must relax in order to function at a higher level.'

This is pertinent advice which shows a shrewd insight into John's character. In another communication, Tom probed deeper and said: 'His weakness is a triple weakness. It is a weakness of guilt, and the guilt then creates another problem with Sir John, for he tries to remove his guilt by doing, and then he begins to build a resentment and a feeling of pity for himself. Sir John, what we are trying to say to you is that you strive so hard for balance that you are always unbalanced, and in that situation those that love you and that you love are the ones that are hurt by you, and when you are in that situation of trying so hard to be balanced, it is when you are easily led astray. You are a paradox, Sir John. At times you are overly generous, and then the goodness that you have done on the one hand you wipe out on the other. It is your constant attempting to balance. But if you will not try to balance, all of a sudden you will be balanced.'

Andrija, too, has received psychoanalysis and pertinent advice about his personal problems from Tom, and I only need refer the reader to his quarrels with Tom, over Phyllis when they were in Ankara and on the subject of 'sirens' at Ossining in February, to establish the point that by functioning in relation to the three as a teacher and counsellor, one might even say as a guru-figure, and by exhibiting subtle psychological insight, acumen and wisdom in this role, Tom affords us strong evidence of his independent existence. It would be naïve, however, to claim that it is conclusive evidence. In some recorded cases of dual or multiple personality, a secondary personality has shown remarkable insight into the psychology of the primary personality. In the recent and immensely complex case of Sybil Dorsett, for example, one of Sybil's sixteen other selves was so knowledgeable about the other personalities inhabiting Sybil's body that she was able to help the psychiatrist, Dr Wilbur, integrate them all into the 'new Sybil'. I know of no case, though, in which a secondary personality has shown wisdom and insight comparable to Tom's in respect of other people, or made so many statements of wide general relevance exhibiting a profound understanding of human life and character and a consistent moral viewpoint.

Let us pass from Tom-as-teacher to Tom-as-colleague. There are many passages in the communications that sound for all the world like company board meetings with Tom officiating as Chairman. To pursue the analogy, it is as if the company were a holding company, Universe Unlimited, and the meetings concerned primarily but not exclusively with the present problems of its subsidiary, planet Earth. The Chairman has long experience of the problems of the subsidiary, which has not only consistently failed to contribute to the growth of the company as a whole but now is in such a sorry plight that it threatens to cause the company to stagnate or even have to go into liquidation. On several occasions in the past the Management has invested fresh capital in attempts to raise the level of the subsidiary's productivity, and the Chairman can tell you all about these occasions, who was involved in them, what they accomplished at the time and why they ultimately failed. He knows it all, he was there, and he remembers. But he suffers from one of the drawbacks of top management: inadequate expertise in dealing with conditions at shop floor level; and he is bound by the policy of the company not to intervene in the autonomy of subsidiaries. Which is why he needs understanding and active colleagues on planet Earth.

John feels strongly that the Nine have frequently demonstrated an uncanny understanding of the shop floor level in spite of their claims to the contrary, claims which, he believes, 'have been made merely to let us off the hook at times when we were not able to handle what they were telling us about our own weaknesses'.

As an example of the board meeting type of session, I would refer the reader to the discussion of the need for a statement of purpose and programme (pp. 144–6). Here, as in many of the communications, we witness a vigorous and intelligent exchange of the views and attitudes of independent minds. There is genuine give and take. A problem is posed, different feelings and opinions with regard to it are aired, and an understanding is reached through the introduction of a point of view not previously entertained, a point of view, moreover, that is recognisably consistent with Tom's general philosophy and ostensible situation. Authentic dialogue and dialectic are frequently to be found in the communications, and it is this fact, rather than their information content, that poses the biggest challenge to the parapsychological hypotheses. Mental contents are one thing, and mental functions quite another, and when we encounter the latter exercised with versatility, spontaneity and generic consistency it is difficult to resist the conviction that we are in the presence of an independent mind.

So I think we may say, by way of summary, that in relation to Andrija, John and Phyllis, Tom manifests a superior wisdom and psychological insight in the role of teacher, and an originality and dialectical vigour in the role of colleague, that are difficult to reconcile with the view that he is a product of one or more of their own minds.

*Other mental functions and attributes*

As I have listened to the recordings of the communications in sequence over the past months I have been struck by three particular characteristics: Tom's faculty for total and accurate recall of the content of earlier communications, the factual and conceptual consistency of the communications as a whole, and a curious decline in the language of the communications with the passage of time.

These three points may be illustrated with one example. The reader will recall that the very first time Tom appeared was when Phyllis fell into an involuntary trance at Count Pino Turolla's house in Miami and uttered a chant in an ancient language. Tom explained that the language came from some 34,000 years ago, when there were 'Three cultures, three divisions from three areas of the universe. One came with love, one came to own, and one came to observe . . . The one that observed recorded it, the one that possessed controlled the minds. The being that came tried to prevent . . . There was a massacre . . . A much more advanced civilisation began then was lost.'

That was in March 1974. Six months later, in October 1974, Andrija referred back to this communication, and without prompting Tom said, 'We spoke, at that time, of a massacre.' Another year passed, and in October 1975, John again referred to the first communication and asked how it related to what they had learnt since. Tom answered: 'If you will review of those of your communications, it is of a similar. There were of those that began of that of the Earth and that of the seeding. And that of the doctor came in that of the time. And there were of those of the negative forces that came to attempt to control. If you can recall, we have told you of that too. And there were those such as that of Altea and of other higher civilisations, that had of the observation and remembrance of this. And there was of you, and of our doctor, that in truth observed; and that of us.' Then John asked about the massacre and received the reply, 'It was a diminishing of spiritual self.'

This communication is of much later vintage than others in this book, and the decline in the language will be apparent to every reader. Asked to explain this, Tom has said that it is due to a gradual exhaustion of the channelling faculties of 'the Being', and in view of our ignorance of the mechanisms referred to we either have to accept this or put it down to a refinement of cunning on Phyllis's part. If it were the latter, it would be a rather supererogatory refinement and one that would be tedious to sustain.

The chief interest of the above-quoted passage, however, is that it elaborates a communication that antedates it by eighteen months with information received in the interim. References to 'the seeding', the previous incarnations of Andrija and John, the civilisation of Altea, and the attempt of the negative forces to exercise control, both elucidate the original message and are elucidated by it.

This is but one example. Statements like, 'If you review your tapes . . .,' and 'If you recall . . .,' occur constantly in the communications, and subsequent checking has always confirmed that the point referred to has indeed been previously communicated. Tom's faculty of total and instantaneous recall is certainly impressive.

Even more impressive is the consistency of the factual and conceptual content of the communications. There is nothing *ad hoc* about the information, no sense of its having been built up as the communications have proceeded. It carries the stamp of something revealed rather than created, of something that existed *in toto* before the first communication was received. Tom's initial elliptical reference to the three cultures, of which 'one came with love, one came to own, and one came to observe', encapsulated a mass of detailed information that was to be elaborated in later communications. It is information, one feels, that was already there; and to say 'already there' implies the existence of an independent mind, unless we wish to invoke the ancient esoteric belief in the 'Akashic Records', which is a point I shall return to later.

If either of the hypotheses I have categorised as 'transcendental' were correct, we would expect Tom to exhibit ESP abilities. The term, of course, means extra-sensory perception, and as neither a discarnate entity nor an extra-terrestrial would have a sensory system like that of a human being he would not be subject to the limitations of human sensory systems. Tom does, in fact, convincingly exhibit faculties of telepathy, clairvoyance and precognition. Often in the communications he says, 'Yes, Sir John?' or 'Yes, Doctor?' and invariably John or Andrija responds immediately with a question or by making a point that clearly was on his mind and he was waiting to put. They became accustomed to this and it soon ceased to surprise them, and the listener to the tapes, too, tends to become blasé about small marvels when the frontiers of his credulity are under barrage from much bigger guns, but the evidence for Tom's infallibly right anticipatory telepathy and mind reading is convincing and has to be taken into account in any attempt to determine who or what Tom is.

Evidence for precognition is also convincing, particularly with regard to developments in the Middle East political situation, as I pointed out in the final chapter of the narrative. As regards clairvoyance, Tom has often allegedly exercised this faculty in order to report to his colleagues on the deliberations taking place in the higher political echelons in the US, Russia, Israel and the Arab countries, but of course the truth of these reports is difficult to verify. (Though occasionally one can pick up an intriguing hint of a correspondence. For example, within days of the completion of their last mission in Israel, the *Jerusalem Post* reported the visit of a top Russian missile expert to Syria. Also the allegation that the US was considering military action in Saudi Arabia seemed too fantastic when Tom made it in November. But in January Dr Kissinger made a *faux pas* by stating publicly that the use of force against the oil-producing countries would be dangerous, but could not be ruled out. And during his Middle East trip in March he had to make a special visit to the Saudi Arabian capital to explain himself to King Faisal.)

To conclude this section, then: the evidence for the exercise of supernormal (by human standards) memory functions, and of what we would call ESP faculties, together with the inherent consistency of the communications, supports the same conclusion as was arrived at in the two previous subsections of this discussion: that Tom is an independent intelligence of some kind. In other words, it weights in favour of our original hypotheses 4 and 5.

Let us now approach the question of Tom's identity from another angle and consider

*The content of the communications*

In recent years a great deal has been published on the subjects of UFOs, prehistoric civilisations on Earth, the visits and influence of extra-terrestrials, Atlantis, reincarnation, the intelligence of dolphins, the New Age, and the traditions of the Apocalypse. These are also the predominant themes of the communications. Depending on your point of view, you might argue that this correspondence indicates that objective truth is now being revealed to different individuals and groups on Earth, or that it is a case of the exponential growth of a congeries of baseless beliefs powered by man's incorrigible need for novelties and wonders. William James observed that 'The *Zeitgeist* has always much to do with shaping trance phenomena', and he raised the question whether 'all subconscious selves are peculiarly susceptible to a certain stratum of the *Zeitgeist* and get their information from it'. This is a question we should certainly bear in mind when considering the significance of the fact that the content of the communications corresponds with that of a great deal of contemporary popular esotericism. But to speak of getting information from a stratum of the *Zeitgeist* is rather vague. It is not a description of how the information is obtained, but an observation that it corresponds with information from other sources. It is an insight worth pursuing, though, so let us consider the possibilities as to how and whence the information content of the communications is obtained. Again I suggest five possibilities for consideration:

1. That the information is stored in Phyllis's unconscious memory and becomes accessible only when she is in trance.

2. That in trance Phyllis establishes a rapport with the unconscious minds of the sitters and draws the information therefrom.

3. That she draws the information from the consciousness of a distant person or persons, or by clairvoyance from books, etc.

4. That she has access to the cosmic reservoir of information and memories that esotericists call the Akashic Records.

5. That she is indeed 'channelling' information that emanates from a non-human intelligence.

I will make a few remarks on each of these possibilities. With regard to the first, in the critical literature of psychical research the possession of unlikely knowledge is often put down to 'cryptomnesia', or unconscious memory. If the person has at any time had access to the information in question, even by glancing through a book many years before, it is theoretically possible that a 'photographic memory' function of the unconscious may be triggered into action when the person is in an altered state of consciousness such as trance. However, Phyllis is not a bookish person nor widely read, and considering the wide range of subject matter covered by the communications, and also the fact that there is internal consistency between information in different categories (for instance cosmology and the interpretation of Revelation), cryptomnesia seems a highly improbable explanation. It is also, incidentally, one that Tom is well aware of. In one communication he said: 'If one of your channels were a student of the book (the Bible), and then in her channelling or her dream state or her inspirational state she received information as in the book, would you know if it were true or in her mind? . . . It is better for the channels not to have previous knowledge.'

The possibility that Phyllis relays back information which she draws from the minds of the sitters is on the face of it more plausible. Andrija, particularly, is a knowledgeable and widely-read man. There are problems with this explanation, however. For one thing, the range and quality of the content of the communications does not vary with the identity of the sitters. Andrija was not present, for instance, when Tom elaborated his statement about the beginnings of civilisation on Earth (see p. 319), and in the period subsequent to the one covered by the present narrative there have been many sessions in which he has not participated, and some from which John has been absent, but the content of these communications is totally consistent with the rest.

Telepathy is said to work regardless of distance, so it may be argued that Phyllis is still drawing on Andrija's unconscious even when he is not present. But the parapsychological studies that have demonstrated telepathy at a distance have also shown that information thus obtained tends to be fragmentary, discontinuous, imagistic rather than conceptual. There is no evidence that coherent and sustained thought can be conveyed or picked up telepathically. The same applies to the hypothesis of selective clairvoyance. As much of the information is elicited by questioning and not simply given, and as it builds up into a consistent pattern piece by piece over a period of time, in order to support the clairvoyance hypothesis we would have to assume the working of a consistent principle of selectivity and that a multiplicity of channels to different kinds of information would be simultaneously open. This is what Professor Hornell Hart, discussing the survival question, called the 'super-ESP' hypothesis. The acquisition of virtually any information can be attributed to 'super-ESP', and if the communications consisted only of information the hypothesis might apply. But, as we have seen, they consist of much more, and the teaching, the exhortation, the pertinent psychoanalysis, the spontaneous wisdom, the personal criticism and the vigorous dialectic, are all factors that argue against the 'super-ESP' hypothesis.

So again logical considerations weight in favour of possibilities 4 and 5. As for the 'Akashic Records' explanation, the idea that there exists a cosmic reservoir of information and memories that can be tapped by a gifted psychic, there would seem to be little to choose, from the point of view of plausibility, between this and the non-human intelligence hypothesis. It is perhaps relevant to note that the Edgar Cayce material, which has some characteristics in common with the Ossining communications, was said to have been derived from a kind of cosmic reservoir of knowledge, and that in later communications Tom has said that such does in fact exist.

The method of argument by elimination which I have followed in the foregoing pages can only, of course, favour one of several predetermined conclusions, and so it is always open to the criticism that there may be other hypotheses that have not been taken into account. I cannot think of any, however, and I would submit the conclusion that the evidence we have surveyed is compatible with our hypothesis number 5: that Phyllis is channelling information that emanates from a non-human intelligence; whereas it is not compatible with the more obvious psychological and parapsychological explanations.

But the term 'non-human intelligence' could apply to either of our original hypotheses 4 and 5: a discarnate spirit or an intelligent being from another part of the cosmos. Can we now determine which of these alternatives the facts favour? I believe we can consider a few points that are germane to the question, though I am well aware that some readers with a philosophical turn of mind will consider that to attempt rationally to choose between two hypotheses when there is no empirical basis for belief in either of them is an absurd enterprise. For the sake of the argument, we have to assume that both spirits and extra-terrestrials might exist. The reader might recall the conclusion reached by the Columbia Professor of Logic and Ethics, James Hyslop, that 'In a number of cases, persons whose condition would ordinarily be described as due to . . . some form of mental disturbance, showed unmistakable indications of invasion by foreign or discarnate agencies.' The formulation 'foreign or discarnate entities' corresponds with our hypotheses 4 and 5.

So, assuming that they both exist, how would you distinguish a spirit from an extra-terrestrial? Well, for a start, the content of their respective communications might be a pointer. There is quite a substantial literature of alleged spirit communications, but they tend to fall into William James's 'philosophy-and-water' category. As that most critical of early psychical researchers, Frank Podmore, wrote of the Rev. Stainton Moses' *Spirit Teachings:* 'It needed not that a spirit should descend from the seventh sphere to preach views which could be heard from any Unitarian pulpit.' Such teachings, which are usually obtained through automatic writing, generally consist of pious sentiments, exhortations to a more noble way of life, and descriptions of 'the next world', all couched in a pedestrian and woolly language which makes a sarcasm of the term 'inspirational writings', which is often applied to them.

Podmore's remark about *Spirit Teachings* implies, particularly for the modern reader, that Stainton Moses' automatic writing was channelling nothing more than contents of his own unconscious. But this is not a justified conclusion on the evidence of the content alone. If spirits are, as both some of their own alleged testimonies and esoteric traditions maintain, the surviving non-physical part of former human beings reluctant to leave the Earth and its physical attractions, we should not expect them to be wiser or much more knowledgeable than human beings. The only thing they would know more about would be the mode and conditions of post-mortal existence. The content of 'spirit literature' tends to bear this out.

The Ossining communications clearly do not belong to this *genre*. Their philosophy and cosmology are broader than those of any so-called spirit teachings. Tom says at one point, 'What we ask we are asking from a universal point, and not from an earthly or a spirit point. There are many things in which you on the planet Earth are involved that in truth do not have the nature of the universe but only of the planet Earth or of the spirit planes that surround the planet Earth.' The 'spirit planes' of which in spiritist literature there are generally held to be six, with the Earth constituting a seventh, physical plane, have been described in many 'inspirational' writings, but such writings do not offer any description of the universe as a whole such as we get from Tom. Nor do they represent a consistently universal viewpoint. Throughout the communications all problems, all situations, personal, interpersonal, political, ethical, religious, are consistently analysed and regarded *sub specie aeternitatis*. There is no evidence in the literature of putative spirit communications that a spirit would have either the knowledge or the motivation to maintain a consistently universal point of view.

But couldn't a mischievous spirit have invented the whole

thing, and enjoyed improvising and elaborating the story over the years? The correct predictions, the good sense and wisdom, and the implicit morality of the communicators, I think, argue against such a frivolous explanation.

These points also make it unlikely that manipulative spirits should be responsible because the motive normally attributed to these spirits, namely that of gaining control over many souls, is missing. The trio, after all, have never been encouraged to collect followers.

As I have said, arguments by elimination cannot be conclusive, but this discussion has, I think, established that there are strong supportive arguments for the extra-terrestrial hypothesis. Personally, I would be happier with this hypothesis if we didn't have Atlantis, UFOs, Apocalypse, dolphins, ancient civilisations, consciousness expansion, previous incarnations and the New Age all in the same package. But perhaps the *Zeitgeist* of the 1970s really is in touch with the 'unified infinite intelligence'. If that were true, we would surely be on the threshold of a New Age. It would be rather less exciting, however, though not much less remarkable, if something purporting to be the 'unified infinite intelligence' should be in touch with the *Zeitgeist*.

Which brings us to the second key question that I wish to discuss in this Conclusion:

### Is the material of the communications original?

We have already established that the themes are not original but the question is whether Tom's contributions to them are. Before we attempt to answer this, let us be clear about what we might infer from the presence or the lack of originality in the communications.

It is not simply a matter of the more originality the more apparent authenticity. This is true for some types of statement but not for all. We have in the communications statements of various kinds, for instance: (*a*) statements of verifiable fact, (*b*) statements of non-verifiable fact, (*c*) statements of alleged fact, (*d*) predictions, (*e*) exhortations, (*f*) philosophical statements, (*g*) psychological statements, (*h*) moral statements.

The term 'original' implies different things with respect to these different types of statement. It may imply the exercise of supernormal cognition (types (a) and (b)), or mean novel (types (c)), unexpected (type (d)), insightful (type (g)), or without precedent or parallel (types (f) and (h)). Now, originality in statements of types (a), (b) and (d) (for instance: Assagioli had a bad day today (a)); At a secret meeting the Israeli leaders decided to make a foray into Lebanon (b); There will be a settlement between Israel and the Arabs in July (d) is suggestive of the operation of a more-than-human intelligence. Originality in statements of type (c) (for example about Atlantis, the beginnings of Earth civilisation at Aksu, and about the universe and its other civilisations) is certainly consistent with the existence of such an intelligence. But in statements of types (f) and (h) *un*originality would tend to support the extra-terrestrial intelligence hypothesis if the communicators' claim to have been influencing Earth civilisations and using other human channels throughout history were correct. We would, if that were the case, expect to find historical precedents for and parallels with their philosophy and teaching.

And indeed we do.

### Parallels with Gnosticism

I have already remarked that the term 'Aeons', by which Tom refers to himself and his peers, is used with the specialised meaning of 'beings beyond space and time' in certain rare texts of the Gnostic philosophers. Now, Gnosticism is a philosophy and a religious view of man, the world and the cosmos that was widespread throughout the near and middle East before Christianity, and that profoundly influenced certain aspects of Christian thought and teaching. With elements derived from, or corresponding with, Egyptian, Babylonian, Greek, Iranian and Jewish traditions, Gnosticism may be regarded as a syncretic or as a seminal philosophy. Much of its literature was suppressed and destroyed by State Christianity and the Church Fathers in the first centuries of the Christian era, so it is not easy for us to understand how influential and widespread it was. The classic study of Gnostic literature,

G. R. S. Mead's *Fragments of a Faith Forgotten*, is aptly titled. But it is no exaggeration to say that among the tenets of this forgotten faith are some of the oldest, most universal and most tenacious beliefs of mankind.

Tom's definition of the nature and purpose of the soul is pure Gnosticism. He likens the soul to a spark that is 'a particle of us' (the Aeons) and whose purpose is 'to return whence it came'. Now compare this with Mead's summary of the Gnostic myth of the creation of man by the demiurgic angels or nature-powers. According to this myth, at first 'the nature-powers could only evolve an envelope or plasm, which could not stand upright, but lay on the ground helpless and crawling like a worm. Then the Power Above, in compassion, sent forth the life-spark, and the plasm rose upright, and limbs developed and were knit together, that is to say, it hardened or became denser as race succeeded race; and so the body of man was evolved, and the light-spark, or real man, tabernacled in it. This light-spark hastens back after death to those of its own nature, and the rest of the elements of the body are dissolved.'

Gnosticism makes much of the forgetfulness of the soul or light-spark 'tabernacled' in the physical body and of the 'density' of the physical world that the spiritual powers in man and in the cosmos have to contend with. And Tom says, 'sometimes we peer at you and we say, "The three of them have forgotten who they are, and they are trapped in the physical and the thinking of the physical."' The use of the term 'the thinking of the physical' in this context is interesting, for in the Gnostic text, the *Pistis Sophia*, there is an account of the evolution of the soul, which Mead summarises as follows: 'Having descended to the lowest depths of chaos, she at length reaches the limit, and the path of her pilgrimage begins to lead upward to spirit again. Thus she reaches the middle point of balance, and still yearning for the Light, rounds the turning point of her cyclic course, and *changing the tendency of her thought* or mind or nature, recites her penitential hymns or repentances. Her chief enemy is the false light, the desire-nature . . .' (my italics).

Here is another quotation, and I invite the reader to guess whether it comes from the communications or from another source: 'Jesus was born like all other men; he differed from the rest in that his soul, being strong and pure, *remembered*.' In other words, he remembered who he was, where he came from and what his mission on Earth was. The words could be Tom's, but in fact they are Mead's statement of a tenet of Gnostic Christian belief.

While we are on the subject of Jesus, here is another interesting correspondence. In a communication on 4 January 1975 Tom stated: 'The being Jesus Christ was all of us at once. Jehovah came with the perfect goodness that is in each of us. Within us, as within you, there are various elements, but Jehovah had from each of us the most perfect of the elements of us.' Now compare this with Mead's statement of the Gnostic interpretation of the beginning of the Fourth Gospel: 'The Logos . . . contained in Himself the whole substance of the Aeons.'

Jesus remembered who he was, whence he came and what he had to do because his soul was 'strong and pure'. The ideas of purity, purification and refinement are recurrent in the communications. In one of the earliest communications, channelled by Phyllis from 'Ryr', there occurs a statement of the basic Gnostic insight: 'When we return to your physical world, we oftentimes forget the spiritual side of our nature.' This is followed by the statement that souls have 'evolved through processing', in other words through being progressively purified and refined. And Ryr adds: 'The work is not just our work. It is the work of the universe.' This latter idea is interesting, for the outstanding contemporary Gnostic scholar, Hans Jonas, writes that, 'this process [of the evolution of the soul] is part of the restoration of the deity's own wholeness'. Possibly this is the most fundamental correspondence between the philosophy expressed by Tom and Ryr as spokesmen for the Nine, and Gnosticism: the idea that the evolution of individual souls has a cosmic significance, that whatever is achieved by and in the microcosm resonates in the macrocosm. Mead wrote: 'whether we interpret their allegories from the macrocosmic or microcosmic standpoint, it is ever the evolution of the *mind* that the initiates of old have sought to teach us . . . The material mind was to be purified, and so become one with the spiritual mind'. In the communications, this process of evolution of the mind is spoken of as the 'raising of the consciousness of the planet', which Tom defines as bringing souls out of darkness, and further elaborates that 'when we say darkness we do not mean negativity but true darkness, for they do not see and do not understand the cosmic'. So the raising of consciousness, the evolution of mind, is to be accomplished through the communication of knowledge and understanding. This again is pure Gnosticism. The word *Gnosis* means 'knowledge', and in its religious aspect Gnosticism is a belief in salvation through knowledge. And it is to Gnostic tradition that we owe the symbolic equation that runs right through Western thought and literature, of darkness with ignorance and light with understanding.

The poet Kenneth Rexroth, in an Introduction to a modern edition of Mead's *Fragments*, specifies as characteristically Gnostic 'the concept of the universe as a moral battleground, existence itself as the struggle of light against darkness'. In Judaism and Christianity as well as in Gnosticism, he remarks, we have a cosmic drama, focused on man, 'a drama in which the individual worshipper plays a primary role'. In the communications the trio, both as individuals and collectively, are said to be playing a primary role in the cosmic drama currently being played out, which consists of battles being fought out both 'in the spheres' and on the physical planet Earth. The Battle of Armageddon has been in progress 'in the spheres', Tom has said, since November 1974, and the work of the trio on their visits to the Middle East was to prevent a corresponding situation flaring up on Earth. *A propos* this, an explanation of Mead's is interesting: 'The "wars in heaven" precede the conflict of good and evil on Earth.'

Gnosticism, then, teaches the reincarnation and evolution of souls, the forgetfulness that follows entrapment in the density of the physical, the fact that the refinement and purification of the individual soul has cosmic significance, that salvation is achieved through *gnosis*, knowledge, and that the universe is a moral battleground where individual human struggle counts. All these teachings, together with the characteristic Gnostic symbolism of the 'light-spark' of the soul, the opposition of darkness and light, and the cosmic battle, are also to be found in the communications. That the material of the communications is simply derivative from Gnostic sources, through the conscious or unconscious mind of one or more members of the trio, is a possibility that we can discount for reasons already adequately gone into. How, then, are we to explain these parallels? I would like to leave the reader to ponder an explanation suggested by Mead in the Prolegomena to *Fragments of a Faith Forgotten*:

The soul of man returns again and again to learn the lessons of life in this great world-school, according to one of the great doctrines of general religion. If this be so, it follows that when similar conditions recur a similar class of souls returns to continue its lessons of experience. It may well be even that many of the identical souls who were embodied in the early centuries of Christianity are continuing their experience among ourselves today. For why otherwise do the same ideas recur, why do the same problems arise, the same ways of looking at things? They cannot fall into our midst from the *"Ewigkeit"*; must it not be that they have been brought back by mind to whom they have already been familiar?

*Parallels with Esotericism*

Esotericism, which is known to its devotees as 'The Ageless Wisdom' or 'The Secret Doctrine', is a corpus of knowledge and teaching allegedly possessed by the 'Esoteric Hierarchy' or the 'Masters of Wisdom', portions of which have from time to time been released to mankind through various channels. In modern times the two main channels have been Helena Blavatsky and Alice A. Bailey. When Mrs Blavatsky published her *Isis Unveiled* (1877) and *The Secret Doctrine* (1888), the Hierarchy completed the first stage of a three-stage plan for the unfoldment of the Ageless Wisdom. The second, or intermediate stage, was accomplished through the series of books written by Alice Bailey between 1919 and 1949. The third stage, according to the teaching, will be the 'Revelatory', and, beginning after 1975, it will comprise communications on a world-wide scale employing, in addition to human channels, modern media such as television and radio.

Theodore Roszak, who is Professor of History at California State University as well as a most perceptive and eloquent observer of the contemporary cultural scene, has written of the modern esotericists, with particular reference to Mrs Blavatsky, that 'if we search the strange mythological extrapolations of these occult evolutionists to discover the vision they offer of human potentiality, we may, at the very least, find them among the most innovative psychologists of our time. In their work, we see the evolutionary image being used for the first time in the modern West as a new standard of human sanity – or rather as a newly rediscovered standard, for to a degree that far surpasses the work of Nietzsche or Bergson, they remain unabashedly loyal to the schools of the Hidden Wisdom, and so link contemporary thought on human potentiality with a rich basis in tradition.'

You will look hard, outside the ranks of the devotees, for a favourable opinion of the esotericists prior to 1975, when Roszak published this opinion in his book, *Unfinished Animal*. Significantly, the book is sub-titled 'the aquarian frontier and the evolution of consciousness'. The term 'aquarian' is one that has found its way out of esoteric doctrine into popular usage and understanding in recent years. The astronomical fact that in the 1970s the solar system is moving into the sphere of influence of the constellation Aquarius and out of that of Pisces is regarded by esotericists as the most significant cosmic event, so far as mankind is concerned, since the entry into Pisces, which inaugurated the Christian era. A new age, as different from the old as the Christian era was from the age that preceded it, is upon us, and the belief that it will be an age when humanity will take a great evolutionary leap forward is another esoteric idea that has become exoteric recently. At the beginning of the Aquarian age, moreover, the tradition holds that much more of the Ageless Wisdom will be revealed than ever before, for mankind will be in the process of becoming sufficiently evolved to be able to understand it and benefit by it. The tremendously increased interest in revealed teachings and religion of all kinds in the present decade would certainly seem to bear this out.

The New Age, esoteric tradition maintains, will culminate in the reappearance of The Christ, and this event will be preceded by 'the externalisation of the Hierarchy', that is to say, the appearance in the world of a number of great initiates and men of wisdom who, while doing normal worldly jobs, will be serving as guides and spiritual leaders. These members of the Hierarchy, it is said, have long been preparing themselves for existence in the unfamiliar confines of the physical body. Their work of preparation will be assisted by a large and continually growing group of people in all countries and walks of life, who are known as 'the new group of world servers'. The Christ, who last incarnated as Jesus of Nazareth, will return near the beginning of the Aquarian age when through the work of these precursors man has manifested in his political, economic and social relations a will to base his conduct on the principles of co-operation, sharing, goodwill and mutual responsibility. He will return to complete the work begun in Palestine two thousand years ago, which could not be brought to fruition at that time because mankind was not sufficiently educated and spiritually evolved to understand and apply the teaching. With the circumstances prevailing in the present age – a general higher standard of education, widespread awareness of the imminence of a planetary crisis, and the availability of media of mass communications – the task of world transformation will this time surely be accomplished.

The esoteric teachings do not maintain that the Hierarchy hail from elsewhere in the cosmos, but apart from this the message corresponds pretty closely with what Tom says about the New Age, the landing, the preparations for that event, the previous work of the Christ through Jesus of Nazareth, and the raising of consciousness. Let me quote a passage from the teachings of 'the Tibetan', channelled by Alice Bailey, to illustrate how close these correspondences are:

The New Age will bring in eventually a civilisation and a culture which will be utterly different to anything hitherto known. I would remind you here that all civilisations and cultures are externalisations – modified, qualified and adapted to racial and national needs – of the potent, vibrating and planned activity of the world of initiates and disciples who constitute the Hierarchy of the time. Their plans, Their thinking and Their living potency pour out ceaselessly, and affect the consciousness of Their disciples; these latter step down the inflowing energies so that the thinkers and idealists can grasp these new emerging truths more accurately. Eventually the truths thus grasped change the consciousness of humanity as a whole and raise it – if you like that phrase; thus modes of daily living, civilised methods of conduct and cultural developments eventuate. All this is traceable to the group of initiates upon the inner side, who thus serve their fellow men and carry forward, consciously and with intent, the Law of Evolution.

Both the esotericists and the Ossining communications envisage a necessary change in human consciousness being effected through occult influence, by means of energies and knowledge being channelled from a higher source. Both see the preparatory work being carried out by groups of human beings throughout the world who have volunteered to be 'in service', and both express awareness of the hazards and difficulties of working in this way. In the story the present book has related there have been failures, backslidings, wrong turnings taken, interpersonal conflicts disrupting the work, and the reader might have asked on several occasions why the Nine, if they are as powerful and as knowledgeable as they are supposed to be, allow these things to occur or fail to foresee that they are going to occur. Tom has explained this in various places, and when we recall his explanations the following words of 'the Tibetan' have a familiar ring:

They [the Hierarchy] impress the Plan and some suggestion as to its scope upon the mind of some man or some woman upon the physical plane. If that mind is unstable or oversatisfied, if it is filled with pride, with despair, or with self-depreciation, the vision does not come through with clarity of outline; if the emotional body is vibrating violently with some rhythm set up by the personality, or if the physical vehicle is ailing, and concentrated attention is therefore prevented, what will happen? The Master will turn sadly away, distressed to think of the opportunity for service that the worker has lost through his own fault, and He will seek someone else to fill the need – someone perhaps not so fundamentally suitable, but the only one available on account of the failure of the first one approached.

The idea that there exist extra-terrestrial intelligences that are at the present time implementing a Plan for the planet Earth and for man's further evolution, and that the success of the Plan depends upon man's having the imagination to comprehend new knowledge and the will to act on it, are common to both esoteric teachings and the Ossining communications. Other features the two sources have in common are the doctrine of reincarnation, that of the multiple 'bodies' – the physical, the etheric, the emotional, etc. – that man possesses, a cosmology based on the concepts of polarity and balance, and a scientific philosophy and psychology developed around the imagery of fire, light, energy and vibration. The correspondences, indeed, are so close that it is surely not merely idly fanciful to wonder whether the Ossining communications might not be a principal part of the Revelatory phase of the unfolding of the Ageless Wisdom, which esoteric tradition maintained would begin about 1975.

*Parallels with other contemporary communications*

In one of the communications Tom said that there were other groups and individuals in the world who were in contact with other extra-terrestrial units, but stressed that Phyllis was the only channel for the Nine, and that the communications with the Ossining group were the most complete and detailed that were being channelled to Earth at the present time. When I first heard this statement I thought it would be very interesting to try and track down some of these other communicators and see if the information they were getting corresponded with that channelled by Phyllis. If such correspondences were found, this would surely be the most conclusive evidence possible that the information emanated from a source independent of all the groups involved in communications. The problem was how to locate the other communicators. We had one example in the case of Andrew Watson, Lyall's brother, who had been out of touch in South Africa and independently communicating with 'Aragon'. But his material was not published, and our knowing about it was seemingly fortuitous, so it seemed impossible to know how many similar cases there might be and how one could get to know about them.

However, in the course of the last few months, by browsing through bookshops and book catalogues, I have come across accounts by two putative recipients of communications from extra-terrestrials which have striking correspondences with the Ossining material.

The first is related by Brad Steiger in his book, *Revelation: the Divine Fire*. The channel for this material is named Charles, lives in Phoenix, Arizona, and is described as 'a blue-collar worker of modest education'. The communicating entity identified itself by the name 'Ishkomar'. In the following transcription of some of the Ishkomar material I have italicised interesting points of correspondence with the Ossining material:

I was brought to the vicinity of this planet *approximately thirty thousand years ago*, by your method of time measurement. Your planet and the living forms upon it have a specific value to us. Your form of life has a particular value to us. For this reason, at about the time I was brought to the vicinity of your world, *we interfered with the natural development of the species of man that inhabited this planet.* Our purpose was to shorten the cycle of development necessary for the human inhabitants of this planet to be of use to us. We have worked patiently with you *for over thirty thousand years*. The development brought about would have taken, by normal cycles, over two hundred and fifty thousand years. *Our intent, however, is not to control or to rule over you*. Intergalactic law within our group forbids this. We are, however, permitted to guide you. *Your acceptance of us is by your own choice*.

We, however, are not alone in our interests in your world. There is in existence with us another group. Their interests are not necessarily harmful to you, yet their methods are in direct opposition to ours. They also have interfered with the development of your planet. *They wish to reach their ends, not by co-operation, but by control and domination.*

You must reach a high level of mental development and knowledge to be able to understand our purposes. We have attempted to gain your co-operation for thousands of years. *We have been vigorously opposed by the other group. We must achieve our goal by guidance of your kind, but you must desire guidance for us to be of assistance to you.*

*We are using many methods at this time to inform your people of our presence and our immediate purposes. The time is quite near for co-operation between us to begin. Your next step upward will soon begin. Full knowledge of our presence will soon be known to your people. There will be, at that time, great upheavals on your planet.* We regret this cannot in any way be avoided. We, therefore, have warned man repeatedly to prepare for these events, both mentally and physically.

I am sure that the correspondences with the Ossining material, particularly with regard to the points italicised, will be clear enough to the reader to require no further comment. The same is true of some of the 'Mark-Age' material channelled by the medium Nada-Yolanda, a substantial corpus of communications received over the last fifteen years from which I have extracted the following significant passages:

The space people who are here at this time are here to aid the spiritual program . . . The space brothers, both physical and etheric, are here to supplement, not to replace, your own God consciousness, your own intunement with your high Self . . . They can do many things with their equipment in order to awaken and to stimulate certain spiritual centers, to help you along the path. The time is short; and that is why they have come to aid this planet, and the race upon it, to evolve a little bit more quickly.

As you know, coming into this particular aspect of your world and history we can and do desire to *raise your vibrational frequencies* to accept and to utilise properly the new rate of vitality of your present expression or vehicles . . .

You have upon your planet thousands upon thousands who have no idea of spiritual enlightenment, who have no desire or need for psychic explanations, yet they are receiving inspirationally and through mental telepathic guidance our ideas and our future aims. You have them in every walk of life . . .

*You have people who have come from other planets who know no such thing as life on other planets,* who even may not believe in life on other planets. Yet, they are in your Earth's atmosphere waiting, living the life – normal, so-called average, everyday, prosaic lives, according to you who are studying – and they still are receiving. Their teachers are around them. Their high Selves know who they are and what their destiny is . . .

*Within every single human being is a transmitting and sending set of vital energy, which is the vital energy of the universe.* The purpose is that each one of you should be able to be transmitters and receivers of this energy, to perform and create as co-creators with God. This is why we try to make you understand that we are not here to control you or to hurt you. *We are here to help you understand your true roles and to help your true powers, which you have forgotten on this particular planet called Earth.* Although you may have incarnated from very high etheric realms and other planets which have exercised these powers and rights, *while you are in the Earth vibration,* incarnated in this set of vibrations, *you have lost or have forgotten, as though in a dream state, those natural, inherent rights and powers . . .*

When we use this vehicle – for instance, when we use Yolanda's body – it is strictly through the dedication and the free will of the high Self consciousness. *Before incarnating into this life she dedicated her vehicle to these teachers to do this . . .*

We protect and teach and guide you *because you are of us and one of us. But you have volunteered your missions,* we have volunteered ours . . .

You are being taught the meaning of co-operation, co-ordination with every other realm, dimension and planet, because one cannot be out of order or out of character while the others are being geared to a certain role and a certain function . . . If you are not in co-operation with them they cannot move forward with ease and harmony . . . *You are holding them up* . . . If they are hindered or held back to do a role or play a part in your evolution or growth, they cannot expend that time's energy upon their own evolutionary growth . . .

We bring this message through to you at the peak of the cycle known to this unit as the action cycle because it precipitates several plans in the overall program . . . Plan one is space communication, physical and mental, accepted and *presented to the mass media.* Plan two is occupation by space brothers for further illumination of integrated solar federation of planetary brotherhood. Plan three is mass education on the spiritual program known as evolution into the fourth dimensional consciousness.

To say the very least, the parallels and correspondences we have noted in the foregoing pages indicate that the Ossining communications are not an isolated phenomenon or the product of somebody's crazed subconscious. They have links with history, with esoteric tradition and with other contemporary psychic phenomena. Whether they are something more than a remarkable and fascinating psychic phenomenon, whether they really do emanate from an extra-terrestrial source, are questions that we should, by all accounts, soon have unequivocal answers to.

Speaking of the landing, let us give Tom the last word. In a communication held on 11 January 1977, just before this book was delivered to the publishers, John asked whether 'what has been stated in the book fully covers what you want said about the landing?' Tom replied:

'It is important that it be stated in the chronicle of the three of you that there will be physical civilisations that will come to raise the level of this planet Earth, to bring it out of its own contamination, to purify it and to prepare the people to keep it in a pure state so that it does not become in a collapsed state for future generations. This is the most beautiful of all the planets that exist in the universe. It has the greatest variety. That is expressed in the book, but it is also important to tell the readers that there is hope for future generations on this planet. For in truth if this planet may be purified, then it will be the greatest paradise for all souls. It is also important that they understand that each of them is responsible for him or her self, for their neighbours, for future generations and for the universe. And if they believe that they will have life after their physical death, then they must understand that what they do in this life they must undo in the next. It is of the greatest importance that they understand the necessity for the purification of this planet Earth, and that they understand, too, that it cannot be done with their technology, for the time is past for so saving it. This must be told so that they will not create difficulty for the civilisations that will come.'

And ye shall hear of wars, and rumours of wars: see that ye be not troubled: for all *these things* must come to pass, but the end is not yet.

For nation shall rise up against nation, and kingdom against kingdom: and there shall be famines, and pestilences, and earthquakes in diverse places . . .

And then shall many be offended, and shall betray one another, and shall hate one another.

And many false prophets shall rise, and shall deceive many.

And because iniquity shall abound, the love of many shall wax cold.

But he that shall endure unto the end, the same shall be saved. . . .

Immediately after the tribulation of those days, shall the sun be darkened, and the moon shall not give her light, and the stars shall fall from heaven, and the powers of the heavens shall be shaken:

And then shall appear the sign of the Son of man in heaven: and then shall all the tribes of the earth mourn, and they shall see the Son of man coming in the clouds of heaven with power and great glory.

*St Matthew, 24*

# Bibliography

BOOKS ON MEDIUMSHIP AND PSYCHICAL RESEARCH

Broad, C. D., *Lectures on Psychical Research* (Routledge and Kegan Paul, London, 1962)

Flournoy, Theodore, *From India to the Planet Mars* (University Books, New York, 1963)

Garrett, Eileen J., *Many Voices: the Autobiography of a Medium* (Putnams, New York, 1968)

—— *My Life as a Search for the Meaning of Mediumship* (Rider, London, 1939)

James, William, *William James on Psychical Research* (ed. Murphy and Ballou, Viking, New York, 1960)

Leonard, Gladys O., *My Life in Two Worlds* (Cassell, London, 1931)

LeShan, Lawrence, *The Medium, The Mystic and the Physicist* (Viking, New York, 1975)

Prince, Walter Franklin, *The Case of Patience Worth* (University Books, New York, 1964)


BOOKS ON EXTRA-TERRESTRIAL LIFE AND INTELLIGENCE

Sanderson, Ivan T., *Uninvited Visitors* (Spearman, London, 1969)

Sagan, Carl, *The Cosmic Connection* (Hodder, London, 1974)

Sagan, Carl (ed.), *Communication with Extraterrestrial Intelligence* (M.I.T. Press, Cambridge, Mass., 1973)

Shklovski and Sagan, *Intelligent Life in the Universe* (Dell, New York, 1966)

Stoneley & Lawson, *Is Anyone Out There?* (Star Books, London, 1975)

Trench, Brinsley le Poer, *Mysterious Visitors* (Stein & Day, New York, 1973)

Vallée, Jacques, *The Invisible College* (Dutton, New York, 1975)


OTHER BOOKS AND AUTHORS MENTIONED IN THE TEXT

Assagioli, Roberto, *Psychosynthesis* (Viking Compass, New York, 1971)

Bailey, Alice, *The Reappearance of the Christ* (Lucis Press, 1948)

—— *Externalization of the Hierarchy* (Lucis Press, 1948)

—— *Discipleship in the New Age* (Lucis Press, Vol. One, 1955, Vol. Two, 1972)

Blavatsky, H. P., *The Secret Doctrine* (Theosophical University Press, 1888)

Burr, Harold Saxton, *The Fields of Life* (Ballantine, New York, 1973)

Campbell, Joseph, *Primitive Mythology* and *Occidental Mythology* (Viking Compass, New York, 1970)

Crookall, Robert, *Casebook of Astral Projection* (University Books, New York, 1972)

Jung, Carl Gustav, *Flying Saucers* (Harcourt Brace Jovanovich Inc, 1959)

Lilly, John, *Lilly on Dolphins* (Anchor Books, 1975)

Mead, G. R. S., *Fragments of a Faith Forgotten* (University Books, New York, 1960)

Monroe, Robert, *Journeys out of the Body* (Souvenir Press, London, 1972)

Muldoon, Sylvan, and Carrington, Hereward, *The Phenomena of Astral Projection* (Rider, London, 1951)

Nada-Yolanda, *Visitors from Other Planets* (Mark-Age, Miami, 1974)

Russell, Edward W., *Design for Destiny* (Ballantine, New York, 1971)

Steiger, Brad, *Revelation: The Divine Fire* (Prentice-Hall, Englewood Cliffs, N.J., 1973)

## BOOKS BY OR ABOUT PEOPLE INVOLVED IN THE STORY

Carlson, Rick (ed), *The Frontiers of Science and Medicine: Texts of and Commentaries on the May Lectures, 1974* (Wildwood House, London, 1975)

Fuller, John G., and Puharich, Andrija, *Arigó: Surgeon of the Rusty Knife* (Crowell, New York, 1974)

Geller, Uri, *My Story* (Warner Books, New York, 1976)

Panati, Charles (ed.), *The Geller Papers* (Houghton Mifflin Co., Boston, 1976)

Puharich, Andrija, *Uri* (W. H. Allen, London, 1974)

—— *The Sacred Mushroom* (Doubleday, New York, 1959)

—— *Beyond Telepathy* (Doubleday, New York, 1962)

Watson, Lyall, *Supernature* (Hodder, London, 1973)

—— *The Romeo Error* (Hodder, London, 1974)

—— *Gifts of Unknown Things* (Hodder, London, 1976)

# Index

# A SELECTED LIST OF BOOKS
## ABOUT UFO's AND OTHER
## STRANGE PHENOMENA

WHILE EVERY EFFORT IS MADE TO KEEP PRICES LOW, IT IS SOMETIMES NECESSARY TO INCREASE PRICES AT SHORT NOTICE. CORGI BOOKS RESERVE THE RIGHT TO SHOW AND CHARGE NEW RETAIL PRICES ON COVERS WHICH MAY DIFFER FROM THOSE ADVERTISED IN THE TEXT OR ELSEWHERE.

THE PRICES SHOWN BELOW WERE CORRECT AT THE TIME OF GOING TO PRESS (JAN. 79)

*All these books are available at your bookshop or newsagent: or can be ordered direct from the publisher. Just tick the titles you want and fill in the form below.*

CORGI BOOKS, Cash Sales Department, P.O. Box 11, Falmouth, Cornwall. Please send cheque or postal order, no currency.

U.K. send 22p for first book plus 10p per copy for each additional book ordered to a maximum charge of 82p to cover the cost of postage and packing.

B.F.P.O. and Eire allow 22p for first book plus 10p per copy for the next 6 books, thereafter 4p per book.

Overseas customers please allow 30p for the first book and 10p per copy for each additional book.

NAME (block letters) ............................................................................

ADDRESS ............................................................................

(JAN. 1979) ............................................................................